SEA OFFICER

MICHAEL PENNEY, OBE, RD

with Leslie Viney

For the library of Surrey County Council

Michael Penney
16 April 2008

First published in Great Britain 2008

by the author M D Penney

PO Box 35, Virginia Water GU25 4XG

Typeset by Lindley Readett

Black and White Picture Design by Mark Basten

Dustjacket Colour Design by Ashley Kinsella

Printed and bound by CPI Antony Rowe Ltd.

ISBN 978-0-9557562-0-7

For my long-suffering family

and

Those in peril on the sea

Contents

Contents

Foreword

It was my old colleague, Jim Davis, who inspired me to write this account after he had in 2006 published his book "You and Your Ships" which has found many readers. His preface sets down what got him started, and I am following suit.

I chose the title "Sea Officer" because that is what I set out to be, and was. It is an expression that first appeared about two centuries ago and was used to describe a sailor who had accepted higher responsibilities, particularly for the conduct of ships and their sailors.

There is a long list of people who have helped me with this book. It starts with my immediate family who have put up with my being glued to a computer screen. Bunty has spent time proof reading my drafts and eliminating typographical errors. My daughter Lindley has typeset the MS, and both my daughters and grandchildren have guided me through the mysteries of using a personal computer, and I am very grateful to them. It seems to be a world where the younger you are, the more you understand about the machines.

Robin Knight, Chairman of the Old Pangbournian Society, and a professional communicator in his own right, steered me towards Leslie Viney as my editor. Leslie was brought up in Philadelphia, city of the Liberty Bell, and she is both a journalist and lecturer in English. Despite being an enthusiastic yachtswoman, she knew little about the maritime world and its background and history, and this was just what I wanted. Her editorial work has often involved demanding to learn what on earth I was talking about and with her encouragement I have re-written a number of lines so as to be more readable for others. I am greatly indebted to her for her contribution.

Foreword

Mark Basten undertook to design the black and white picture pages and the appendices, and rendered old photographs such that they are clearer than the originals. I now know much better how my grandparents looked. Ashley Kinsella has provided the design of the dustcover and flier. His work has demonstrated his skills in the practical artistic world and I am sure he has a great career ahead of him.

No less than fourteen old colleagues have assisted in the capacity of "sub-editors". These are people who shared some of my experiences in years gone by and they either corrected inaccuracies or dealt with serious omissions in my first drafts. I do still have many documents to help me, but not enough, which means having to fall back on a memory which is not always perfect. They all made serious contributions.

Lionel Stephens, Honorary Secretary of the Old Pangbournian Society, provided input about WW2 and Pangbourne for Chapters 1 and 2. John Owen was my shipmate in Chapter 3, which was a momentous day for us both. Commodore Michael Bradford was very helpful with Chapters 7, 8 and 12. Commodore Ian Gibb and I were shipmates in Chapter 7. Jean Constantine née Childs was my part time secretary in Chapter 9. Her husband Willie contributed to Chapter 12, as did Paul Ogden. Chapter 13 was a life highlight for Paul Ogden, Stan Mole and for me. John Crossman made major contributions to Chapter 14. My daughter Victoria shared experiences with me reported in Chapter 15. John Hampton assisted with Chapter 17 after many years in his fleet manager's job.

I extend to them all many thanks for their wonderful assistance.

Chapter 1. Seafaring Ancestry

I am the fourth generation seafarer in my family, as far as I can trace. My great grandfather, Captain Peter Penney was an East Coast Master in Sail, but there are no details of his life available, as far as I can trace.

My grandfather was Captain Stephen Penney, JP and a Trinity House Pilot. Born in Yarmouth in 1846, he went to sea as a young man, and became a master mariner. Later he set out for a career as a Trinity House Pilot in the South Channel (of the Thames Estuary) Outward.

Trinity House pilots were self-employed. Although it was a long haul to the top it was well worthwhile if you made it. There was a six month apprenticeship period without any income, shipping with a licensed pilot, learning and committing to memory every buoy and light in the Southern channels. After passing an examination, the apprentice was granted a licence as under-draughtsman which allowed him to pilot ships drawing 16 feet or less. Fee levels were geared to draft; the deeper the draft, the higher the fee. Once pilots began to earn fees, they had to contribute to the cost of the pilot office on Gravesend pier and to the cutter cruising off Dungeness.

To start with, my Grandpa Stephen had to be a turn pilot, meaning that he had to take his turn with other pilots, to take ships as they appeared, so that when he reported in to the pilot office he did not know when he would work and earn a fee. He was required to live within five miles of Gravesend pier so that he could reach the pilot office quickly. As the years went by, he progressed to full draft and also to choice pilot, which meant he no longer had to wait a turn. Choice pilots were taken on by the large shipping companies, and he started as P&O's Number 2 choice pilot, before becoming Number 1. This was his target, because the P&O mail ships sailed from London every Friday afternoon which meant that he could be back home on Saturday or Sunday. By 1900 he was earning £3,000 a year, then a very good income.

Being back home in Gravesend on Saturday or Sunday allowed him to moonlight as a magistrate, sitting on the Bench each week, Monday to Thursday. He was also involved with other maritime activities including the Safety of Navigation at Sea Act and the Pilotage Act. He also wrote a book with sailing directions for the River Thames which is in my library. In 1877 he married Jane Posgate, daughter of a mariner and pilot, and as was not unusual for his times they had a big family of five sons and three daughters. All five sons were educated at Ardingly College in Sussex.

In 1912 my Grandpa retired to Worthing after the loss of P&O OCEANA which was in collision with a German 4 masted steel barque, PISAGUA, of the famous P Line.

OCEANA had sailed from London, and was proceeding to Southampton to embark her passengers. My Grandpa was in pilotage charge and off Beachy Head, in thick fog and a moderate North Easterly wind, OCEANA was stopped and was rammed amidships by the 4,000 ton barque, soon sinking. Two sailors were lost and the remainder scrambled ashore from boats. There was no official inquiry, but under the rules "Steam gives way to Sail", he felt responsible. OCEANA was equipped with a good steam whistle, whilst PISAGUA had only a hand operated fog horn, as required by the rules, but not really enough for a 4,000 ton steel ship. I also suspect that a square rigged sailing ship was making the best of a North Easterly wind to clear the Straits of Dover and reach the broader waters of the Channel before the wind backed Westerly. The wreck of OCEANA is still there and has a web site. My Grandpa died in retirement in Worthing in 1918, before my birth, so unhappily, we never met

My Pa, Stephen Leslie Penney, MBE, known either as Leslie or Tuppence, was born in Gravesend in 1890 and he went to school at Ardingly College. He was very short sighted, so there was no way

Seafaring ancestry

he could follow my Grandpa as a mariner, which was a matter of disappointment to the family. The eldest son was a barrister, and the other three were electrical engineers. My Grandpa, who was very impressed with the style of P&O, persuaded my Pa to join as a clerk, which he duly did in September 1908. At that time P&O was chaired by Sir Thomas Sutherland, who had developed P&O's activities greatly, and was very highly regarded in the shipping world. Under his hand, P&O had its own offices in all the major ports of the Far East and Australia, manned by staff from London working four year tours of duty. The senior hand in each office was known as The Agent, who was supported by between two and four clerks from London, plus others recruited locally.

If they fitted in, new clerks of 18 years of age could express a wish to serve abroad as No.3 Clerk, and this typically happened at age 25. This meant back to London for six months leave when they were about 29, to be followed up with a second overseas posting, probably in another place, and perhaps as No.2 Clerk. This signal of approval meant more pay, enough to support a wife, and with six months to find one to take overseas with him. A good performance could lead to an appointment as The Agent, who returned from overseas service aged about 52, was usually comfortably off. On return, the Agents either retired or went on to a senior management position in London. It all made for a very clubby place in which to work.

My Pa reached age 24 and WW1 broke out. Like every young man in the office, he immediately volunteered to join the army.

Since he had difficulty in seeing a rifle without glasses, let alone knowing where to point it, he was appointed to the Pay Corps and spent four years in Hounslow Barracks. This less stressful lifestyle was in complete contrast to his WW2 experiences later on when he was in his fifties.

In 1918 he returned to the office, to find everything had changed. Sir Thomas, who had retired, was followed by the First Earl Inchcape whose management style was quite different. All the

Sea Officer

Agents and their staff were recalled, and were replaced by Mackinnon Mackenzie & Co or MacDonald Hamilton & Co, private partnerships of which the First Earl was a member. My Pa had to face up to the fact that he was a poorly paid clerk without prospects who could not afford to marry. There is one good story of the First Earl's dealings with suppliers of his ownership, and gin. From the Chair he noticed that the consumption of gin in the Company's ships was enormous but it was all supplied by the big battalions - Gordons, Gilbeys, Plymouth etc. He sent a staffer to locate a distillery for sale and found one in the West Midlands, being sold by a temperate wife who had just lost her husband, on the condition that the family brand name was not used. The Earl agreed, and arrived in his Rolls at a broken down large shed. He was shown round by two Brummie foremen in cloth caps and appeared to be pleased with his purchase. Before leaving he asked them their names, to which they replied "Burn m'lord" and "Turner m'lord". "That's it" said m'lord, "our brand name is Burn and Turner". It was still served in the 1950s, and was very good, but I think it has disappeared today.

Unhappy in his work, my Pa soldiered on until 1926, when an escape route appeared. The 1920s saw an upsurge in the building of passenger and other ships, to replace those lost in the war and to cope with trade expansion. The passenger numbers per ship increased, as did the workload of the purser. So my Pa went to sea, joining in the family tradition at last. He was deputy purser for one voyage in P&O MALWA, and later was purser in a number of ships, until he retired in 1951. This provided him with the where-withal to marry, which he did almost immediately to Ivy May Smith, one from a large family of five girls and one boy in Richmond, Surrey, where the newly weds set up house. My Mama was 31, and a trained secretary working for a stockbroker in the City. The family lived in Richmond for five years and I was born there in 1929, followed by my sister Shirley Mary in 1934. In 1935 the family moved to Witham in Essex but my Mama had no friends there and after eighteen months we moved back to Surrey to a large house in Horley. In WW2 Horley turned out to be a waypoint on

Seafaring ancestry

the Luftwaffe's track from France to London. In WW1 my Mama had experienced the Zeppelin raids on London and she was very ARP minded.

Pre WW2, my Pa served in NARKUNDA, MALOJA and STRATHAIRD as purser. Whenever his ship was in Tilbury he would take his whole family to stay on board for a few days which certainly encouraged my fascination with seafaring.

As a Purser my Pa was obviously popular with his passengers, many of whom became friends and gave him a number of gifts. The most significant was a large solid silver cigarette box, inscribed inside with the eleven facsimile signatures of those who dined at his table during a voyage homeward from Japan in MALWA in Jan/March 1928. They include some important names, especially Jack MacGregor, a taipan from Hong Kong who had a firm grip on most of the top liquors imported into the colony (in 1956 the family continued that grip), and Admiral Boddam-Whetham. The admiral had just hauled down his flag as CinC Far East, and was returning to the UK to retire at age 60. In 1939 he "returned to the colours" to spend all of WW2 as a convoy commodore, mostly sailing to Russia. On one such trip, when he was wallowing along in the Norwegian Sea at seven knots, he announced "Don't like this bloody ship, I'm transferring to that one". Halting a convoy for an hour in an area heavily populated with U boats was a hazardous performance. The escort commander was reported to be jumping up and down in frustration, but the admiral had got it right. His original ship was torpedoed and sunk at dawn next day.

When WW2 broke out, my Pa was in STRATHAIRD, which had been converted for trooping. In June 1940 she was ordered to Cherbourg to evacuate refugees. This was accomplished. However Cunard's LANCASTRIA, tasked to do the same, was found and sunk by the Luftwaffe at anchor off Cherbourg, and 9,000 lives were lost, the biggest loss of life in one incident in WW2.

In January 1942, STRATHAIRD was ordered to Singapore to evacuate non-combatants. The Japanese Army had already gained a foothold on the islands so things were looking very bad. Some dispirited Australian troops, exhausted from retreating the length of Malaya and learning that the ship was bound for Sydney, tried to rush the gangways, and the redcaps had to open fire on them. As the Japanese air force was fortunately still concentrating on military targets STRATHAIRD steamed to safety.

Later in the year my Pa was transferred to STRATHALLAN, built in 1939, the fifth of the Straths. She was included in the troopships required for operation TORCH, the invasion of French North Africa and the graveyard for so many P&O passenger ships. In October she made a round trip to Oran without undue incident and sailed again with reinforcements. In early December her convoy had nearly reached Oran when at 0225 on a clear and moonlit night she was torpedoed in the engine room. She had on board about 4,000 troops and 250 QA nurses but none of these was lost. Only four of her ship's company were lost, being two engineer officers and two of their ratings. She stayed afloat for hours and was taken in tow for Oran, but a fire aboard grew steadily worse and she sank only 12 miles from Oran. My Pa found himself in a boat full of QAs for 14 hours whilst the escorts hunted the U boat. Finally picked up by a destroyer, he was at last able to visit her heads!

My Pa came home as a passenger in Canadian Pacific's DUCHESS OF BEDFORD and took leave. Normally when he came home on leave he was smartly dressed in uniform and was accompanied by two large suitcases of goodies for his family. These were items of clothing and food unobtainable in the UK. On this occasion it was different: his uniform was a total mess, he had lost his cap and been lent another, three sizes too small and without its P&O badge. A small cardboard box secured with string contained all his possessions not lodged in his house. His family were all deeply shocked.

After leave and rest, he was appointed to RANCHI, which had been an AMC but was now converted for trooping. The ship was very busy in the Mediterranean, helping the Army in their work to take over Southern Europe. I can only remember one incident which occurred in the Gulf of Sirte when the convoy was attacked by aircraft and RANCHI took a bomb in the vicinity of No. 2 hatch. It did not detonate, leaving the ship through the ship's side, but the impact started rivets. One of these killed the bosun, as he sat in the heads, adding one more name to add to P&O's long Roll of Honour.

He left RANCHI in 1947, and joined CARTHAGE at Alexander Stevens shipyard, in Linthouse on the Clyde, where she had been built originally, and where she was restored in a year for her peace time role for the UK/Hong Kong trade. He was originally due to retire in 1950 aged 60, but was asked to stay on for a further year. Compared to the Straths, the ship was quite small, but it suited him very well for his "run down" years. When later I was 4th Officer in CANTON, also in the UK/Hong Kong trade, we would pass each other at sea twice every three months. If the two ships passed in sight of each other I could send him a message by signal lamp. In addition to this, the staff of agents at the way ports were used to carrying messages.

He was also granted a free round trip to Hong Kong with my Mama as passengers, which was much enjoyed. He had certainly earned his MBE, an award which he greatly appreciated. On retirement my parents sold the big house in Horley and moved to Lymington.

Chapter 2. Schooling

My first recollections of school are from about 1935, when I was six. The family had moved from Richmond, Surrey to Witham, Essex, where Ena, a spinster from Chester-le-Street, joined us to do household chores and to be our nanny.

I was enrolled in the junior department of Colchester Royal Grammar School. As there was a door to door bus service available, I started as a dayboy, but soon became a weekly boarder. Later, when my family moved back to Surrey, this time to Horley, I spent a term as a boarder and enjoyed it. However, I did not appear to be learning very much.

I was therefore transferred to Wavertree Preparatory PNEU School in Horley. It was in fact just across the road from our house, but I became a boarder again. Not only did I enjoy being a boarder, but with my Pa away at sea my Mama found it a relief that my unruliness at home only had to be borne during the school holidays.

Wavertree School was quite small, catering for about 35 boys. It was run by a husband and wife team: Mr and Mrs Moore, both PNEU teachers, with Mr Moore a Latin scholar. Their teaching was excellent and I really began to make progress. I had made up my mind I wanted to join the Royal Navy and to attempt the Dartmouth entry examination on reaching 13½ years, i.e. in December 1942, and my parents approved. Both Mr and Mrs Moore took my target on board and steered me steadily in the right direction. At age eleven I was invited to translate Caesar's Gaul into English, a big step up from the exercises in the Latin text book. I enjoyed all the usual sports, without shining in any except for swimming.

Things started to change in the early summer of 1940, with the fall

Schooling

of France and the Battle of Britain. We watched the skies and witnessed many dogfights. Gatwick airport, located nearby and very small in those days, was taken over by the RAF and equipped with Spitfires, Hurricanes and transport aircraft. The old Gatwick Racecourse, which abutted the airport, was also taken over by the RAF as an extension and was equipped with damaged aircraft as decoys for the enemy bombers. The Moores decided to evacuate Wavertree and found a large empty house at Hele, just outside Taunton, and prepared to start there in September 1940.

My Mama became a volunteer ARP controller, working shifts in the local control room located in an arch of the road bridge at Horley station and switching the air raid siren on and off several times a day. At our house a local builder strengthened the ceiling just outside the cupboard under the stairs, to be our shelter.

The Battle of Britain was at its height during our summer school holidays in August and September. Both my friend Peter Stockman and I had "O" gauge railway sets, which we used to pool for a big track layout, using his parents' large garden, with a perfect lawn at the back of the house, next to Horley church. But I was also the proud owner of a real steam locomotive, which used methylated spirit as fuel, and took just a few minutes to produce live steam. One day the sirens had sounded "All Clear" for the second time, so we fired up the boiler, and squatted while awaiting results. We became aware of the sound of a low flying aircraft approaching, not an unusual sound so close to Gatwick, but on looking up we found it was a Heinkel bomber, badly damaged and descending to crash land. Its guns started firing (not at us), so we jumped into the Anderson shelter in the vegetable bed. The Heinkel was fired upon by Canadian troops in vehicles stopped on the A23 and crashed on the racecourse with a bang. All this excitement took a few minutes of course, and we emerged from the shelter to see my loco racing down the lawn and pulling four coaches. When the loco and rolling stock came off the track at a bend, the methylated spirit doused a dry lawn setting fire to it. All just part and parcel of being a junior railwayman, but the lawn looked very sad. Peter's father was a retired army colonel, recalled to work in the War Office, and he commuted daily. His return a bit later was to prove a lot more frightening than a crashing bomber. He dismissed as nonsense his wife's report about us being fired at by a Heinkel, and I was told never to bring my loco to his house again. Back to the clockwork locos.

During the winter of 1940/1, there were air raids nearly every night, targeted on London. Our cat and dog, and my sister and I slept in the cupboard under the stairs, whilst my Mama and Ena dozed in easy chairs just outside, trying not to listen to the droning of engines above us and the banging of AA guns. Horley was never a proper target, but occasionally was hit by jettisoned bombs. In 1941 the Stockman's empty house was practically flattened by a land mine behind the church, which lost all its glass, but left the stone building still standing.

Wavertree continued to operate well in Somerset and there were many schools around for sporting fixtures. In a soccer match against Taunton School, I actually managed to shoot a goal past the keeper, who turned out to be a son of Emperor Haile Selassie of Abyssinia. But in early 1942, when I reached 13, disaster struck when the Moore's only child, Desmond, fighting in the Army in North Africa, was killed in action. They were absolutely devastated, and it was soon apparent that their grief was badly affecting Wavertree's performance as a school. It was a critical time for me, the Dartmouth entry exam was only seven months away. My parents decided to move me at the end of the summer term, and in the middle of August I was sent to Babbacombe, Torquay, to join a crammer, run by the Skinners, who specialised in preparing fourteen and eighteen year olds for entry into the Royal Navy. Incidentally Dorney Skinner had been in the Royal Navy in WW1.

As August 1942 was a hot month, the authorities decided to re-open some of Torbay's beaches, closed in 1940 when invasion loomed. With their usual ineptitude, the UK Press showed pictures of beaches crammed with sun worshipping holidaymakers, duly noted

Schooling

by our enemy. A few days later the Luftwaffe appeared in the form of four ME 109 aircraft armed as fast fighter bombers, bombing the gasworks, and shooting up the area. One bomber was shot down on Torquay beach, but the others escaped back across the Channel to France. I had just arrived at Torquay station and was trying to find a scarce taxi, when two overflew the station, banging away with their cannons, before bombing Preston gasworks. Happily the station was built in Queen Victoria's time and could not be pierced by 20 mm cannon rounds, so I and many others were safe inside.

Dorney Skinner and his wife, who was fluent in French, took me in hand, arrested the decline, and crammed away, with some success. I sat the exam early in December and apparently produced very good papers, largely thanks to them. Unfortunately I failed the Admiralty Interview Board, so could not go to Dartmouth. Another young man I know failed Dartmouth at 14, and he too was sent to Pangbourne and entered the Royal Navy at 18. He later became an admiral, and Second Sea Lord, which demonstrates that the AIB was not chaired by the Almighty.

My parents decided I should attempt entry to Pangbourne and my Dartmouth papers were forwarded and accepted. My Mama took me to Pangbourne for an interview with Sir Philip Devitt, Chairman of the Board of Governors and one of the co-founders of the college ashore, after the family abandoned their fleet of sail training ships.

In his small office, only recently demolished to make room for the new ILLAWARRA Division, he was a lot more fun and human than the AIB in Whitehall. We chatted away for about 20 minutes, and then he told my Mama he would be delighted to accept me. Turning to me, he said, "If you are to be a sailor Penney, you must always keep your weather eye lifting". One of his eyes was what is known as lazy - by a quirk of nerves it could point all over the place. As he delivered his small homily, his eye shot straight up to the ceiling. I did not then fully understand his homily, but I thought the action of his lazy eye was perhaps a part. What a super interview.

Sea Officer

I joined the Nautical College, Pangbourne in February 1943, in the middle of the Spring Term, joining PORT JACKSON, the junior Division, and was placed in Form 4c. It was a very good experience. Looking back I have felt sad that I never got round to thanking my parents properly for this schooling. With taxation at a very high level, and my sister being privately educated as well, they made a big sacrifice to sponsor me. I cannot recall the level of Pangbourne's fees in 1943, but in 2007 they are £20,000 p.a. plus the cost of uniform.

Jock Lefevre, his distinct Scottish accent not matching his Channel Island name, was my guide for a few days to show me the ropes. He retained the accent throughout his long career in P&O, and even when captain of CANBERRA. All Pangbourne's divisions were named after the sail training ships, and in September 1943 I moved up to a senior division – MACQUARIE, and to Form 5c. The following June I sat the School Certificate examination, obtaining the five credits necessary to exempt me from Matriculation. I had intended to have another shot at the Royal Navy in the Special Entry at 18, but my Pa believed that with the end of the war approaching, I would be better off in P&O in peace time. Increasingly I was beginning to see myself as a maritime sea officer, comfortable with both the Navy and the Merchant Marine, so I took his advice and joined the Merchant Navy Form for my last two terms. I became a P&O apprentice at the end of March 1945, with a First Class Leaving Certificate. In my last term, I was promoted to Cadet Leader for the customary half term.

I believe it was the naval staff who shaped me into a responsible teenager ready for sea service at 16. They included the executive officer, retired Commander McIlwaine RN, who also taught navigation to a very high standard. The three instructors who reported to him were retired RN Chief Petty Officers, and were dressed as warrant officers at the college. They took charge of us for all the times we were not in classrooms with our academic teachers. The senior hand was "Gnarley" Bill Stamper, a seaman, whose face appeared to have been carved from mahogany. He was assisted by

Schooling

"Poppa" Henning, a slightly built PTI, and "Chas" Sewell who was a yeoman of signals and master at arms. The top button of his coat was never fastened because it had been stitched on in such a way that it could not be fastened. This was to remind all and sundry that he had fought at the battle of Jutland in WW1. They taught us Seamanship, Signals and Rule of the Road, Parade Training, Rugby, Hockey, Cricket, Running Cross Country, Boxing, Fencing, Swimming, Pulling and Sailing on the Thames.

There was also a full set of teachers for academic subjects, led by the Director of Studies, who also reported to the executive officer. The Chaplin, Sammy Shields, was a very likeable man, who was a Doctor of Science as well as Divinity. He had majored in Hydrostatics, and much preferred experiments with ship models on the large water tank to lecturing us about the evils of sex. "Robo" Robinson taught Mathematics with flair, and Bevis taught French until 1944 when he was called up as a major in the Army to become a Town Major across the Channel. "Rat" Davey, a diminutive Welshman, taught Physics and a year of his teaching in Form 5c not only prepared me for a sailor's life, but also for so many machines and electrical gadgets that we use in this modern world.

I participated in and enjoyed all of the sports and was in the Colts XV, but my real love was "messing about in boats" on the river. I learned to pull in the 8-oared gigs for racing and sailed in RNSA dinghies, X class, and a Montagu whaler. Our boats were all really past their shelf life, and replacements in the middle of a war were unobtainable, but the boatkeeper and Gnarley Bill kept them going. Subsequently I sailed all my life, believing it was part of being a blue water sailor. Beating up river in the whaler was quite an accomplishment because missing stays under the trees and tearing the mainsail meant the punishment of extra work. We also swam and took our lifesaving examinations in the river.

Founder's Day arrived in June 1943 and we all fell in by Divisions and Watches. Our inspecting officer's name was released only ten minutes before he arrived, and it turned out to be HM King George VI, accompanied by a teenager who is now our sovereign. It was a truly remarkable day, and its memory is enhanced by the skills of the Pangbourne photographer, who succeeded in capturing all eight watches of 30 cadets of the college, from both ends, so that nearly every cadet had a picture of himself in the company of his King. His Majesty also chatted to Pangbourne's staff, particularly Bill Stamper. They had been shipmates when HM was a lieutenant and Bill a young petty officer. Bill was completely overcome to be told that he had taught HM just about everything he knew.

But in 1943, not everything was good. Of course it was war time and food was strictly rationed, but the college's messing arrangements were dreadful. At a time when our strength was heavily taxed by continuous exercise we were just not fed enough. We never walked anywhere, we either marched or ran. For good measure there was a run and a cold shower before a miserable breakfast. Our meals were taken in the dining hall, with waitress service. Mary (known as Bloody Mary) was a Lancashire lass and in charge of the young girls recruited to wait on us. When a cadet rebelled at what was put before him, the girl slipped away to fetch Mary, who quickly appeared, breathing fire, and shouted her staff solution to the problem, "You've had your ration", and that was it. Some cadets received tuck parcels from home. Others like me visited Pangbourne's shops where, without a ration book, for 6d we could buy a small Hovis loaf and pot of Shippam's fish paste, devoured undercover in Pangbourne's woods.

In July 1943 and January 1944 I completed a two week course in the gunnery ship in London and the firing range in Shoeburyness, organised by the Royal Navy for Merchant Service officers, to learn how to use AA weapons. One of these turned out to be a new weapon designed by Churchill's own team of scientists, to shoot down Stuka dive bombers and later kamikaze aircraft. As it never went through RN gunnery tests, the Navy disowned it. It consisted of a small thin steel igloo-shaped hut which could be trained (turned) by foot pedals.

On either side was a rack holding 10 2 pound rockets, which were also laid (elevated) from inside. The crew consisted of three men, with the gunner imprisoned inside and two loaders outside under cover. A 300 knot gunsight was provided, but the rules of engagement provided that it could only be fired at an aircraft flying directly at the ship and not at aircraft crossing. This took into account the fact that many gunners in merchant ships were too inexperienced to get the aim-off right. At Shoeburyness I was allowed to fire off one rocket from each side. Whilst not fitted to the P&O ships to which I was appointed, this weapon was installed in a P&O Strath (there is a photograph). It was generally regarded as very dangerous for the gunner, especially if rockets did not fire. At the end of my course I was granted a certificate that states "This officer is capable of taking charge of the armament of a Defensively Equipped Merchant Ship". Amazing, as I was only 14.

In my last summer holidays, and badly in need of some funds, I found work with a team of foresters at Merstham, just North of Redhill, and cycled there daily from Horley. We worked on the estate of Sir Jeremiah Coleman, the mustard magnate, cutting down trees and clearing the land. The timber was all required for the war effort - great beeches for plywood for Mosquito aircraft, Douglas and silver firs used for telegraph poles and pit props, oaks and pines for general usage. The team consisted of two very experienced foresters, a reserved occupation which excluded them from joining the armed services, a young commando subaltern working on the land to recover from battle shock, and six Jehovah's witnesses, who were conscientious objectors. The pieces of equipment we used were all hand tools, there were no chain saws. The foresters had no time for the "conchies", but were very kind and helpful to the subaltern and to me, taking great pains to teach us the trade. I learned to use a 7lb felling axe and an 8' crosscut saw and how to use my body, not arms, to fell a great tree at one end of the saw. I was paid 5s 0d per day, but after a fortnight was sufficiently useful to join the piecework team, and earned a lot more. When a really big tree was ready to fell, the two foresters bet each other £5 (to me a huge sum) on the exact place the very top of the tree would finish up. We lesser mortals watched the exciting measurement exercise to determine the winner and it was always very close.

Sea Officer

My last night at Pangbourne came in March 1945, and that night we all behaved disgracefully, singing lewd sailor's songs. The next day I went home for 10 days leave. My Mama and sister were on their own, because Ena had been conscripted to staff a big NAAFI canteen. There she was paid a lot more than the 17s 6d, plus keep, that she earned in the family. She was a very nice person, and was soon married and settled down. I kept in touch with her for long afterwards.

Chapter 3. First Day in the Job

The journey to my new job really all started the previous evening, when I said goodbye to my sister, and my tearful Mama took me by train to London from Horley, Surrey. Encumbered by a large fibre suitcase containing all my kit and books required for six months, and equipped with a single ticket from Horley to Glasgow, we duly arrived at Euston Station in plenty of time for me to catch the 2000 overnight train, which at 1930 was already full. Along with many other young men and women, I crammed myself plus case into the corridor. Happily, on reaching Carlisle at about 0230, some seats became vacant, so the next four hours to Glasgow were more comfortable, and I did not mind a bit that the girl soldier in the next seat went to sleep with her head on my shoulder.

At Glasgow Central I met up with my Pangbourne classmate John Owen and his Pa, who came from Weston Super Mare. Owen Senior was concerned that we might be bored sitting around in a ship, (little did he know), and thoughtfully purchased a book for each of us. We walked with our kit to the P&O office in Bothwell Street, where we reported to Captain George Bridge, the P&O superintendent, who told us we were to join CORFU, currently berthed at a buoy in the Gareloch. This was great news, as security considerations had meant that we could not be told earlier to which ship we had been appointed - and mail from home had to be addressed to a ship. Further single tickets were issued from Glasgow to Gourock, and we joined a very slow train along the South bank of the Clyde. We then walked down to Gourock pier, where the sea transport officer examined our papers, and issued us with a pass for a Motor Fishing Vessel, saying that the MFV would appear in about an hour.

The time waiting enabled us to study the anchorage at the Tail of the Bank, which is where the Clyde widens opposite Greenock and Gourock, and which was packed full of every type of ship. Some had just arrived in a convoy, and were awaiting a berth up the river in Glasgow to discharge their cargo or undergo repairs, and others were waiting to join an outgoing convoy. The U boats had not been totally defeated, and there were some still active in the Firth of Clyde, including one reported to be lurking off Arran. There was a boom and gate across the river just downstream from Gourock at Cloch Point. John confided that he had not seen real ships before, apart from the White Funnel paddle steamers that plied the Bristol Channel, and he was absolutely amazed.

Jumping into the MFV at last, it seemed that we had to visit many of the ships anchored at the Tail of the Bank before entering the Gareloch, to arrive at last at CORFU's gangway, falling aboard at about 1500. Also boarding was an elderly gent in plain clothes, who immediately assisted John in lugging his portmanteau up the narrow gangway.

CORFU was one of six P&O "C" class ships built in the 1930s to service HMG's mail contract. She provided a fortnightly service from London to Yokohama, via all the other Empire posts en route. About 13,500 GRT (Gross Registered Tonnage) and with a service speed of 18 knots, she carried 190 first class passengers and 200 tourist class, served by a ship's company of about 240, and for this service carried about 6,000 tons of mail and cargo.

At the outbreak of war in 1939, all six of the ships (and many others) were taken up by the Admiralty and converted into Armed Merchant Cruisers. They were re-named HMS, and manned by the Royal Navy to protect merchant ships from German armed cruisers. They were equipped with (very ancient) 6 inch guns as the main armament, plus other smaller weapons for AA defence, which were almost totally ineffective until replaced by the 40 mm Bofors and 20 mm Oerlikons. She was not equipped with Asdic (Sonar) to detect submarines underwater, nor with the weapons with which to attack them.

20

First Day in the Job

The ships continued in this role until they were converted to ferry large numbers of troops from the UK to India after the Kreigsmarine's surface fleet had been beaten. The AMCs were therefore converted to troopers, lost their HMS, and were manned and managed for His Majesty's Government by their owners. CORFU was converted in Mobile, Alabama. All the cabins were double bunked for officers and NCOs, and the lower hold and tween decks fitted with pipe cots for the troops. A mess hall was created in a tween deck to complement the two dining saloons, and salt water showers installed. On a three week voyage to Bombay the capacity was limited to about 2,800 troops, but on a five day voyage from Rangoon to Singapore for the invasion of Malaya they carried about 3,200, which is surely where the term "sardine class" originated.

After arriving safely aboard the ship with our kit, John and I were escorted by the quartermaster to meet the chief officer, Gavin MacLean, in his office under the bridge. "He must be forty if he is a day" I thought, "and probably past it". I could not have got it more wrong - he was a ball of fire. The first thing asked of us was where we were from. On replying "Pangbourne, Sir" he replied "Thank God for that, we have two signalmen". He then set out in great detail what was expected of us, in regard to sea and harbour watches, taking sights daily at sea, day work on deck and in the boats, stations for entering and leaving harbour, attending the Captain's Church Service, our school course on board, keeping our cabin and our clothes clean, writing home each week - the list was endless and it seemed to add up to about 80 hours a week. We would start the next day at 0600 until 2359 daily, one of us always on watch for signals from the signal station on Gourock pier from where all the operational signals to the ship came, sent in the Morse code by signal lamp.

Thanks to Charlie Sewell, the Pangbourne yeoman, this was a doddle, even if the quartermaster from Stornoway on watch with us was not too good at "writing down". The last duty to be spelled out for us was to "look after" the Indian crew, comprising about 40 seamen (kalassis) from the West coast, and 40 firemen (agwallahs) from the NW Frontier. What on earth did he mean by "look after" I wondered - we were too inexperienced to be working bosses? It turned out to mean personnel welfare management etc, checking they got the right rations, clean blankets, assisting in disciplinary matters and checking their quarters for cleanliness.

"Have you got your Malim Sahib's Hindustani?" Gavin MacLean asked, referring to a paperback language primer costing 1 shilling and 3 pence, "Yes Sir" we replied, to be told that we had three months grace in which we might speak English to the crew, after which it must be in Hindi. Our Schoolie was Third Officer "Wong" Drysdale, whose Hindi syllabus started with English nursery rhymes, one which I still remember today. John would "look after" the seamen, leaving the firemen to me.

Storming out of his office, Gavin MacLean led us aft to meet our crews. I stood back whilst John was introduced to the deck serang, after which it was my turn to meet the firemen. Approaching the engine room serang he said "Salaams Serang" and pointing at me said "Penney Chota Sahib" (Chota = little/small). The Serang, a grave and thoughtful man old enough to be my grandfather, six feet tall in his sandals, dressed in denim trousers, jacket and cap, removed his cap and said "Salaam Chota Sahib". Whenever I recall this meeting, it is very humbling, summing up the Indian Empire in these three words.

After 24 hours of near trauma, at 1900 a transformation occurred, called dinner. In the First Class Saloon a Goanese steward served us four large and sustaining courses on a table with gleaming white table cloth and silver cutlery. This was repeated and copied at all our meals. It was a far cry from Pangbourne and ration books. There was yet another big surprise when John's porter from the gangway appeared and sat down to dine at another table, but this time he was in uniform as our master, Captain Charles Parker,

John and I explored our cabin, located under the bridge. It was 8' x 6', and contained upper and lower bunks, a wardrobe, small chest of drawers and desk, but no running water. We shared the junior officers' heads for fresh water basins and salt water baths, and laundered our clothes in a hand basin with bars of Sunlight soap. But this was almost heaven compared to the lot of a private soldier sleeping in a tier of pipe cots six high in no.2 lower hold!

After a week or so at the buoy in the Gareloch, we shifted berth to an anchorage at the Tail of the Bank. Next day our troops, about 2,800 of them, appeared with their baggage in a succession of tenders, and that night we weighed and proceeded, out through the gate in the boom, to join a number of other troopships forming into a well escorted 14 knot convoy in the Firth of Clyde. Our destination was Bombay. The convoy steamed West, round Malin Head in Ireland, then turning South after 300 miles of the Atlantic, and broke up after rounding Cape St. Vincent in SW Spain. We proceeded independently to Port Said in Egypt and the entrance to the Suez Canal. The convoy had been fully darkened at night, with urgent signals sent using a dim torch with a Morse key on it. Collisions in the convoy were only avoided by the extreme vigilance of the watch-keeping officers. After St. Vincent, and into the Mediterranean, we switched on our steaming lights at night.

At Port Said CORFU secured to buoys on the canal's West bank, taking on both fuel and fresh water whilst waiting to join the next southbound convoy. The first time out of the UK for both John and me, it all looked strange and attractive. When the chief officer pronounced that we might go ashore for an hour, we jumped at the chance, but he first cautioned us not to buy a watch from a street trader. There was no need for the caution as we had very little to spend. Once ashore a local in a robe and red fez approached us and said "Psst, Mister, want to buy a watch?" Looking back, he bore some resemblance to another trader from Egypt that we hear of in the UK most days. A great uncle perhaps? We politely declined. In a few moments he was back. "Mister, how about a nice jewel for your lady?" We did not have girlfriends, let alone ladies (nor much cash). He would not go away. "Mister, I get you a nice girl, guaranteed virgin". It was time to go back to our ship.

Sea Officer

As we steamed across the Indian Ocean to Bombay, there came VE Day and the war in Europe was at an end. Whilst families and homes were now safe, our young British soldiers knew that they were going to a nasty war in the Far East, which might go on for years.

At Bombay we berthed first at Ballard Pier, Bombay's passenger terminal, where the troop trains were drawn up to take them on to their barracks in India. Later we moved berth, locking in to Alexandria Dock, where we were to stay for a few days. All I can recall was the really terrible smell, not just Bombay and the heat of May, but the impounded water of the dock, into which all the ships berthed discharged their untreated sewage. After a few days we escaped back to sea, having embarked a few troops, and proceeded back to the UK, as an independent ship, and using our lights.

Chapter 4. The Invasion of Malaya

In South East Asia, Admiral Mountbatten's original plan was to remove the Japanese from Malaya in an operation codenamed Zipper. This used armed landings which involved moving thousands of troops and their equipment from India for what was expected to be an opposed assault at various points, including Port Dickson and Morib, not far from Kuala Lumpur. In the event, General Slim's brilliant Fourteenth Army routed three Japanese armies in Northern and Central Burma, then raced South to take Rangoon before the SW monsoon broke in July. As a result, the Japanese were forced to give up in SE Asia, although small pockets of their troops, with few rations and little ammunition, struggled to cross the Sittang river and escape into Thailand. They were left with few forces in Malaya. At a meeting in Rangoon between Mountbatten and Lieutenant General Count Teryauchi, the Japanese commander, a cease-fire in SE Asia was agreed, although the general could not guarantee that isolated units would surrender, in view of their individual oaths to their Emperor to die first. The assault forces went ahead on a reduced scale, meeting no serious opposition. In early August the USAF used nuclear bombs on Hiroshima and Nagasaki, and this really brought about the end of the war.

The scale of events taking place was way beyond the ken of a teenage apprentice. I have no personal notes or diaries, and cameras were forbidden, but I do have some sharp memories of what occurred in CORFU. On looking up the official records, they do not coincide with my memory, so I have not tried to put dates on events.

As a troop ship, CORFU was still quite heavily armed, particularly with close range AA weapons. The 6" guns for surface targets were gone, to be replaced with a 4" on the poop. The four dual purpose

3" guns were retained, to be supplemented with a Bofors 40/60 in each bridge wing, and eleven 20 mm Oerlikons in single gun pits on the Boat Deck. We carried a DEMS (Defensively Equipped Merchant Ship) contingent from the Royal Navy, led by a lieutenant, and about 20 ratings. Our own ship's company was used to bring the gun crews up to strength as loaders. On passage out from the UK, we had a practice shoot, which provided an impressive barrage. Our OC Troops offered to augment it with troops firing Bren guns from his armoury, but our gunnery officer was not impressed, believing the soldiery would knock bits off the ship before they struck the enemy.

In CORFU we sailed (from the Clyde again) in June carrying about 2,800 British troops to Bombay. After dropping them there, we soon left for Rangoon without troops and, rounding Sri Lanka, we again darkened ship at night. We zig-zagged at 18 knots in the Bay of Bengal, where Japanese submarines were still operating. The Royal Navy's last ship loss of WW2 was an Ocean Minesweeper, torpedoed off the Andamans at the end of July.

We spent two or three weeks in Rangoon swinging round a buoy. The city was badly damaged, but was the centre for British POWs released from Japanese camps on the railway, who needed a lot of attention from the 14th Army's medical teams. The misery ashore increased when the monsoon broke. There was a victory parade in Rangoon, and Merchant Service officers and men marched with the Armed Services. We had to wear our long white uniforms instead of shorts and shirts, and I will challenge anyone to get Rangoon's red mud out of white trousers and white shoes with Sunlight in a hand basin. The Navy wore black shoes and black gaiters!

Eventually Convoy Charlie formed off the river entrance. It consisted of about 40 ships in eight columns, a mixture of troop ships and cargo ships, which meant the convoy speed was 7 just knots. The port column was ordered to Penang, and the remainder to Singapore. CORFU joined the port column, and Captain Charles Parker asked to be last in the column, because CORFU steered like a bathtub at slow speeds. As far as we could see in the complete dark, so did the other troopers. There were some hair-raising near-collisions in the dark but apart from that the passage was uneventful. Off Phuket the port column hauled round to port, and proceeded to the anchorage off Georgetown, Penang.

We carried about 3,200 troops from the Indian Army, three infantry battalions from different parts of India, and their three quite different smells! It was hot and very humid in the troop decks, there was no air-conditioning, and the punkalouvres delivered hot wet air. I later learned that a human being generates about 40 watts of heat, equivalent to 128 kilowatts from all our 3,200 troops.

After a few hours at anchor, we were told that as there were no significant enemy forces around an infantry brigade was not needed in Penang or Butterworth. We were therefore to proceed to Singapore, led by HMS RACEHORSE, a destroyer, and followed by two cargo ships with military stores and transport. In the Malacca Strait there was a minefield, no swept channel had been marked or identified to us. We were to follow close astern of RACEHORSE. Having gained minesweeping experience later in life, I do not believe there was a swept channel. There was merely a route which the Royal Navy would use with live ships in the hope that nothing would happen. Mostly it seemed to work.

Halfway down the Strait there appeared a line of warships right ahead of us with destroyers leading two battleships: NELSON, wearing the flag of Vice Admiral "Hooky" Walker, and the French RICHELIEU. We passed very close, "port to port", and it was an exhilarating experience to be almost alongside such titans. About 20 minutes later, when they were below the horizon astern, there was a very loud bang, which we later learned was RICHELIEU setting off a ground mine. It did not sink her of course as she was too big and strong, but it did persuade Captain Parker to race to the voice-pipe to give minute by minute instructions to the quartermaster to keep dead astern of RACEHORSE.

At the time we were all busy with many things, but in later years I did start to wonder why two battleships were steaming North towards the Bay of Bengal, when fighting was still raging around the Japanese islands in the Pacific, and somehow I found out. It transpired that the Japanese military governor in Penang was a rear admiral in the Imperial Japanese Navy, reflecting the importance of Penang as a base for Japanese submarines, and a way port for U Boats en route to Tokyo. By now he had no fighting troops and only a few base staff, but he refused to surrender his personal self to an officer who was junior to a vice admiral, particularly since, after WW1 when he served as CO of a Japanese destroyer in the Dover Patrol, he had been awarded the Royal Navy's Distinguished Service Cross. It is always useful to have a spare vice admiral on hand for such occasions.

Eventually we arrived in good order to anchor in the old roadstead, just off the shoreline of the Maidan. This whole area is now part of the Singapore Port Authority's huge container yard. There were a few other ships anchored in the roadstead, including HMS BULOLO, the Royal Navy's command ship complete with CINC Far East, and from where our orders came. Landing craft soon appeared to take off our Indian Army guests, and BULOLO's first signal just read "Bake Bread". CORFU's small bakery was designed to cater for about 550 passengers and crew, but in the troopship role it coped by firstly being excused from providing exotic pastries, and secondly by working on a 24/7 basis, usually with army bakers supplementing the crew, but we still managed 24/7 with just our own crew. There was no shore leave and our troops were required for dealing with civilian unrest.

In Singapore the galley wireless told us that we were to take aboard a full load of released POWs and return to the UK. But there were no military POWs in Singapore, they were all up North on the railway. There were however about 600 civilian internees languishing in the old jail at Changi. This provided a full load for MONOWAI, a trans-Tasman ferry (owned by P&O) rigged up as an assault ship, and CORFU was ordered to return to Rangoon for the POWs.

I personally read the long signal from BULOLO that sent us on our way. In addition to general instructions, such as darken ship and zig zags, we at last were given full details of the so-called swept channel.

The Invasion of Malaya

This consisted of a complete list of alter course positions between Singapore and Rangoon, together with courses and distances between them, and covered two large pages of signal pad. It was difficult to read in Morse, being a jumbled collection of letters and numerals. But Charlie Sewell's training was so thorough even a 16 year old lad could read it. After all, we could read encrypted five letter/digit groups, get one character wrong and it would not decrypt.

I took the signal to 2nd Officer Eric Spurling, who took it straight to Captain Parker for approval, and then returned to the bridge, got out the charts and laid down all the courses. We weighed and proceeded along the track with some care and there were no nasty bangs.

Looking back over the years, it now seems incredible that my signal reading was never checked by an experienced officer for accuracy, it was assumed to be correct. The credit really goes to Charlie Sewell for his untiring work. There was so little public recognition for him that in 2005 I sought to commemorate him and his two naval instructor messmates, "Gnarley" Bill Stamper and "Poppa" Henning, by joining with 21 other Pangbourne classmates of 1945 and providing a silver bugle for Pangbourne's band, duly inscribed as the "Instructor's Bugle".

Chapter 5. The Happy Return

Back in Rangoon, we prepared to embark troops for home. Originally it was intended that all of them would be ex POWs. But when the 14th Army heard about this there was a near mutiny ashore, because so many of the soldiers were way past their demobilisation dates, and after three or more years in the Far East under extremely difficult conditions they were really desperate to get back to their homes. Vice Admiral Mountbatten, using his considerable charm, promised them that CORFU's embarkation would be 50 percent 14th Army, and 50 percent ex POWs, and this was seen as satisfactory. It was also a sad fact that so many of the POWs needed further hospitalisation, and CORFU's medical resources were pretty limited.

I think that all troopships carried a small permanent military staff. Ours consisted of a colonel, supported by an adjutant and medical officer, plus a few warrant officers and senior NCOs. The colonel was known as OC Troops, and he was just that, the CO of all troops on board. His staff made sure that all the troops were properly berthed and fed, and were responsible for their military discipline. The ship's chief officer was the troop officer, and he worked very closely with the OC Troops.

When our agreed 50/50 split of troops became known, Rangoon's sea transport officer issued instructions to the OC Troops that the two contingents should be berthed separately, so that the 14th Army could wait upon the POWs. This must rank as one of WW2's most stupid orders; the concept of one lot of soldiers trying to wait on another in the crowded confines of a troopship was idiotic to say the least. OC Troops totally ignored the order, and arranged for his staff to mix all the troops up as much as possible, because he believed that being close their own kind was the very best medicine for men completely debilitated by years in the camps. OC Troops got it right, and the POWs' shattered morale improved quickly.

The long horrible war was over, we sailed with all our deck lights on. The air was full of joy and relief, it was making the voyage more like a champagne party. CORFU carried four radio officers who for years had only been able to receive WT as their two Morse keys were padlocked. But now that the keys were unlocked, they were able to send personal message traffic to the families of those on board. It was usual in a troopship for all the soldiery - officers and men- to keep well clear of ship spaces such as the bridge, engine room, radio room etc, but things changed. On the bridge at 0300 there was Supernumary Second Officer Eric Rose, chatting up a couple of soldiers, and telling me to get them some tea and toast from the galley. In the radio room a young ex POW Royal Signals captain was sitting tapping away at a Morse key, exchanging technical chatter with the 4th Radio Officer, and healing himself almost visibly in the process.

Once clear of the Bay of Bengal, it became apparent that we were racing MONOWAI to be the first home, but neither ship knew which UK port was their destination - it was "Lands End for Orders", the standard voyage instruction before a specific port had been decided upon. Captain Parker became enthused with the race, and broadcast daily what he thought were our two positions. It turned out that both ships shared the same Northbound convoy in the Suez Canal, so from Port Said onwards the heat was really on. The race would be won by the first ship to berth alongside in the UK. I noticed from the bridge propeller shaft tachometers that we were making a lot more revolutions than Chief had previously said were possible, and wondered why the daily fuel consumption was so high?

About halfway across the Bay of Biscay, our destination ports were revealed - CORFU to Southampton, MONOWAI to Liverpool. It was really good news for us that the Southern UK ports were open for business at last, having been closed for five years whilst there was any chance of receiving a visit from the Luftwaffe. Most people lived in the South, and it meant that we would no longer have to spend all night standing in the corridor of a train when travelling to and from our homes for a few days leave.

Turning to the race, we appeared to be neck and neck, and the distances to Southampton and Liverpool were not much different. However someone thought to consult the Tide Table. CORFU could berth in Southampton's New Docks at any state of the tide, whereas MONOWA could only lock in from the Mersey to Liverpool's docks on the last of the flood. Steaming up Southampton Water with everyone in a euphoric mood, Captain Parker announced that we had won the race, adding much to the general mood on board.

Most docks were still working to war-time security rules and there were very few on the quay to welcome us except Army teams to assist with the disembarkation. At the back of the quay shed, there were lines of Army vehicles lined up to take everyone to transit camps on Salisbury Plain, where they could be issued with the required paperwork, identity documents, ration books and other necessities plus uniform items suitable for the UK in autumn. For many there would be a demob suit.

As the vehicles trundled away out of the docks and reached the streets of Southampton they met the real welcoming party, which included most of the population of Southampton and beyond, who cheered them like mad, and bombarded them with flowers, a very proper heroes' welcome.

Later that Sunday evening, when the ship was quiet again, my cabin mate Alan Bennett and I decided to have a short run ashore, in search of a pint. As we crossed the Boat Deck, we noticed Captain Parker, leaning over the rail on his deck above. "Are you lads going to church then?" asked our captain. "Yes Sir" we replied, lying through our teeth. "I expect that will be the one where the prayer books have handles" said the captain, grinning broadly. It was proper that a Happy Return should be conducted by a Happy Captain.

Chapter 6. Indentures completed

At the end of our first voyage together, my friend John Owen left CORFU and was transferred to her sister ship CHITRAL. We had been two very junior cadets together, and P&O preferred one senior cadet on board. CHITRAL was converted in Bombay to carry small landing craft in her davits in place of lifeboats, and joined the invasion convoy to the Morib beachhead. This was the beachhead that turned out to have serious mud beneath a thin layer of sand, and most of the vehicles sank into it and were lost. Fortunately the landing was virtually unopposed. In CORFU I was joined by Alan Bennett, in his third year as cadet.

I made one more trooping voyage in CORFU, and early in 1946 was transferred to her exact sister ship CARTHAGE, spending the best part of the year trooping in the Far East in her. Whilst the war was over, there were still thousands of British troops to be moved out or home, but we also carried Indian troops back to India from the Mediterranean, Italian POWs back from India to Italy, and took Indian troops to Mombasa in Kenya. It was mostly very routine seafaring, with nothing of the excitement of being in convoy and at war.

One incident did raise a few hairs. Returning to Karachi with Indian troops, we berthed to much acclaim from the local people and a large military band playing on the quay. We sailed next day for Bombay, and the following day the Indian Naval mutiny took place at the same quay, with shots being exchanged and quite a lot of blood spilt. This was in the lead-up to the creation of India and Pakistan as two separate independent countries, and tensions were running high.

However I spent a lot of time improving my seaman's skills. At sea I stood two watches each of four hours every day with either the supernumary second officer or the third officer, and learned how to use my eyes. At Stations for Entering/Leaving Harbour, I was either on the bridge, or with an officer on the foc'sle or aft with the mooring parties. At sea each morning at about 0830 I had to take a sun sight and another at noon, to fix the noon position, and slowly I started getting it right. Off a coast I learned to fix the position on the chart required every 30 minutes or less by taking bearings of 2 or more fixed objects ashore. In addition to this, I spent about three hours a day (except Sunday, Captain's Church Service) on doing manual work, cleaning, painting or checking the lifeboat equipment, stores and fresh water. CORFU had 10 lifeboats and a collection of large life-saving rafts to cope with troop numbers and these all had to be checked on a regular basis. On Saturday mornings at sea the captain inspected crew quarters, so I had to ensure beforehand with the serang that they were up to scratch, for if they were not, I was the first to be blasted. In the dog watches between 1600 and 2000 each day it was school again, writing up my apprentice's journal, completing the correspondence course provided by P&O, or a tutorial with the third officer.

One night while I was deeply asleep in CORFU about 0200, I got a shake from the quartermaster, telling me I was to get dressed in uniform and report to the chief officer in his office without delay. When I arrived I found Gavin MacLean sitting behind his desk together with Chief Engineer Charles Maybe. Standing to one side was the engine room serang with one of his pani wallahs (water-men) sporting a shocking black eye. On the other side stood a fourth engineer. Gavin MacLean had his Official Log open on his desk in front of him, so this looked like a discipline job. Arriving I was told to stand next to the pani wallah and proceedings commenced.

It transpired that the pani wallah had entered the boiler room singing quietly to himself, in a high falsetto voice as typical Pathans are wont to do. What he sang was "Humara baldi kitha hi" which translates as "Oh where is my bucket?" The fourth engineer was from the Merchant Navy Pool, not a company Sahib, so could not be expected to understand Hindi. But he was a Geordie, and had succeeded in reaching his 26th birthday without a hair on his head. He thought he was being insulted when he heard the word "baldi"

Indentures completed

and decided to strike first and talk later. In punishment his name was entered in the Official Log and he was fined a day's pay. The meeting broke up and I went back to my bunk.

Thinking about it later I was a bit miffed to have had to lose valuable sleep for something I did not have to take part in. On watch with the third officer the next morning I recounted the proceedings and expressed my concern. "Wong" Drysdale just said that it was a lesson in the administration of discipline from which I should learn. Later I realised it was just a case of the P&O system which took its Indenture obligation to teach me the business very seriously.

Of course I had Indenture obligations too. One of these was not "to frequent taverns, alehouses and houses of ill repute". I often mulled over these words and particularly "frequent". Presumably it meant that the odd one-off visit was allowed and perhaps an elderly lawyer drafting the indenture remembered his young tearaway days. In CARTHAGE the chief officer allowed us to buy the odd bottle of beer at age 17 and on reaching 18 we were allowed a daily beer purchase provided we could pay for it.

Despite not being paid much we were really not badly off. P&O provided our board and lodging. Whilst the lodging was a bit claustrophobic, the board was extremely good. During the war we were issued with cigarettes and afterwards we could buy them cheaply duty free. Uniform clothing was expensive but my Pa paid for my initial outfit, including a shore-going suit.

In Bombay the tailors offered tropical clothing at half the price of London, and very good it was too. At the end of our Indenture we had to provide for ourselves ashore in London for three months whilst at the 2nd Mates' school so savings were necessary.

Pay under the Indenture consisted of £2 per month for the first year, £3 for the second, and £4 for the third. From this, 1s 6d per month was deducted and paid over to a Seamen's Friendly Society. This was to provide sailors with a small pension in their old age but was overtaken in the late 1940s by the National Insurance Fund as a result of the Beveridge Report. (Much later the DWP agreed my

NIC contributions ran unbroken from 1945.) In addition, I was paid War Risk Money as were all seafarers, £5 per month for the first year, £10 per month thereafter and this could be drawn as earned in the ship.

The worst aspect of my first two years was the total absence of any recreational or social life. If there were no soldiers on the Boat Deck, playing deck quoits was possible but rather tame. My great love of sailing had to be restricted to the ship's boats which were dreadful sailers but I did achieve my Lifeboatman's Certificate, a professional requirement. There were no girls, parties, dances or beach picnics, because all the Far East was recovering from the War. There were no British people established ashore to invite us to dinner. Occasionally there was a film to watch, either on deck or ashore, but life was otherwise all work. Leave at home was infrequent and short. I did have a very nice girlfriend, Anne Wall, a friend of my sister's who lived down the road in Horley. We enjoyed ourselves as best we could but life was austere with food and clothing rationed. The Horley cinema was still operating, but Great Britain was virtually bankrupt and everyone was engaged in making something which, if it was not nailed down, was exported to achieve export earnings. My next voyage was to last for five months during which time Anne attracted other admirers, which was hardly surprising. But my social life was about to change.

In the New Year of 1947 I left CARTHAGE and joined PARINGA. It was a bitterly cold winter not helped by a serious shortage of coal and gas and frequent power cuts. Many of PARINGA's tank sounding pipes were frozen solid and there was difficulty in determining how much fresh water was on board.

PARINGA had started her life in 1936 as ESSEX part of the New Zealand Shipping Company's fleet and all part of the P&O Group. She was a refrigerated cargo ship for the trade to Australia and New Zealand and carried no passengers. She was powered by two Doxford diesel engines that gave her 16 knots and was manned by an all British crew berthed amidships. In volumetric terms she was about the same size as CARTHAGE but her GRT was less since the uppermost cargo deck, known as the Shelter Deck, was not

Indentures completed

refrigerated and was excluded from the GRT. This gave a saving on various sorts of dues. She had six hatches, each with lower hold, lower and upper tween decks and shelter deck. She survived WW2, but only just. As part of a fast convoy carrying many items required in besieged Malta, which she reached well enough, she took a bomb straight down the funnel when in Valetta.

I was no longer a Chota Sahib and needed no Hindi, since I was just an extra pair of hands on deck along with three other apprentices. We were usually up to our eyes in muck. There was no dinner at 1900 in a four star saloon, it was high tea in the greasy spoon caff at 1800 at sea, 1700 in harbour. The fare was generally terrible, and portions often ran out.

But I did learn a lot about old fashioned break-bulk cargo work and not just how to stow it, but also what it consisted of, where it came from and where it was going to. This became an interest that has endured all my life. Basically, we carried a great mixture of UK goods to Australasia to create revenue to pay off the country's debts and returned with foodstuffs to feed the population and wool and hides to clothe it.

Captain Cyril Pollitt was in command and it turned out to be his last cargo ship command before moving on to passenger ships. He was tough, but fair. John Kerridge was chief officer and sometimes referred to by the crew as a "Bucko Mate", which he needed to be with the crew we had. Wally Eade was 2nd officer and cargo officer. He had just finished six years in the Royal Navy as an RNR submariner in command where his moment of glory was that he had succeeded in relieving a U boat captain, who surrendered to him, of his superb Plath sextant and Zeiss binoculars. Gordon Blythe, son of Douglas Blythe in the London office, was 3rd officer. My cabin mate was Derrick Bolas, who became a great friend, and Roger Game. a Pangbourne class-mate and ex Chief of the College, was another shipmate.

We had a large number of engineers, headed by Chief Harry Roper, and three refrigerating engineers. Apart from our Bosun, Mitch, and his brother who were both excellent, the rest of our crew were

Sea Officer

from the Merchant Navy Pool and were a rough and unruly lot. The seamen and stewards were mostly Londoners, the greasers were Northern Irish except for their PO Donkeyman, Mr Pepper, who was a cockney. We sailed from London and about four weeks later reached Fremantle in West Australia, which was our first discharge port, travelling via Marseille and Suez without incident. We were allowed ashore in the evening, and two of us went to a dance hall in Fremantle to sample the delights of Australia. It did not go well for me. I found a partner and after dancing her around the hall once she said "You can't dance you old bastard, can you?", which was disconcerting to say the least and I gave up.

Much more serious was the fact that nearly all the crew got roaring drunk that night. Another cadet witnessed two of our Glasgow Irish greasers, both of them blind drunk, assaulting Mr Pepper and holding him out at the top of the engine room, threatening to drop him all the way down to the bottom plates. Worse still, they were encouraged by two ladies of the town. The cadet ran off to fetch the chief officer but the combatants had moved away. They did not drop him thank heavens but they beat him up most severely and the scars were still showing three months later. But Mr Pepper did not forget the incident.

From Fremantle we sailed round the coast to Adelaide, Melbourne and Sydney where we completed discharge. The Australian wharfies worked very slowly, and our port stays were quite long. In Melbourne and Sydney the cadets had family contacts ashore, and we began to learn about the generous hospitality that seems second nature to so many Australians. There were parties, car trips, dances and beach picnics. It was all marvellous and made up for the hardships of PARINGA and the lack of a social life in previous ships. I remember my first steak - it extended over the edge of the plate at both ends.

At Sydney we learned we were to load a full cargo in Auckland so we crossed the Tasman Sea. Loading took five whole weeks and Kiwi hospitality was fully up to Australian standards. There was no cargo work on Saturday afternoons or Sundays and we made friends with a lot of Kiwis of our own age group and had a great deal of

Indentures completed

fun. I was beginning to catch up on all those lost teenage years.
After five weeks the ship was absolutely full of butter and
telescoped lamb carcasses, scoured and greasy wool, plus strongly
smelling hides.   Two cadets worked with the refrigerating
engineers, checking the temperatures of incoming cargo, and
rejecting it if they were too high. Our reward was to be allowed to
store our food purchases for home in their icy-cold evaporator
room. On the weather deck bales of greasy wool were loaded 6'
high on to the hatches and secured with tarpaulins and lashings.

The Auckland dockers had a similar work speed to their Australian
cousins but a different system. Gangs were arranged in two halves,
with each half working for one hour followed by an hour off.
Daywork was from 0800 to 1200 and 1300 to 1700. If overtime
was required by the ship, there was a shift from 1800 to 2100 but
for dock workers it was voluntary and no work was possible unless
gangs were at full strength. Overtime gangs were often short
handed. Here right under our feet was the answer to the financial
strains of lots of partying. We could carry out our normal ship work
from 0800 to 1700, have high tea, and work from 1800 to about
1920 as a docker. We were paid immediately for three hours work
in cash and so could be cleaned up and ashore by 2000. Three
hours at the overtime rate was quite a lot of money. What a deal.

We sailed for home via the Panama Canal and Curacao for bunkers.
The trans-Pacific leg took three weeks and we settled down to
watch keeping, checking the temperatures of every refrigerated
compartment every four hours, and to ship maintenance. Like her
sister ships, PARINGA had huge areas of wood in her
compartments and insulated hatch covers. These were frequently
damaged by boisterous dock workers and needed a lot of
maintenance. Our Chippy, James, was always busy and quite often
two cadets were allocated to assist him. One day after days at sea
Derrick and I were in the Chippy's shop, receiving instructions.
Derrick, who was not very tall, had taken about 6' of 4 x 4".for a
job and it was over his shoulder when into the shop came a very
large AB, who was not a very nice character, and who walked
towards Derrick.   There was something odd about the AB's
appearance - predatory perhaps - that looked wrong. Derrick was

wide awake, and turned his body slowly, clocking the AB's head with the 4 x 4". Not hard, or hurriedly, just enough to rattle his teeth, followed by "Oops, so sorry". He turned and left without delay.

Rounding Ushant on our voyage home we received instructions to discharge first at Hull, completing in London, where we would pay off the crew. At Hull it took only a week to remove 80 per cent of our cargo and we moved to London where we completed discharge and with great relief paid off. . We started loading a general cargo for Australia again and a new crew signed on. A couple of days before sailing, we had a visit from two plain clothes officers who asked for assistance with their inquiries. They were investigating a very serious assault on a Glasgow Irish man by then in hospital at East Ham who had just regained consciousness after ten days, and had been able to give his name and employment details. We recognised the name of course but could not help them, even if the galley wireless did report that he had met up with a few of Mr Pepper's friends from Bermondsey soon after he had left the ship.

PARINGA made another voyage to Australia, on this occasion loading homeward in Australia for London. One particular joy for me was an outward call at Brisbane where we completed discharge. Brisbane was the home of the Butt family - Uncle Ray, Aunt Elsie, and my cousins Ron, Maurice and Brenda, all about my own age. In WW1 Ray, trainee accountant, joined the Australian Army and went to fight in the trenches in France. He survived and on an R&R visit to London met my Mama's sister Elsie, who was working voluntarily in a club in Richmond for the armed services. They kept in touch. When he was properly established in Brisbane, he asked her to marry him so she booked a passage to Brisbane and tied the knot. Ray, just about the kindest man I have ever met, had lots of things organised for me to do. The family had a large old American Ford which was comfortable with six passengers up. I saw a lot of Brisbane and its surrounds and caught small crabs on the beach in Moreton Bay which we cooked and ate. They certainly were determined to make me welcome and succeeded completely.

We started our loading homeward in Townsville, berthed at a long pier on to which the trains from Mount Isa, 400 miles inland, could move. The trains brought two thousand tons of lead ingots, ideal for our bottom cargo. PARINGA, like most ships of that era, had poor stability characteristics and so lead was most welcome. It was followed by frozen beef, consisting of huge hinds wrapped in gunny. Temperature control was a nightmare in hot and humid Townsville. Get it too cold in the holds and the dockers refused to work. Get it too warm and our refrigerating engineers would go berserk.

Townsville's dockers were even more unfriendly than in other ports. They made it very clear that they would not let their daughters go out with "pommy bastards from the meat boat". It was not quite like that however. John Kerridge sent for me and sitting in his cabin was the Chaplin of the local Missions to Seamen. John informed me that, with another cadet, I was to attend a party at the Mission that evening (no point in trying to argue with our chief officer). Oh dear, I thought, this will be tea and small cakes, hymns, prayers and Bible readings. I was totally wrong. It was a trip in a launch to Magnetic Island, with girls, beer, portable gramophone, dancing on the beach and swimming, all conducted by the Chaplin. The Mission had enlisted my support for the rest of my life. We went on to load more meat at Gladstone, even smaller than Townsville, and then Sydney, Melbourne, Adelaide and Fremantle, before heading home via Suez.

Our new crew were a considerable improvement on their predecessors. When working on deck, Bosun Mitch always liked to separate us so that we worked with an AB, not a fellow cadet. There was one AB I particularly liked. He was a cockney from Bow and I believe he only shipped as an AB when the Met were getting too close because he preferred to be a barrow boy (without a licence). Whilst he enjoyed fleecing the general public on London's streets, he was intensely loyal to his shipmates and they could do no wrong. While painting PARINGA's long steel decks, he would instruct me in his modus operandi, drawing with his paintbrush streets and crossroads, positioning the barrow, and avoiding the coppers.

Sea Officer

Returning to London early in 1948, Derrick, Roger Game and I left to sit the Second Mates examination. For this we attended the Sir John Cass School in the Commercial Road. There were many young men doing the same thing, Great Britain was rebuilding its merchant fleet as fast as it could, and desperately needed young officers. The Merchant Service casualty rate in WW2 had been horrendous and on a percentage basis was much higher than all three armed services. The sea service required for Second Mates had been reduced from four years to three, and the minimum age from 20 to 19. (My Pangbourne Leaving Certificate was considered as the equivalent of one year's sea service.)

With our homes not in London, we had to have local accommodation, at least during the week. All the cabins in the School were occupied so we crossed the road to the four storey Sailors' Home. There we got individual cabins without facilities and on each floor there was a heads and washbasins block. Methylated spirits was the cheap tipple for alcoholics and the stench of it once it had passed through a human body was horrible. On the other hand, the School had a very good and cheap cafeteria for our meals.

The East End of London was a pretty rough place, which was confirmed by my cousin Wharton, who was a fourth year medical student just down the road at the London Hospital in Whitechapel. At Wapping on the river there was an excellent pub - The Prospect of Whitby - but to go there you needed quite a few mates and doctors to form a convoy for a visit and we certainly could not go alone.

The school coached us very well for our examination in both the written papers and the much dreaded oral Seamanship examination. The examiners and their foibles were well known to our tutors. There was one who opened proceedings by flinging some rope at a candidate as he came through the door. The staff solution to this gambit was to grab the rope and turn up one end on the door handle. In the world of sailing ships and many ropes, loose ends were not tolerated and must be made fast immediately.

Indentures completed

In the week after my 19th birthday, we both passed the examination, and were given a chit to confirm it. Our copperplate certificates would follow in the post. My oral was conducted by Captain Wallace, a large man in his forties sitting behind his huge desk on which stood a small fleet of models with different arrangements of lights. It all went fairly well until I hesitated in my answer to a "How is she heading?" when he banged hard on his desk with both fists making all the models jump up and down. The question required two dimensional mental arithmetic, and was all in points and quarter points of the compass. "You are heading NE ¼ N, the wind is SW, you see the red of a sailing ship 6 points on your starboard bow, how is she heading?" But after an hour and ten minutes he passed me. If it had gone on for an hour and a half I would probably have failed. If it had lasted for two hours I would have been sent back to sea for six months. He really was quite a bully.

Years later, when I was an experienced 2nd officer, he visited my ship to examine about 20 Goanese stewards I had trained as lifeboatmen. Afterwards I invited him for a drink and lunch. He said he did not remember me from the 2nd Mates' examination, which was hardly surprising given the numbers of candidates he dealt with every week. After a glass of gin I asked him why he found it necessary to put the fear of God into candidates. He was quite unabashed and he said it was intentional. He was required to spend about an hour with a young man he had never seen before, and in that time to decide whether he was fit to be on his own in charge of a ship in the middle of the night. If he crumpled in the examination room, he would probably go to pieces when shouted at by a bad tempered Master appearing on the bridge in his pyjamas. I think it was fair comment.

Chapter 7. P&O Matey

Having obtained a 2nd Mate's Certificate, the next thing was to race to P&O's office in Leadenhall Street and apply to join as 4th Officer. Speed was of the essence so as to get my name on the seniority list before others. Derrick Bolas, whose name began with a B, had been examined and passed the day before me. The seniority list was the basis of all future promotion, usually known as "Dead Man's Shoes". Many officers had joined it as the most junior 4th Officer and left as Commodore. I attended the Officers' department, and was received by B W Turner, its head, and his colleague G Copeland, who signed me up without delay. I was now a P&O Matey. This slang word covered every rank from 4th Officer to Chief Officer, all of whom were "Masters' Mates", a term that had been around for a few hundred years. I was told that a sea appointment would shortly be sent to me and given a chit to take to the purser's cash department, which ran the sea staff payroll. They took down all my details and, knowing full well that new 4th Officers were penniless, immediately offered me an advance on my monthly wage of £29 2s 6d.

Before anything else, there were social obligations to enjoy as my life had reached another step on the ladder. Whilst we had been at school it was possible for Roger Game and me to spend the weekends in our homes, but Derrick's home was at Churston Ferrers, in Torbay, where his parents owned and managed The Dormie House Hotel. It was too far away and expensive to reach. for a weekend. To escape from the Sailors' Home, Derrick often spent weekends with either Roger or me. The Bolases were out-going and hospitable and invited both Roger and me to spend a few days with them to return our hospitality. Derrick and his sister Diana organised several lively parties with their circle of friends, and we had a great time. One of Diana's friends was Bunty Riley (known as Bunny by her friends in earlier years), the middle of three daughters of Bill and Irene Riley, Yorkshire folk who had moved to Torbay in the 1920s to enter the hotel business. In WW1 Bill had joined the Yorkshire Regiment, had fought on the Somme, and had been badly gassed. The effects of the gas were to last a lifetime but it did not stop him having a successful career and he lived until he was in his 80s. The top hotel that he and his wife had built up in Torquay, the Astwell Hall, was requisitioned in WW2 and not returned to them in 1945. He managed to acquire the Park Hotel on the front in Paignton, which had just been released as an RAF billet and was in a mess, but he started from scratch again. Bunty (known to her friends as Bunny in her earlier years) and I took a shine to each other and started to correspond regularly and to meet when we could.

On returning home, there was a letter appointing me to P&O CANTON. She was the newest of the C Class and slightly larger than her sisters. She had been fully restored to carry both first and tourist class passengers, plus mail and cargo, and was deployed, with CORFU and CARTHAGE, on a four weekly service from London to Hong Kong. My uniform wardrobe was the worse for wear after a year in PARINGA, and I needed a great deal of clothing for a peace time passenger ship, so headed towards naval outfitters S W Silver & Co in the City. The least I could order was a new blue uniform, plus cap and shoes, a mess undress - jacket, waistcoat and trousers - four long white uniform suits, plus shoes, white mess jackets and cummerbund, and last but not least, a lounge suit. Silvers produced it all in about a week, and the bill was about £120. Not having any cash, Silvers invited me to make a standing order to them, and when I asked if an amount of £5 per month was acceptable, they were well pleased. It seems incredible today, but in the 40s it was the usual practice, besides which P&O Mateys were very credit worthy.

I joined CANTON in London's Royal Albert Dock, and spent three voyages in her. She ran very well, and the voyages were without major incident. Malaya and Hong Kong were still British Colonies, and nearly all the expatriate staff from the UK travelled to and from their posts by sea, regardless of the beginning of jet flights by Comet aircraft. The expatriates ranged from senior officers from the three Services through many officials employed by the Colonial Office, such as police, postmasters, district officers, marine and civil aviation officials, to the senior UK staff in the large trading houses. Our customers were from the great and the good, and it was usual to have an HE aboard with his lady. There was still a lot of mail that went by sea since airmail letters were expensive and the diplomatic mail could only be handled personally by a ship's officer. Outward cargoes reflected the growth of the UK's manufacturing capability and there were cars both belonging to passengers on board, and for sale through local dealers. Other commodities included bagged sugar, together with high value cargo such as banknotes and coins stowed in the bullion room. Homeward cargoes were agricultural products, tea, stem ginger and cotton piece goods from Hong Kong. From Malaya came rubber, latex, palm oil, tin ingots and tropical hardwoods, with pepper, spice and sago flour from the East Indies transhipped to us in Singapore. From Colombo there were large chests of Broken Orange Pekoe tea.

Whilst it did not affect the ship, while we were in Malaya there was an emergency caused by communists in the countryside seeking to take over the country and terrorising villagers. They were beaten by the High Commissioner for Malaya, Malcolm MacDonald, and General Templar, the GOC Land Forces, who managed to concentrate the agricultural community into large villages where they could be protected. Whilst this was in progress there were quite a few bangs as trains were blown up. During a 24 hour call at Penang I was invited with the 3rd Officer and a couple of our passengers to a typical noisy Straits party at the bungalow of the postmaster. Amongst other guests, we joined five young British police officers from Butterworth just across the water.

At about 2340 one of them addressed his team saying they must leave to catch the last ferry back to Butterworth. They went first to another room to collect their kit. They emerged to say goodbye all armed to the teeth with sten guns, hand guns, and lots of ammunition. We sailed next morning via the South Channel and as we cleared the channel our pilot pointed to a Penang beach on our starboard quarter on which a few people could be seen lazing around. I was told that this was a communist R&R centre but that they never bore arms in Penang. The beach is now part of a large holiday resort development.

The captain was Geoffrey Stable, his chief officer was Tommy Tucker, and his 2nd officer and cargo officer was Eric Waghorn. In three voyages we had three supernumary 2nd Officers. I only remember one, Terence Healey, who had spent WW2 as an RNR submariner. He was the younger brother of Dennis Healey, the Labour Minister, who came aboard in London to visit having just been demobilised from the Army, and taken up his seat in Parliament.

At sea I was on watch with the 2nd Officer. The captain stuck strictly to the rules and I was not allowed to be on my own on the bridge for one second. At Harbour Stations I was also on the bridge, working the engine room telegraphs and keeping the log, minute by minute. But it was a good place from which to watch how the ship was handled by the pilots, for I was intent on learning how to do it. I was particularly impressed by the Singapore pilots when they berthed CANTON in Keppel Harbour stern to tide to save time in not turning round. It was quite contrary to my text books, and the ship's twin geared steam turbines were not the most flexible of power units. They did it very well, and later I copied their technique with success to the astonishment of an examiner from the Royal Navy.

On short leave between voyages I was able to meet up with Bunty again but she also appeared alongside CANTON in a local Torbay launch to wave to me when we made a brief call homeward on our way to London to embark colleagues from the passenger and purser's cash departments and our Thames inward pilot. At least she was learning to be a sailor. We were spending more and more time together when I was in the UK, and it was not long before we became engaged. Quite contrary to the usual parental expressions on such an occasion my Mama told me that Bunty was much too good for me whilst Irene Riley told her daughter that I was much too good for her, so naturally all was well.

Sea Officer

In 1949 I was promoted 3rd Officer, and appointed to P&O KARMALA, a cargo ship employed in the trade from the UK and the Mediterranean to Colombo and the Bay of Bengal. She had been built in the USA in only 60 days as a standard Victory ship and named SHEEPSHEAD BAY VICTORY. The Victory ships were the successors to the Liberty ships, mass produced by the Kaiser family for the war effort. They were very good dry cargo ships for their time, with first class cargo spaces and gear, and their single steam turbine gave them 16 knots. Their main drawback was that they were very hot in the tropics. In the accommodation areas all the doors and furniture were made of steel and there was no wood to provide insulation in sight. P&O had just purchased KARMALA when she was no longer required by the USA.

I made two round voyages to Calcutta and back, with many intermediate ports of call. Outward, the cargo was the usual mixture of manufactured goods from the UK, Northwest Europe, Marseille and Genoa. Homeward, our cargoes were mainly agricultural products, especially jute, and vegetable oil in our deep tanks. The voyages were uneventful, but there was much for a sea officer to learn.

My captain was Reggie Cowell, an outstanding sea officer, later to become P&O Marine Director. He was also a Captain RNR, with his last appointment being Captain MCM for Eastern Scotland, responsible for several minesweeping squadrons sweeping the whole coast. Returning to P&O he had to rejoin as chief officer but soon returned to command. His chief officer was "Daddy" Woodroe, and a wild Irishman, Fergus Kell was 2nd officer and cargo officer. He too had served in the RNR in WW2 but a FLOWER class corvette made him so sick he arranged shore appointments. One of these was in newly liberated Antwerp where he became a sea transport officer. As the traffic through Antwerp increased, so did his staff including a party of Wrens. One of his tasks was to find billets for the girls. He found a barracks for the ratings, and the empty second floor of a small hotel for their WRNS officers. The ground and first floors were in use as the hotel and the patronne looked after her naval guests very well. All went well until visiting top brass learned that the hotel was in fact a brothel. There was hell to pay and the WRNS officers had to move to another billet.

Reg Cowell always made it clear that he trusted his officers from the start. As 3rd Officer I was the junior watch keeper and in charge of the watch for eight hours a day. Our first passage was from London to Hamburg via the NEMEDRI swept channels with quite a few separate legs. Dropping our pilot at the Sunk Light Vessel at about 2000 I took over the bridge as watch keeper for the very first time. Reg spent 20 minutes or so with me, ensuring I had checked the chart and knew where to go, then left the bridge, not to return in my watch. This was a refreshing contrast to CANTON, where I was not allowed to be on the bridge alone at sea for one minute. It was not very difficult. I met and passed quite a few other ships and kept mine on track. The visibility was about normal for the North Sea, i.e. not very good. At midnight, feeling very pleased with myself, I handed over to Fergus Kell, and so made a start to the sea time required for my next examination.

Calcutta was not a nice place to stay in an all steel ship in the monsoon and midsummer. Of about 30 ships in the impounded docks there always seemed to be one with a jute fire, caused when the moisture content and high temperatures produced spontaneous combustion. Once burning, they were the devil to extinguish, on no account add water since it makes matters worse. However, getting into and out of the port or shifting berth required really expert pilotage, ship handling and seamanship, so there were many professional lessons to learn. It took two days to reach Calcutta from the pilot cutter at Sandheads, moving up the River Hooghly and anchoring for the right tide level, carefully avoiding great mud banks. A number of wrecks on the banks provided plenty of visual encouragement to get it right.

At Calcutta the river is quite narrow, and the current flows strongly. In addition to the docks, there were river berths at which to work cargo. The river is subject to bores. If a high one was spotted up river, ships at the river berths had to take refuge in the docks for a day or so, double banking on other ships. Securing to a river berth was a very long process. The ship had to end up with two crossed anchor chains at each end; one of each pair secured ashore, the other to a buoy off the berth. Mooring (and unmooring) took at least six hours of hard and sweaty work, hanging off both anchors, and breaking out lengths of cable and sending them aft. My harbour station was the foc'sle, and I learned at the sharp end. The pilots were expert ship handlers, and at the river berths were supplemented by two experienced local gangs of about 10 sailors per gang, who assisted the ship's company with all the heavy cable work. Thus taking refuge in the docks involved two mooring and unmooring operations, and locking in to and out of the docks. It seemed I lived on the foc'sle. But I admired the skills of the pilots, and their seamen teams, and learned a great deal.

Amongst Reg Cowell's many sound beliefs, one was certainly to look after his sailors. KARMALA's programme changed almost daily as we were delayed or diverted to another port "with inducement". To receive mail from home, it was important for our families to know where to address it. Radio messages were charged per expensive word. Reg and his wife both had commercial brevity code books, so when our programme changed he sent her a very short radio message. She decrypted it and posted a copy to our families - there were 15 British officers - and we shared the cost.

After one voyage Reg Cowell left KARMALA and was relieved by Captain G K Fox, another experienced officer with whom I got on very well. We made a voyage to Calcutta and back. In my early days as a watch keeper I still had a lot to learn. One night in the Red Sea on passage from Aden to Massawa by way of the West Channel, which was not well charted or lit, I thought I was lost. Whilst I checked everything, an important light had not come up when it should. One of the jingles we learned was "When in danger, when in doubt, always call the Old Man out". So I did just that, he appeared, checked everything himself, and seemed relaxed. A few minutes later the light came up. I expected to be blasted for dragging him from his bunk, but he commended me, remarking that I had done the right thing to justify his confidence in me, a lesson never forgotten.

One task allotted to me in KARMALA was quite unexpected - the doctor. It was actually the chief officer's job, but he did not like doing it. The total crew was about 65, and apart from the 15 officers, the rest were kalassis and stewards from India, agwallahs from Pakistan, and two Chinese fitters. I took over the small hospital and surgery, with its big numbered bottles of medicines, and a marvellous book entitled "The Ship Captain's Medical Guide". In clear and very simple terms it told you how to do anything and left me wondering why it was taking 6 years for my cousin to add MD after his name. I did have a St. John's Ambulance First Aid Certificate, a requisite for the 2nd Mates' Certificate, but little else to qualify me for the job.

However the job got me very close to our crew and their gratitude for getting their insides moving in the right direction with a dose from the right large bottle was a major factor of man management. I did a whole lot of small things, and they seemed to work. The pantry man nearly cut off the top of a finger in a slicing machine, and it was hanging by a thread. (It was just before lunch, and the sautéed potatoes in our dining saloon were studiously avoided.) I used old fashioned iodine quite liberally, stuck the top back on, and bandaged him up. There was a lot of pain from the iodine, but it soon subsided and the MRSA did not stand a chance. Two days later he visited a shore doctor in Aden and returned delighted that the "graft" was working. The Chinese were rather strange. I had to treat a nasty burn on the arm of one of them, caused by superheated steam. He was clearly in great pain as I laid on the sulfa patches, but his cabin mate, who I thought was there to support him and see fair play, was laughing like a maniac. I never understood why, but apparently it is an old Chinese custom to laugh at the pain of a friend; perhaps it is believed to ward off evil spirits. In Suez Bay I stitched up a coolie whose forehead had been slashed by a cargo sling hook opening up, and he survived.

I left KARMALA in January 1950, and Bunty and I arranged to marry on 8 February. She had taken a job as nanny with a family in Bickley in Kent, to be closer to the Thames, but returned to her parents for the wedding. Although she was domiciled in Paignton we both much preferred St. Luke's church in Torquay, and particularly its vicar, the Reverend W H Ryder-Jones. Apparently the CoE is very territorial about these matters, insisting that one of those being married must be resident in the parish. Bunty soon settled that by leaving a suitcase full of clothes in her Granny's house in Torquay. We had a very great day, and I was only saddened that my Pa was at sea. I was well supported by my Mama and sister, plus cousins, and Robson Raw, a P&O Matey, was my best man. My new father-in-law provided the wedding breakfast in his Park Hotel. Everyone seemed to enjoy themselves, the waitresses got drunk and we left by car in the traditional style to go to Newton Abbott, having tea at the famous Madge Mellors café. We then caught the train to London, where we stayed the night, going on to Paris the next day for our honeymoon. On return Bunty went back to work in Bickley and I received a ship appointment but we managed to find a small flat in a nice old house in Shortlands, Kent, and so set up our first home.

My next ship was to be P&O which was nearing completion at Vickers Shipbuilders in Barrow-in-Furness, where I joined her as 3rd Officer. An appointment to a new passenger ship fitting out was a mark of approval, although I had to serve as junior in the 1st Officer's watch. This was disappointing after I had already been a watch keeper on my own and it only counted as half sea time for my next certificate. But the big compensation was to witness at first hand how ships were built, because the BoT certificates included a paper on ship construction. Vickers Barrow enjoyed a good reputation for building first class passenger ships, and CHUSAN was no exception.

CHUSAN was to be deployed in both the trade to Japan, and in the summer as a cruise ship from Southampton. She was 23,500 tons GRT, carried about 1,000 passengers in two classes, plus cargo and mail. She was powered by twin geared steam turbines, for a top speed of 25 knots, and a service speed of 21.5 knots. Her ship's company numbered about 500, and was of the company's standard type. In June we sailed, under Vickers flag, to carry out our sea trials in the Firth of Clyde, in a spell of perfect June weather. Trials were successful except for one item of equipment, the fin stabilisers. These were supplied by Denny Brown of Edinburgh, and CHUSAN was the first big ship to be fitted. A good swell was needed to test them. In the Firth of Clyde and Irish Sea it was absolutely calm - not a ripple. It was agreed that Denny Brown's engineers would be allowed to take manual control and make the ship roll which they did very successfully, up to 20° each side, to the amazement of a few yachtsmen who probably decided to be abstemious thereafter. The 3rd Officer got a new task, keeping a special stabiliser log of their operation. Out in the Atlantic later on, they certainly suppressed any roll but seemed to increase pitch.

We sailed to Southampton and there was a small ceremony as the P&O house flag replaced that of Vickers, who handed over the ship to our Chairman, Sir William Currie, and Captain Tunbridge. The former handed over a big cheque for the final instalment of the cost. About a week was spent in Southampton preparing for our first cruise passengers during which time Bunty and other wives were allowed to live on board. It was of particular interest to her that some of the artists who had provided their work to adorn our bulkheads were still busy with minor improvements and after-thoughts.

Prior to WW2 P&O had carried out years of cruising with their passenger liners in the summer months. In the summer the passenger traffic to Australia and the Far East always declined because ships without air conditioning were extremely hot, especially in the Red Sea. One solution was to send the ships on Mediterranean cruises for a week or two and this type of employment was successful. Despite having few of the facilities available in the floating real estate of today, passengers really enjoyed themselves, and there were few complaints. Cruises were seen as good value too. In CHUSAN in 1950 we had a lot of Jewish customers, who know a good deal when they see one, so much so that in the fleet CHUSAN was nicknamed Kosher Flyer.

From June to September we made 14 and 7 day cruises from Southampton to the Mediterranean and Atlantic Islands. It was time for great sightseeing in a beautiful surrounding. There was no cargo work for the mateys, but quite a lot of time was spent on the gangways assisting passengers to get ashore for their organised excursions.

Captain Tunbridge provided a lesson for me that I never forgot - the Captain's eyes are the best in the ship, which is a practical judgement, not an ophthalmic one. It meant that it was not just good eyes that mattered; it was the years of training that counted. Steaming South down the Portuguese coast towards Lisbon on a bright clear day, he had left orders with the 1st Officer to call him once the Burling Islands were sighted. I was keeping a sharp look-out, seeing nothing. My captain appeared beside me without a summons, looked over the dodger, and said "Ah there they are". And they were too.

I left CHUSAN in September, took leave (the leave entitlement had been increasing steadily), and was soon to receive a promotion to Supernumary 2nd Officer, and appointed to MOOLTAN.

MOOLTAN, and her sister ship MALOJA, were enigmas. In 1921 Harland and Wolf received an order for two transatlantic passenger ships from an owner who went bust before their completion. P&O purchased them uncompleted, making some minor alterations, and in 1923 deployed them in the Australian trade, where for 10 years they were extremely popular with passengers. In the 1930s they were somewhat eclipsed by the five new Straths but they soldiered on. They both survived WW2 as troopships, and after the war they were re-fitted as tourist one class, and returned to the Australian trade, carrying mainly passage-assisted migrants and young Australians, in addition to cargo and mail. They eventually went to the breakers after 30 years, when P&O was introducing three brand new 28,000 ton ships.

It really is surprising that the two ships should do so well when you considered that so many bits of their technical make-up were quite dreadfully wrong. Harlands were notorious for building very heavy ships, and MOOLTAN was deep drafted, to put it mildly. One consistent difficulty was her very small single plate rudder making her difficult to steer. It was rumoured that some Suez Canal pilots always reported sick when she or her sister were approaching. The problem was compounded by the two propellers which ran at only 66 RPM to achieve 16 knots with a coarse propeller pitch to produce this. It meant that if the two shafts were out of synchronisation, steering was affected and the small rudder had to struggle to compensate.

Her machinery was from the previous century, consisting of two quadruple expansion steam reciprocating engines, each of about 6,750 SHP. The low pressure cylinders were the size of a block of flats. The eight boilers that supplied the steam were of the out-of-date Scotch fire tube type, each holding a great tonnage of water. If one was drained for repair she immediately took on a list.

Her stability was minimal, and required careful watching but it gave her a nice slow roll. Approaching a major bunkering port and low on both fuel and water, her stability would go negative about five days before arrival requiring 400 tons of salt water ballast in a double bottom tank to correct it.

She was equipped with two low pressure steam turbines which used the exhaust steam from the engines to generate electricity for the sea load, a fuel saving arrangement. In harbour, two more independent generators provided the load. The arrangement was called "the drive" and changing over was quite a tricky job. Trying to balance a fluctuating load often resulted in complete black-out. Of course none of the mateys could understand the problem. At the side of each engine was a handle marked "drive", with two positions: "in" and "out". This seemed simple enough, but was not. Fortunately the chief electrician, 15 years in the ship, always restored power in the end. On deck the windlass and capstans were steam driven, with the unique aroma of oil and steam mixed together. The small deck cranes were hydraulic, served from a big pressurised water tank in the engine room. When pressure was lost they would slowly sink down like flowers that were dying. This was the time to stand well clear, since when pressure was restored they recovered very fast.

During my six years at sea, I had followed the lead of my captains and senior officers. These were generally very good but there was one area that began to give me doubts, being the inter-departmental relationships within a ship. Of course, most large and existing organisations suffered from departmental rivalry but in the small world of a ship this started to look plain silly. In MOOLTAN there were two small events that convinced me that things should change. Many of my seniors preached the doctrine that the deck department was the only one that mattered and engineers and pursers were second class people. Alongside Station Pier in Melbourne, with a Strath in the next berth, Captain Peter instructed me to call on the Strath's captain, and invite him for drinks and dinner that evening. (Even a 2nd Officer recognised that he was captain's messenger when need be.) The Strath's captain was a very difficult martinet, but I was aware of his regime.

I therefore stood in silence in his open doorway for 2 minutes until he looked up from his desk. He said "Sorry Penney, I thought you were a purser". This was not only an insult to me (in his book), but also to my Pa, whom he knew well, and who had more years in the company than he did.

Another incident occurred during the same voyage. Rounding Ushant in the middle watch, I had four very difficult hours with a combination of poor visibility, coastal navigation, and many ships using the same alter course positions. My 3rd engineer colleague also struggled with his antediluvian machinery below. When we exchanged bridge/engine room information at 0400 he invited me to his cabin for a beer once I had completed upper deck rounds. With his two watch colleagues, we drank quietly a couple of glasses and I left to return to the bridge flat about 0445. Who should I meet up with en route but the chief officer who was always about early and who asked me in pointed tones if I had been drinking with the engineers.

Our managing directors quite often sent us a circular stressing the importance of departmental co-operation, although stories circulating and visits to the office suggested that they were not much good at instigating it right under their own feet. However they did start to create spaces for junior officers' smoke rooms/ wardrooms with their own bar and barman, and this idea slowly took hold. The move certainly encouraged co-operation between departments, and reduced cabin parties.

P & O Matey

I made two round voyages to Australia, under Captains Turner and Peter, carrying passengers and cargo. On one voyage we went to Brisbane, so I was able to re-visit my cousins, and again was made very welcome. Throughout this time I had charge of a watch without a cadet to help, and in May 1951 I left the ship with sufficient sea time to sit for 1st Mate. This examination was not difficult and so meant I was able to spend a lot of time with Bunty. After my leave expired I spent about two months in the Dock staff in the UK, engaging in ship-keeping whilst the ship's officers took leave which also meant quite a lot more time at home. Bunty and I decided we had outgrown our small flat, and we wanted to buy a small house. We found a bungalow in Sidcup that we liked, priced at £2,495. We chose Sidcup because it was fairly close to both the Royal Docks in London and Tilbury. Other P&O couples lived nearby so Bunty had friends when on her own. With a little help from both sets of parents we scraped up the necessary 20 per cent deposit plus buying expenses and so owned the home where we lived for five years.

My next sea appointment was STRATHMORE, as 2nd Officer, another step up, and in the next 16 months I made five round voyages to Australia. I continued in the graveyard watch, but now had a 4th Officer to assist me. STRATHMORE was a very handsome ship, built at Vickers Barrow in 1936 and considered the best of the five Straths. She was launched by the Duchess of York, daughter of the Earl of Strathmore, later to become Queen and then Queen Mother. On board there was a charming photograph of the Duchess taken in the 1930s by Dorothy Wilding. A troopship in WW2, STRATHMORE was refitted after the war to carry 1100 first and tourist class passengers, plus mail and cargo. She was 23,580 tons GRT and her 24,500 geared turbines gave her 18 knots service speed.

We carried a number of notable passengers, ranging from a new governor for South Australia to the English cricket team en route to contest the Ashes. Two of the team were the Bedser twins, Alec and Eric from Surrey CC. In return for playing deck tennis with them most evenings they gave a signed copy of their cricketing story book to both John Crichton, the supernumary 2nd Officer, and to me. John and I realised very quickly we could not play Strathmore vs Bedser because there was no real contest as both the Bedsers were seriously expert catchers. Their hands were so big that neither John nor I could deliver a successful spinner, so both teams split up to provide some very good games for us all.

My first captain was Cyril Pollitt, whose first words on seeing me after four years were "My God, it's Penney again" but he was not unfriendly, providing I got it right. Watchkeepers were expected to keep their watch in the open on a bridge wing and not in the wheelhouse, notwithstanding heavy and almost horizontal rain. To keep the rain out of my eyes I used to wear a large cotton sun hat with a big brim purchased in Madras and whilst this caused a bushy eyebrow to raise, it was not objected to. In my time in the ship there were quite a few officer changes, but two 4th Officers became lifelong friends. Tony Barrett, aka Smiler, in view of his sunny countenance, went on to become both Commodore RNR and Deputy Lieutenant of London. John Blackburn joined me in the Box Business in 1969, and retired as a container ship Master.

After three voyages, Captain Pollitt went on leave, and was relieved by Reg Cowell. His broad and innovative approach found a lot more scope in a top class passenger ship. On the long and lonely haul from Colombo to Fremantle the watch keepers were on duty for one watch in four instead of one in three, something never heard of in P&O but a little less work and very nice break. His attitude to passengers was very positive, and quite different from many other masters. There was an old P&O tradition that a ship was run for the benefit of the Captain and Officers and passengers could join as long as they behaved themselves. This needed to change and Reg pointed the way. When in the Mediterranean he would close the coast to within a mile or so giving passengers the opportunity of gazing at the coast instead of continuous blue water. Close to, the Mediterranean coast is a marvellous mix of things both natural and human, and the passengers were delighted. Reg Cowell left after one voyage, and moved on to be Assistant Marine Superintendent, being replaced by Captain John Paice. After five voyages I left, having been granted leave to undertake initial training in the Royal Navy, which is described in Chapter 8.

P & O Matey

My next appointment, seven months later, was to ARCADIA as 2nd Officer, joining her at John Brown's shipyard in Clydebank on 2 January 1954. She became my best ever ship as a matey. She was not ready for us to live aboard so I joined Chief Officer James Dunkley in a local guest house where the landlady took it upon herself to make sure we did not go hungry. She provided a good breakfast and high tea when we returned from the shipyard for the day. This was followed by mountains of scones and cakes with tea late in the evening. For lunch we visited a pub just outside the dockyard gates for a pie and half pint. These modest habits were in complete contrast to our shipbuilders, who could be seen knocking back a few double scotches, each chased down with a pint. Clutching my half I wondered how on earth they could afford it but noticed there were children in Clydebank who were barefoot in winter.

There were quite a few problems in completing the ship on time and we did in fact take a large gang of finishing tradesmen for a round voyage to Australia. John Brown did not have a follow-on passenger ship order so their shipbuilders sought to spin things out. Added to that, the new Royal Yacht BRITANNIA was nearing completion. It is well known that Her Majesty and HRH Prince Philip regarded the yacht as the only home they were able to create from scratch for themselves and they set out to achieve this with loving care. This meant that Prince Philip appeared in Clydebank from time to time to inspect progress, and perhaps change a few things. When this occurred, all the shipyard managers deserted us as they were quite naturally more interested in the next ship to us in the fitting-out berths and our completion fell back again. In the meantime a first class team of officers was assembling on the Clyde, including John Blackburn, and it was not long before we moved to live on board followed by the rest of the crew , making a total of 716.

Our captain was Commodore Geoffrey Forrest, who shared with Reg Cowell many ideas about how a ship's company might be re-trained to look on the passengers as our customers. His Staff Captain was Douglas Armstrong, who had been in command of the destroyer HMS MAORI and led the night torpedo attacks just before the battleship BISMARCK met her end in the Atlantic. The next day, when it was all over, MAORI and two other ships were rescuing survivors from the cold sea. MAORI's lookouts spotted a small smoke plume and it had to be assumed it was a U boat so the three ships broke off their rescue operation, steaming away at high speed and leaving many sailors to drown.

In very cold January weather, we sailed down the Clyde to go for sea trials. At the Tail of the Bank, there was a total electrical failure. After three freezing hours on the fo'csle, I had just been told to pipe down the anchor party and return to the bridge when all on the bridge starting waving and shouting at me to return to the fo'csle and let go the starboard anchor. We were drifting helplessly towards the beach. This accomplished, a few minutes later power was restored and we weighed and proceeded to the wider waters of the Firth of Clyde where very successful sea trials were held. We then headed to Liverpool, arriving in heavy snow to undergo dry docking and inspection, and from there to Tilbury, where it was also snowing. The usual handover ceremony was held, and ARCADIA was now a P&O ship so we prepared for our first passengers and cargo.

ARCADIA was a splendid addition to the fleet, of 29,871 tons GRT and powered by twin geared steam turbines to provide a top speed of 25 knots and a service speed of 22 knots. Her passenger capacity was 679 First Class and 735 Tourist Class and she still had 320,000 cubic feet of cargo space. We sailed for a maiden round voyage to Australia on 22 February with our much respected Chairman, Sir William Currie, and Lady Currie on board with us to Aden. The night before Aden they were invited by the junior officers for a pre dinner drink in our new wardroom, and it was special for some our most junior members to be able to meet and talk to our Chairman over a drink.

At midnight I took over the watch and piloted the ship through the Strait of Bab el Mandeb. I was a bit on tenterhooks, not in respect of my immediate duties, but because I was fretting about news awaited from home. Bunty was staying with her parents in Paignton and awaiting an important birth. About 0130 there was a radio message from my sister-in-law to say that our daughter Lindley Jane had arrived safely, and both mother and child were doing well. Becoming a father was quite simply celebrated with a cup of tea from the bridge tray.

For our visit to Australia there was a lot of comment and acclamation at all of our ports of call. As a ship's company we were settling down well and becoming close knit. Our brand new wardroom which had forward looking windows in the bridge front bulkhead was working well. It was a province of the junior officers, since senior officers had their own table in the two dining saloons and were expected to entertain passengers in their cabins and the public rooms. The mess was run by a small elected committee, but the most senior of the junior officers in each department - the 2nd officer, 3rd engineer officer, and senior assistant purser, each had some responsibility for the discipline of their departmental juniors. It was important that they worked together without any formalised authority. The trio of us in ARCADIA got on very well with each other which was noted by the large number of juniors in the ship.

Now homeward bound, the commodore discussed with me his navigational requirements for our coming cruising season which followed our maiden line voyage and was to last from May to September. It provided 16 cruises of one, two, or three weeks both in the Mediterranean and to North Cape of Norway. He wished to provide "close coasting" whenever there was anything to see on every cruise and provided it did not interfere with the ports programme. This involved me in preparing a complete book of 16 chapters, with each chapter setting out all the alter course positions, courses and distances, port timings and daylight hours. The initial positions were one mile or more from the shore marks, but if conditions were good on the day he would decide to go closer, usually 0.5 of a mile, and steaming around large bays. This required a lot of accurate and detailed work on the charts, drawing the track including turning part circles and using alter course positions which were easy to use quickly for an accurate fix. The ship's new radar was of great assistance for providing both bearing and distance off. To sail really close needed other safety pre-cautions. The bridge and engine room teams were beefed up, the main engines were slowed to about 17 knots for faster man-oeuvrability, the watertight doors closed, the anchors were cleared away, and an anchor party closed up. But it was all worth it.

About half way on passage from Fremantle to Colombo, a stretch of the Indian Ocean where it was unusual to sight another ship, without warning we received an XXX (urgently require medical assistance) message and ten minutes later a cargo ship hove over the horizon. We went to Accident Boat Stations and prepared to launch a sea boat, of which I was in charge. The ship was in fact British India's PENTAKOTA, part of the P&O Group, en route to Australia from India. She was one of a class of four new ships, but BI did not buy fast ships, and her sea speed of 11 knots earned the class the nickname of the Quick Ps. The emergency arose because the 2nd engineer had slashed his own wrists in a suicide attempt, and as a cargo ship she did not carry a doctor. Our "sea boat" was in fact a motorised version of our lifeboats, which could each accommodate 100 persons so it was very big for the job. The boat's crew consisted of me, a 4th Engineer, our doctor, the Yeoman of Mails, a deck petty officer who acted as Bosun's Mate when not engaged on mail, two British quartermasters, who failed to turn up at Stations, a 3rd Tindal and five kalassis. ARCADIA in fact carried two doctors which included the senior, who looked after the passengers, and the junior, who had just become MD and attended the crew. I was surprised when Doc Jewson, the senior, turned up because he was a rather portly man in his late 40s and I foresaw the need for a fit person if I was to put him aboard PENTAKOTA. But it was his decision.

We manned the boat some 40' above the water and, with ARCADIA stopped dead, the Chief Officer lowered away until we launched making sure that the falls overhauled, so that we could achieve an unhook at both ends simultaneously. PENTAKOTA had a pilot ladder ready for us and Doc prepared to jump. The South Easterly trade was blowing about Force 6, and there was a swell of about 6 or 8 feet. With the boat scending to the swell we banged about against the ship's side. I told Doc to await my word before he jumped so that I could gauge when we were approaching the top. On the third "JUMP" he did so successfully and quickly clambered up. I hauled off to stop the noisy banging and to await events.

About 20 minutes passed whilst Doc tended to the patient and strapped him into a Neil Robertson stretcher. PENTAKOTA swung out their small gangway cat davit. I went alongside again and he was lowered into the boat and taken into care by a number of pairs of hands. I hauled off again until Doc appeared on the pilot ladder, went alongside again, and then gave Doc three jump offers. He accepted the third and was dragged into the boat. He brushed off the many pairs of hands, and went straight to his patient, not entrusting him to a gang of rough sailors.

We set off back to ARCADIA, only half a mile away, but only visible when we were on the crest for the really difficult part - recovery. I approached the falls unable to appreciate the fact that the ship was moving slowly astern so the 120lb steel fall blocks moved quickly past our heads. The Commodore had been man-oeuvring ARCADIA to give me a good lee but when he rang down for an ahead movement to check the sternway there was another total electrical failure and no response. I hauled off and went around again, by which time the electrical failure had been rectified and the ship was stopped dead. The second approach went better. The absolutely crucial matter of timing was to ensure that both ends were hooked on simultaneously. If only one hooked on it was likely that the boat's crew would end up in the water. There was no need to tell the kalassis about this, as they knew about the risk factor. The other big risks were heads being banged by the heavy steel blocks and fingers being lost between the hooks in the boat and the steel ring attached to the block, or one end coming unhooked again when the boat was on the crest. They got it right first time without accidents and the chief officer on ARCADIA's boat deck started to hoist away. Once clear of the water, the boat started to bang heavily against the ship's side and we had no fenders. ARCADIA's fin stabilisers could not work when she was stopped and she was only rolling about 5° each side but with long falls this achieved a lateral movement of several feet, decreasing as the boat was hauled up. The BoT staff solution was to lay the boat's oars across the boat and bear off, which was helpful but one loom became trapped under a side plate landing, and broke the oar with one end flying up and cutting the tindal's face and just missing his eye. It was our only injury, and a small price to pay. One fall having a turn in it we were bowsed in and secured at the Promenade deck. Our patient was carried down to the hospital, and the boat's crew disembarked clearly experiencing both relief and pleasure to have a very solid ARCADIA under their feet.

Under the care of our two doctors and two nursing sisters PENTAKOTA's 2nd Engineer recovered the health of both his body and mind. I began to see Doc Jewson in an entirely new light. It turned out he was not just a figure sitting at his desk, giving advice to passengers and stuffing their fees into his desk but there was a great deal more to him than that. A couple of months later we received a letter from Head Office, telling us that the board of BI were providing a payment of 100 rupees for our tindal by way of compensation for his small wound. I went aft to tell him the news. He was clearly over the moon but what mattered were his first words to me "Can we take away the sea boat tomorrow Sahib?"

The Commodore had put his thinking cap on and James Dunkley started to prepare a report and recommendations. Clearly there was a big hole in the Life Saving Appliances regulations that needed attention. If you look at a broadside picture of any of today's huge cruise ships you will see in the middle of a row of very large lifeboats a very small dirigible and inflatable sea boat, launched and recovered on a single wire fall. It was unusual in peace time to have to send away a sea boat, but the unsuitability of large lifeboats also became apparent about three years after the incident described above, when STRATHEDEN lost her sea boat in the Eastern Mediterranean. She also lost the boat's crew, lead by 3rd Officer Jim Bowman, plus three of the five Greek fishermen who had been rescued from their foundering trawler JASON.

We made recommendations about the many desirable charact-eristics of a sea boat, including size, the fitment of air cooled diesel engines, instead of water cooled petrol engines, faster recovery winches, fendering, and the provision of hand held radios in both ships and their boats. Another provision in existing tonnage was 5" nylon strops with a soft eye for hooking on during recovery.

P & O Matey

We returned to the UK without further incident and I was able to take a few days leave travelling down to Paignton to meet up with my family and to meet my new daughter for the first time.

It was very exciting. I was impressed to say the least but for my part I did not make a good impression. However I did slowly gain credence in Lindley's eyes. Bunty had been busy arranging a proper christening for this new and small person. She decided she was ready to take up residence in our house in Sidcup again so I escorted her back and helped her to straighten it out before rejoining my ship.

There were to be a lot of anchorage ports using the ship's boats in our cruising programme. Four of our standard lifeboats were landed and replaced by smart and powerful diesel launches which we referred to as the Rolls Royces, but they were also fully certificated as lifeboats. Our two original motor lifeboats were also used to ferry passengers ashore and they were known as penny buses, with no intention of a pun. Twelve apprentices joined the ship to provide coxswains and were placed under the orders of the 1st officer, and John Blackburn, 3rd officer, for whom there was no cargo work. Also embarked was the Commodore's personal 12' fibreglass sailing dinghy which he placed in my care. He sometimes sailed with me to crew for him but if he was busy elsewhere I could use the boat as I wished and was encouraged to teach the cadets to sail. Somehow he had got the idea I liked messing about in boats.

The boats were also used for crew recreation when appropriate. The Commodore was well aware that the satisfaction, or dissatisfaction, amongst our passengers could be affected very much by the performance of their table and bed cabin stewards in providing a personal service. He was also aware that these ratings worked very long hours for days at a stretch and, if they were worn out, their standard of service would suffer. His innovative approach was to arrange beach picnics for 100 at a time. In a port such as Naples, where we berthed alongside, about 95 per cent of the passengers were ashore on excursions all day. Over-ruling the protests of Chief Steward Maxy Perch, who had visions of conducting a large scale operation cleaning acres of ARCADIA's glass doors and windows, two Rolls Royces were launched on ARCADIA's off side. They were loaded with stewards, sandwiches and beer, and towing the dinghy we set off for the delightful small island of Ischia, which was then almost unknown and whereon it was unlikely that we would run into our customers. At first the crew were a bit iffy but when they had experienced a day in the fresh air, sun and sea, they returned visibly refreshed and we repeated the exercise whenever it was convenient.

Our cruise programme was very successful and it was clear that our passengers had thoroughly enjoyed themselves. I got to see Norway, and steaming up Narvik Fjord at 0200 with a bright sun in my eyes was breathtaking. The scenery was splendid throughout and I never wanted to turn in to sleep.

One incident occurred that was definitely not on my happiness register. It concerned our newly introduced nylon mooring ropes. We still had the traditional natural fibre ropes made of hemp and sisal, along with wire ropes, but now we were trying nylon rope, especially for our first line ashore, because it was very light in weight and easily handled. The breaking strain of a 5" nylon rope was said to be twice that of a 6" sisal. But it had some very nasty disadvantages which were not evident at first sight. Firstly, it was very slippery, and even with more turns on the drum, under strain it could suddenly slip. In fact this had happened when I was in STRATHMORE and securing to the Suez canal bank. Being aft I did not witness it but when it slipped, the Chippy was standing in a big bight and it happened so fast that there was no time to jump. It picked him up and chucked him into the air and he broke his arm on returning to the deck. Berthing in Bergen, a more serious accident occurred. Normally the matey in charge of a mooring party used his own judgement with a mooring rope under strain, easing it a little if he thought it was about to break.

This was difficult with nylon because it gave none of the signs displayed by fibre ropes that it was about to part. The only indicator was that, as it stretched, the diameter decreased noticeably. Quite apart from this, at a port previous to Bergen I had used my own judgement to ease the line a little at a time when the bridge had ordered us to heave. Later the Commodore tore some strips off me for neglecting his order. His words still rang in my ears as we berthed at Bergen. I was standing on the top of the fairlead through which the rope was led. Inspection revealed a declining diameter but the bridge still ordered us to heave. We had found an answer to the slipperiness problem, which was to take the rope from the drum and put a couple of turns on the bitts, attended by two kalassis to take up the slack.

The rope parted with a bang and in the flash of an eye the inboard end streaked along the deck hitting Hussain, the first kalassi, and boring a great hole in his body, killing him outright. It also threw him back bodily and he knocked over his mate who was slightly injured from his fall. Some of the kalassis rushed to their assistance whilst the remainder prepared another rope. I reported to the Chief Officer when we were finally secured and he told me the Commodore wanted a word. He asked me for a verbal report, said nothing, and avoided looking at me. I spent the rest of the day feeling thoroughly miserable, completing a written report and the BDM (Births, Deaths, and Marriages) form in front of the British Consul. In the afternoon I went with a small party to bury him at a cemetery on a hillside just outside Bergen. It was a very long way from his home on the West coast of India.

We were nearing the end of our cruising season when there were two minor events. At about 0100 one night the Senior Night-watchman appeared on the bridge with a couple of passengers. The man said that their daughter was missing. My first fear was that she had gone overboard but the woman said that she had gone to meet an engineer so I promised them a search. As they left the bridge, I picked up the engine room telephone and spoke to 3rd Engineer Philip Westgarth. Philip had the girl back with her parents in five minutes after which the miscreant experienced some very harsh words. But that was an end of the matter and it was an example of good team work.

The other event that took place highlighted that we were not making the best use of the modern equipment we carried. Our new radar was excellent but it was only switched on when seen to be required. This was supposed to prolong its life but I don't think this was the case at all and later a stage was reached where it was left on at all times at sea. ARCADIA was steaming North off the Portuguese and Spanish coasts, and approaching Finisterre, in what was a busy shipping lane. At midnight it was extremely clear and we could see lights 30 miles away. Two hours later and without any warning we entered a dense fog bank at 21 knots and could not see our own fo'csle. Bringing the ship to the appropriate readiness state the 4th Officer dived into the chartroom and switched on the radar. It took about two minutes to warm up and start painting but as soon as it did he sang out that there was a ship right ahead, on our heading marker, about three miles away, and closing. With radar it had become the practice not to reduce much speed in fog and we later calculated the ship ahead was doing 17 knots. This produced a joint closing speed of 38 knots whereby three miles was run in about five minutes. Knowing this it was easy to make a bold alteration to starboard and within a minute there was no risk of collision but it illustrated that consideration of timing was important. As we finished our cruise programme, I completed my sea time for a Master's certificate. ARCADIA was my "best ever" ship and I was sad to leave. To my complete surprise, I learned that the Commodore had asked the company for me to stay and take the 1st Officer's place which was just becoming vacant but the company stuck to their rule that I must pass for Master to be promoted.

So I left, and was able to live with my small family for a few months. It was easy to join the city gents and commute each day to the Master's School in the City, besides which it allowed me to spend all my weekends at home.

I passed for Master in the middle of November 1954 and it was not very difficult. The examiner for the orals was polite and friendly, in complete contrast to his predecessor in 1948, and we spent an hour together having a chat between professionals. He was particularly interested in the fire fighting arrangements in large passenger ships and as the conversation progressed I got the impression I was providing information rather than being examined. Perhaps that was why he passed me.

P & O Matey

There had been high hopes in the Penney family that I would be at home for Christmas, but this was not to be. P&O was expanding its fleet and experienced officers were in demand for sea billets. In early December I was appointed to CHUSAN again, this time as 1st Officer, and so my junior officer days were over. I was the ship's senior watch keeper and cargo officer. On watch the 3rd officer was my junior. As a senior officer I had my own table in the dining saloon and five passengers joined me. I shared a servant, who was provided by the deck serang, with Roger Cutler, the chief officer. At age 25 I became thoroughly spoilt with personal service.

In CHUSAN I made two round voyages to Japan in the liner service, the first with Captain Ferraby and the second with Captain Bodley, the regular Master. The cargo officer's job was particularly onerous and absorbing. The ship had a cargo capacity of 481,000 cubic feet bale, only a little less than our newest fast cargo ships. As a major passenger ship she had to stick to a strict schedule and there was no question of sailing an hour or two late to complete cargo work. If we got it wrong we had to over-carry, or short-ship, neither of which appealed to our freight customers. There was a great deal of special cargo requiring officer attendance on the spot, but there were four junior officers to assist. Our port stays in Malaya, Hong Kong and Japan were a maximum of two days and we worked cargo all night and every night. We did not break sea watches for the whole voyage and spent a lot of time very short of sleep.

A young man named Derek Bradley joined us as 4th Officer for his first passenger ship appointment. At sea he kept the graveyard watch as junior to 2nd Officer Michael O'Connell. In harbour he added to this working for me on special cargo. Going to his tiny cabin to call him out he was usually sitting in a small chair hunched up into one corner and trying to nod off to recover lost sleep. I nicknamed him Cuddles and this name stuck. Writing to Captain Derek Bradley 50 years later, I thought it would be discreet to omit the nick name, but it did not matter, he is still called Cuddles.

Visiting Japan was a new experience, and many new cargoes were added to my list. In 1954 Japan's exports were still simple commodities, such as plywood, prepared timber and canned mandarin oranges - the TV sets and cameras would appear later. In Yokohama I met for the first time Jim Davis, who had joined P&O's graduate entry scheme and was called a learner. (Indian clerks had sometimes mis-typed this as "leaner", not thought to be inappropriate by old P&O hands.) Jim had spent 12 months in P&O's London offices getting experience in all departments. He was now in the middle of a three year tour of the East and spending eight months as a steamer's assistant, relieving another assistant for home leave. We got on very well and I managed to stow all the cargo he had booked, although my paper work was clearly an enigma to him. He liked Japan and its people (which I did not at this stage), and was learning to speak the language with alacrity.

On our homeward voyage we called at Penang, rightly called "The Pearl of the Orient", to load and embark passengers. Our cargo included the usual Malayan products: rubber, flour and tin ingots, but cargo work was hindered by heavy continuous rain and the hatch tents had to stay on for most of our stay. Our local office had booked 50 tons of tin ingots from a customer for Bombay, a new destination for this commodity, and stressed to me the importance of the shipment. We were due to sail at 0700, but by 0300 it was still pouring down and the tin was still in the transit shed on Swettenham Quay. There was only one thing for it which was to load it manually through CHUSAN's side door at quay level without removing hatch tents and trundle it along the crew working alleyway, using the purser's stores trolleys, to the Bullion Room in No. 2 hatch. This was accomplished in good time, and we sailed at 0700 with all the tin on board. Later that morning, at sea, Captain Ferraby sent for me, following his daily meeting with his heads of departments, to report that the purser had protested very strongly at my use of his equipment. My captain stressed that on no account was this exercise to be repeated but it was said with a smile on his face. What neither Captain Ferraby nor I knew was that the senior in the Penang office, Pat Ritchie, was already writing a letter of commendation to the managing directors which was later to stand me in good stead.

I had begun to think seriously about my future career. So far I had been promoted rapidly, entirely due to the P&O fleet expansion, which meant that there was always a challenge present in mastering a new job. But I had calculated very roughly that I would be a chief officer for at least 10 years before being in command, and it was the prospect of becoming bored that really made me think. I had sailed with able officers who had spent 15 years as 2nd officer and it seemed to me that the more able they were, the more they deteriorated, especially towards alcoholism. I had no wish to do that. I had of course watched with interest P&O's Learner scheme and wondered if I might join it despite not being a graduate. In early March 1955, whilst taking a few days leave between CHUSAN's voyages, and with a lot of support from Bunty, I wrote to the managing directors, without mentioning learners, to inquire whether there were any opportunities for me to transfer to the shore staff to gain experience of the management of the business. To my surprise I got a reply by return, asking me to call on Chairman Sir Donald Anderson.

This of course took place and Sir Donald put me immediately at my ease. We had quite a long chat during which he asked me lots of questions. Much later I learned that Michael Thwaites, one of the two managing directors, had received Pat Ritchie's letter and had suggested to Sir Donald that I should be interviewed. At the end of the meeting, Sir Donald announced he would give the matter some thought, and get in touch. The day before CHUSAN sailed again Captain Bodley sent for me and in his cabin sat Sir Donald. My captain discreetly withdrew from his own cabin and the Chairman invited me to join the Learner scheme as soon as CHUSAN returned in May. He suggested I should try it for a year on the basis that if it did not work out for either P&O or me I could return to sea with no loss of seniority. This was a very generous offer that I could not refuse. He confirmed it with a very friendly letter in a few days.

I made my last voyage as a Sea Officer in P&O. There was certainly a lot to think about and hopefully to look forward to. In Yokohama I broke the news to Jim Davis, who welcomed me to the Learnership, and admired the typescript of Sir Donald's letter, typed on an IBM Executive electric typewriter. But on the voyage home I began to think about the shipmates I was leaving. The officers I expected to see again in the course of the company's business, but it was unlikely that I would be in contact with the Indian and Pakistani ratings whom I had liked and admired so much..

Chapter 8. List 1, The Royal Naval Reserve

Ever since King Henry VIII wisely decided that his island kingdom needed sea power to become rich and powerful there was always a close affinity between the sailors of both fighting and trading ships. In Lord Nelson's times, it was the officers who held a King's Commission and who led the fighting and managed the men, whilst the officers who held Admiralty Warrants supplied specialist skills - the Master and Mates, Surgeon, Purser, Gunner and Sailmaker. In practice it was inevitable that the two classes exchanged skills when they were shut up in a ship for long periods. In creating a truly maritime power, both sets of skills were essential.

As the Royal Navy evolved in the 19th century, it decided to bring about more formality to the association and the Royal Naval Reserve was formed in 1859, which recruited both officers and men. This was sometimes seen as seamen learning how to be gentlemen. Nearly 50 years later in 1903, with tension rising in Europe, the Board of Admiralty foresaw that even more manpower would be needed. They added a fisherman class to the RNR and created the Royal Naval Volunteer Reserve, recruiting men who liked to go to sea for pleasure, such as yachtsmen. This was seen as gentlemen learning to be sailors.

Both reserves proved themselves in WW1 and WW2, and the RNVR grew to be a major force. Their worth is particularly note-worthy in the disastrous landings in the Dardenelles in April 1915. No less than seven Victoria Crosses were awarded to the Naval Services. Two were to officers of the Royal Navy, two to officers of the RNR, two to ratings of the RNR, and one to an officer of the RNVR.

I had always believed that all sailors were important in the maritime world and had great respect for the Royal Navy. At the end of

Sea Officer

WW2 the RNR entry lists were closed as the Navy slimmed down. Six years later they were re-opened and so, with P&O's permission, I joined as Probationary Sub Lieutenant. I had many reasons for doing this; the principal one was to widen my professional experience, having noted the skills of P&O's RNR officers when I sailed with them. To start with, they were all good ship handlers, something I hoped to be. They also seemed always to take a broad view and were good at man management.

At much the same time, the Admiralty decided to create the unified reserve. The RNVR name (but not the spirit) was dropped and the new RNR was divided into a number of Lists each comprising different classes of officers and ratings of both sexes. List 1 was for professional seafarers, List 2 for fisherman whilst List 3 was the old RNVR. There were other lists for people with other skills that the Navy would need in a war. The "Rocky" and "Wavy" uniform cuff lace stripes that had previously distinguished reserve officers were swapped for straight lace worn by career officers but with an "R" in the curl.

Fifty years later these changes looks like a good move. The only thing that does not look quite right is the lack of watch keeping skills in the younger Royal Navy officers. Small blunders have resulted in front line warships being returned ignominiously from around the world atop a Dutch barge at great cost. If mastering the complexities of 21st century weapons and sensors must be a priority for the warfare officers, perhaps it is time to go back 200 years and appoint masters and mates for the ship management skills, if indeed such people can be found. For fifteen years at the turn of the 18th century the Channel Fleet lost only one ship with a broken rudder whilst blockading Brest on a rock-strewn and very dangerous lee shore. This was mainly due to the competence of the masters and mates in the handling of the unwieldy sailing ships that could barely sail to windward.

My initial training was a series of courses lasting 20 weeks. This was a scaling down of the Navy's Sub Lieutenants courses, because we were already experienced seamen, navigators, and visual signalmen. There were six separate courses and in five we had examinations. These were important and there were three grades of pass - 1st, 2nd and 3rd - plus a "fail", the latter resulting in dismissal from the RNR. If 1st class was achieved throughout, twelve months seniority as Lieutenant was granted; 2nd class brought six months seniority and 3rd class brought none. The seniority awards stemmed from each course result and the total could contain a mixture of class result. The purpose of the course was to prepare us for service in the ships of the Royal Navy so that at the end we were fit for a typical Dormant Appointment of "for watch keeping duties in destroyers and below". This was apt and meant that if a war broke out we were immediately available to beef up naval manpower and could do a useful job. Along with 19 other classmates, at the beginning of July 1953 I joined the four week Communication Course in HMS MERCURY which was in a beautiful Hampshire country house near Horndean just North of Portsmouth. It was short of cabins so we were accommodated in barracks in Portsmouth, commuting each day in an ancient "Pussers Tilly", a sort of bus, grinding its way up Portsdown Hill.

From visual signalmen we were upgraded to communicators in a much wider sense, encompassing W/T, cryptology, fleetwork, confidential and secret books, and how to both make and manage signals. It was fascinating stuff of great use both at sea and just about anywhere else. It all went well for me and I got my first 1st Class certificate.

Our next course was for two weeks in Portsmouth barracks at The Divisional Officer's Course. This was to teach us how the Navy went about man management. The system was to split all the sailors into divisions of about 30 each, having an officer to head them. Their DO was responsible for holding the individual records, ensuring they were kept up to date. It was his responsibility to watch out for opportunities for advancement, and further education, and bring them to a sailor's attention, encouraging him if appropriate. If a sailor was a defaulter the DO attended the Captain or XO's "table" to see fair play and act as "prisoner's friend". He also attended the request men's table to help further the request. He counselled sailors about their family matters when invited to do so.

It was a formal and efficient system, introduced as a result of mutinies, and DOs needed to be familiar with a lot of rules and paperwork. It was far more complex than the man management prevailing in merchant ships but then mutinies are usually more serious than strikes. But strikes are also unwelcome too and many of the features of the system in simplified form could be incorporated in merchant ships. To impress our class with what happens when things really go wrong, we spent a morning in the Detention Quarters (navy speak for prison) in the Dockyard, where things were really tough. We also learned how to run the defaulter's system without incurring the risk of appearing in the Daily Mirror.

But first it was necessary for the class to receive some man management. Not all our uniforms were quite right and needed attention. My cap badge (from Pangbourne) contained a King's crown and I had to buy a new one with a Queen's crown. We were taught how to carry a dress sword - not as easy as it looks - and how to salute with a drawn sword.. This was also difficult, with our PO GI explaining that when going from "Present" to "Salute" it was essential not to cut off the admiral's coat buttons. We were also lectured on the laws and customs of the Navy, and how to behave at dinner in the wardroom mess. It was a very good course, and I notched up another 1st Class certificate.

Our next course was to be Part I of our Torpedo and Anti Submarine (TAS) training. The first part took place in HMS VERNON, the torpedo school in Portsmouth. VERNON was a waterfront property with its own berths for small warships and right next to Portsmouth Harbour Station. It was an attractive place with a delightful wardroom building, complete with croquet lawn. Unhappily this has all gone, the site was relinquished by the Navy to be taken up by Portsmouth Council, who offered it to developers. The latter created a new shop and restaurant area in the inelegant modern style. No more vicious croquet games in mess undress after a mess dinner on a summer's evening, trying to compete with the Commander, a skilled torpedo man who knew when and how to shoot.

List 1, The Royal Naval Reserve

The course was equally divided into torpedo and mine warfare. All the torpedo study was undertaken in buildings and sheds, but for mine warfare there were two days at sea in an Algerine class Ocean Mine Sweeper. Whilst in VERNON we were visited by two officers from HMS DOLPHIN, the submarine training school, who called for volunteers to undertake submarine training. I had always liked the idea of serving in submarines and quite a few of my P&O Mateys were submariners so I put up my hand. I had a short private interview with the visiting officers who encouraged me to go on. This involved spending a day at sea in a boat which I found amazing. Later I found out that the real purpose of the sea day was to allow the CO to watch me when the diving klaxons sounded. If I turned green I would not be a suitable submarine candidate. But I stayed the same ghastly colour and all was well.

Following this was a one week course which felt like being on holiday because there was no examination at the end. We joined HMS DAEDALUS, the Royal Naval Air Station at Lee-on-Solent, for the Junior Officer's Air Course. This was strictly a familiarisation exercise and there was no intention of training us as aviators, although one member of our class was so comfortable in a Meteor jet trainer that he was offered a full time position in the Fleet Air Arm on the spot. The place was full of characters. I spotted two four stripe captains who both looked not a day over 35. That was about their right age I was told. As teenagers they had both taken part in the successful raid on the Italian Navy's battle fleet in Taranto in November 1940, flying Swordfish aircraft armed with 18" torpedoes from the carrier HMS ILLUSTRIOUS.

Our time was taken up with a few lectures and films outlining naval air tactics, and a great deal of flying. It was the latter that provided the opportunity for the birdmen to get their own back on the fish-heads and they did it with laconic gusto. Five of us were summoned for a flight in a small twin engine transport plane painted in admiral's barge blue and it was of course the aerial equivalent. It consisted of a small cockpit for two pilots and a cabin furnished with four large armchairs. I jumped in first and took the second cockpit seat whilst my four classmates pretended they were flag officers and lazed about aft. We took off and over-flew the Solent and Spithead at about 3,000 feet observing a stunning view. The pilot, a laid back Lt Cdr, who spoke infrequently, suddenly said "I will now stop the starboard engine". He did so and it was so still I could read the propeller maker's name. He then re-started the engine and repeated the operation with the port engine. After restarting it he then said "I will now reduce the speed of the aircraft so that it can no longer stay in the air". He eased back both throttles until it stalled, diving towards the ground until it picked up enough speed to fly again, when he re-opened the throttles and returned to level flight. At least I had some idea of what was happening, but my classmates did not and were looking pretty white around the gills. I clocked up a total of 6 flights in different aircraft types, enjoying the holiday. A particularly memorable one was in a two-seater fighter at night when we went over the coast to Brighton and back in the middle of the summer holiday when all the resorts were full of holidaymakers and the coast was well lit with bright lights.

In its training establishments ashore the Navy worked a five day week so my weekends were free. Sidcup was less than three hours away by train, allowing me to spend every weekend with Bunty. I was home by Friday evening and, by rising very early on Monday, I could catch the 0545 train from Waterloo to Portsmouth (known in the Navy as The Drunks Express) and be on Divisions in uniform by 0800. Bunty did visit Portsmouth for a couple of days to see it all for herself and to join me at a party but we could not afford a longer stay. Being under 25, I could only receive a senior rate's marriage allowance, which was half the officer's allowance of 19s 6d per day. We stayed at the old Keppel's Head on the Hard at Portsmouth, an historic resting place for naval officers and their families. From the steps in the Hard very many officers had set off by boat to join their ships at Spithead so the place had an atmosphere all of its own. I was a member of the Royal Naval Club nearby and its dining room was very good but a bit expensive for us. No matter, the barman had a special dish he prepared for sub lieutenants which cost 1s 3d and was called a "toast and hammy cheesy eggy topside". Fortunately Bunty still prepares it for me today. My exciting new world had obviously done something to my metabolism because Bunty announced she was pregnant and our doctor had pronounced she was very well with it.

My next course was in HMS PEMBROKE at Chatham barracks in Kent. Three of my classmates lived within two or three miles of Sidcup and one had an old Rover car. We decided to live at our homes whilst on the course for 6 weeks in Chatham, sharing the car expenses. I joined the gunnery school, which provided an exhausting mix of the mental and the physical. There was a great deal of detailed engineering to understand about the Mark 19 twin 4" dual purpose mounting on which we trained and there was a lot of homework to do in the evenings. It contained mainly of gunnery terms that were quite new and had to be learned and Bunty got involved in helping me. One was "gun canted, trunnion correction" which she still narrates more than 50 years later. Another, "latch retaining, BM lever locked, breach mechanism closed" remains with me. We carried out our live surface firing in an Onslow class destroyer at sea off Shoeburyness, manning the whole system. This included the director, transmitting station and the turrets, each with a 4.7"gun. We all changed places after a few rounds. It was a very noisy day and I can still hear it. But we had a good course officer and his PO GI was as smart as paint.

Most days we had to undertake parade training, marching and marching around PEMBROKE's huge parade ground. There were other courses under training doing the same thing and the parade ground was always heavily populated with Chief and PO GIs finding fault with everyone and shouting at them. We were not treated as officers and none of them addressed us as "Sir" when we were under instruction, although they did so meticulously off the parade ground. One Chief treated us very harshly, saying things like "Yer think I don't like yer, don'tcha, yer wrong, I flippin' 'ate yer". They were not all like that and some were very informative and often amusing. The PO GI who taught us about ammunition was both of these and taught us about the Navy as well. The high explosive inside shells was the "gravy", and the steel plating of destroyers was "ticklers tins". Tickler is a cigarette. Teaching us about the Royal Marines he said "Yule orlways treat them royals with respeck genelmen, their job is to stop the mutinuss crew from murderin' the capnorfficers". It was a long course, but I got another 1st Class certificate at the end.

After this I attended a two week course in HMS PHOENIX, the Atomic, Biological, Chemical and Damage Control school, and we were quartered in barracks. This meant we could dine in the barracks wardroom for Trafalgar Night Dinner. It was a truly splendid occasion and about 220 officers sat down to dinner, 14 of them admirals, three of whom made speeches. A Royal Marine orchestra played throughout dinner. It was a very long night, and I forget how many times the port was passed.

On the course, apart from the damage control instruction which entailed being shut in a huge steel tank with water pouring in everywhere and having to shore up beams and plug holes, I just could not get on with the ABC sections. The Atomic scenario was too horrific for words and I was left wondering whether there was any point in learning how to defend a ship under attack. The Bacteriological and Chemical sections were little better and I objected to having an evil substance smeared on the back of my hand, and being told to get it off quickly using an antidote. We were shown films about the wounds that could be inflicted on persons and three of our class actually threw up on the spot. For me it was not a good course at all, and I was not surprised I dropped to a 2nd Class certificate.

By this time there were just two more weeks left to the end of my courses. Bunty and I decided to let our house and she moved down to Paignton to stay with her parents. I suspected that a sea appointment with P&O would appear soon after the course ended. We had enjoyed ourselves together during my courses and thought we could afford another week together on my very last week in Portland. I booked a room for the week in a pub on the road from Portland towards Weymouth. The publican was a Chief Writer in HMS OSPREY working out his last six months in the Navy before retirement. This was helpful for me because we both had to rise early and he not only cooked my breakfast with his own hand but drove me to the dockyard gate in his car. Bunty spent her days

List 1, The Royal Naval Reserve

taking exercise by walking all over the stony Chesil Beach.

I joined HMS OSPREY for part two of my TAS course. The first week was spent learning all about the three sonar sets that were needed to detect a submarine and the SQUID mortars that could destroy it. In OSPREY our instructors always had in the front of their minds how nearly we had lost WW2 to the U boats and it was truly an anti submarine ambiance. We soon started work in the A/S Trainers. These consisted of about 20 double-decker buses that stood in a car park. Whilst our class only used two, the remainder were fully mobile to go anywhere in the country to train up A/S teams. They were compartmented to replicate the inside of a frigate - a bridge with CO, NO, OOW and Yeoman, and an A/S office with the sonar sets, TASO and three operators. Two further compartments housed the instructors directing the game and playing the submarine, and the RAF aviators overhead, who provided information and bombs. We spent two days in these trainers, each of us taking the different roles in turn.

For our second week we spent three days at sea and the class split into two halves with each half going to a Castle class frigate in Portland. I joined HMS TINTAGEL CASTLE. A friendly submarine also known as the clockwork mouse took part. The exercise consisted of each ship in turn running in to find the submarine by sonar, establish its position, course, speed and depth, and then fire the mortar. This had to land the bombs in the water 300 yards ahead of the ship and on the new estimated position of the submarine, set to detonate at its depth. The submarine tried to evade the attack by changing the position characteristics above. For the frigate the trick was to keep its target pinpointed and make corrections to the attack plan to thwart the submarine's evasion efforts. Success depended upon the ability of the frigate's bridge and TAS teams to work together very closely and quickly. Each day both ships made many runs with their class changing roles for each run. Each run was carefully recorded in both frigate and submarine for later analysis at the final course wash up. By the third day most of our runs were spot on, proving the value of the training. I was in my element, greatly enjoying the challenge of marrying eyes, ears and brain, and controlling successful runs. My examination in Part I yielded only a 2nd Class certificate since I had not tried hard enough in the mine warfare section but OSPREY marked me "exceptional" for ability in Part II. Our courses were completed, and we broke up.

It was four years before I could find time to undergo further training, by which time Bunty and I were living in Hong Kong. In the Far East the military situation was fraught with tension as the Communist Governments sought power over the whole area. China and the USA had no diplomatic ties and, lacking an embassy, the Americans had a very large consulate in Hong Kong from which to monitor China. For the whole of our two and a half year's stay, there were always two Super Constellation aircraft at Kai Tak airport ready to evacuate consular staff. At sea between Taiwan and Hong Kong there was a fleet of 60 or 70 US warships, comprising carrier groups, escorts, assault craft with marines, and fleet train; their purpose was to protect Taiwan and some smaller islands from China. From time to time, two or three ships would visit Hong Kong for a week of R&R, much to the delight of the shops, bars and brothels in the colony. The USA blocked all Chinese imports, enabling Hong Kong traders to enrich themselves by issuing Hong Kong certificates of origin for goods they both imported from China and then exported to the USA.

The UK faced its different threats from its main base in Singapore which housed its most senior official, an admiral who was CinC Far East. There were always quite a few RN warships around, augmented by the navies of Australia, New Zealand and Canada, and the naval dockyard at nearby Johore was operational. The CinC's fleet commander was a vice admiral. In Hong Kong we had an army GOC with several battalions of troops and a Commodore for the Navy. The Hong Kong squadron based at HMS TAMAR, the Hong Kong base, consisted of six "Ham" class inshore mine sweepers. At Kai Tak, the RAF operated their aircraft in support. In China, just across the border from Kowloon, there was a huge Chinese People's Army and the Pearl River hosted a couple of squadrons of Chinese fast gunboats. GOC's considered opinion was that he could hold out for four days if the Chinese army crossed the border.

It was against this background that I was able to take local leave from the office for a fortnight, and the Admiralty sent me instructions to join HMS CAVALIER in Hong Kong, for two weeks at sea. She was a modern CA class fleet destroyer and with CHEVIOT formed the 8th Destroyer Squadron. She was typically armed with four 4.7" guns, four 21" torpedoes, sonar and Squid, plus close range AA weapons, and could make 30 knots. Her ship's company numbered about 240.

I joined her whilst she was berthed in TAMAR and reported to Lieutenant William Staveley, First Lieutenant and XO. He took me to meet the Captain, Commander "Ginger" Cartwright, who was sitting at his desk. I passed him my training record, which he examined, and then he asked me how much watch keeping experience I had. I told him it was 10 years. His next question was whether I had a Master's certificate and I replied that I did. He rose from his chair grasping my hand and saying "My dear chap, please do sit down, I need another watch keeper, glass of gin?". It was a far cry from meeting the Captain of a P&O ship. I found it very difficult to understand his plight, because the wardroom seemed to be full of able officers.

We went to sea straightaway and spent a whole week in a five ship formation in the South China Sea, carrying out just about every exercise known. Vice Admiral and FO2 Durlacher was at sea flying his flag in the 6" cruiser NEWFOUNDLAND. In company were the New Zealand 6"cruiser ROYALIST, the Dutch destroyer DELFT and the 8th DS ships CHEVOIT and CAVALIER. I was invited to do a lot of ship handling. I watched one Replenishment At Sea and took the con for the next three. In merchant ships, getting up close and personal with another ship just does not feature at all but for a RAS it is necessary. With both ships doing 10 knots we had to close and pass the RAS gear. In a night encounter exercise the force was split into two parts after which each part tried to sneak up on the other to attack. The ships were all darkened and in the small Ops Room I conducted the plot (with both Captain and

NO standing very close). This turned out to be a task using just radar, which required a lot of concentration and vigilance with ships dashing around at 30 knots. Later we broke up in the Singapore Strait and followed CHEVIOT into the Johore Strait, berthing in the dockyard.

Next day was the official Queen's Birthday and at about 0700 the two ships' companies, all of us dressed in long whites, plus medals and swords for the officers, climbed into buses at the dockyard and were taken into Singapore for a parade on the maidan. At that time the maidan was on the sea front overlooking Singapore roads and was attractive for that. Today it is about half a mile inland with the reclaimed land in use for the container base and some of the charm has gone. But the war memorials are all in good shape since the tidy Singaporeans do not wish to deny their colonial heritage. At the maidan we were joined by parties from the other Services making a lot of smart looking people on parade. We were inspected, marched past, and had prayers, but it was not long before the clerk of the weather remembered that we were honouring our reigning Sovereign and opened the taps. We all got soaked in heavy rain which was not uncomfortable in Singapore's temperatures but deadly for best uniforms. We were bussed back to Johore, and leave was piped.

Next morning we again sailed early, following CHEVIOT to an anchorage in Singapore Roads and joining the carrier BULWARK and the NZ cruiser ROYALIST for Operation SHOW BOAT. Malaya was approaching independence and the creation of Malaysia (including at that time Singapore). Her Majesty's Government was worried that independence might bring in a Communist government and CinC FE thought it appropriate to convince all and sundry that the UK was still a major military force. Many of the top politicians had shown Communist sympathies, as had young under-graduates in the university who for some reason were referred to as school children, despite being in their 20s. The Navy was to take them to sea for a day and demonstrate what it could do. BULWARK took a large party of senior people aboard and about 120 "school children" were shared between the cruiser and two destroyers.

List 1, The Royal Naval Reserve

The operation was to use a great deal of live ammunition in order to achieve lots of noise and visual effects. We were uncertain of the best place to locate our passengers and ensure their safety on the upper deck of a destroyer without blocking their view of events. The fo'csle and quarterdeck were clearly inappropriate since there were four guns on them and the torpedo deck had lots of knobs around that our TASO did not want touched. The fore end of the squid deck was finally selected and the passengers were stationed there, clutching their bags of sandwiches and bottles of coca cola.

Arriving in clear water to the East of Singapore, the first demonstration was given by BULWARK's jets which flew off in great style and bombed a fog float towed by ROYALIST at long stay. The aviators destroyed it very quickly but our Kiwi colleagues had plenty of spares for further demonstrations. The next serial was a throw-off shoot on BULWARK with the two destroyers putting salvoes of shells into the water just ahead of the carrier. CAVALIER had been fitted with Flyplane 5, an early computerised gun control system which both laid and trained the guns whilst layer and trainer sat in their seats as safety numbers, ready to open the firing circuit if anything was amiss. It was quite a good system, but was prone to occasional computer glitches causing all the guns in unison moving quickly off target and back. One thing not fully known on the bridge and in the gunnery director just behind it was that at the time members of the ship's company were going down like ninepins from a virus acquired perhaps from wet clothing, or their run ashore. Fortunately the computer was on its best behaviour and there were no bricks through BULWARK's bridge.

There was no clockwork mouse in the force but the destroyers together attacked a pretend submarine each firing six live squid mortar bombs at the same point in the sea. The mortars fired their bombs in a ripple and forward over the bridge to land 300 yards ahead of the ship. The bombs are quite large and are immediately visible in flight to those on deck which came as a surprise to our passengers who were certainly impressed, if not terrified. On the way back to Singapore, BULWARK's helicopters took off and played an intricate game of cops and robbers in the sky to bring an amusing and quieter end to the day.

There appeared to be no noticeable reaction to SHOW BOAT but the new Malaysia did not go Communist. Indeed, in a few years time Malaysia asked for help from the Royal Navy, when Indonesia decided it wanted to take over the peninsular by infiltrating troops across the Strait of Malacca. The Royal Navy responded resolutely with frigates and coastal mine sweepers. A friend who was CO of a coastal minesweeper told me they had to contend with fast praus, powered by large outboards and armed with high velocity .22 rifles. This does not sound hazardous but the rounds could go straight through the wooden planking of a coastal and then ricochet around inside. The Navy's response was to resuscitate old and stripped down Lewis guns, kept ready on the bridge.

My time in CAVALIER was at an end. I could not believe how much I had been trusted to carry out tasks that previously I had only dreamed about. I had also carried out a lot of graveyard watch keeping, for which my Captain thanked me, and gave me a good chit. On the bridge at night I was greatly helped by the signalmen who not only showed me where all the right buttons were but created outstanding kye (cocoa), using an electric kettle and blocks of chocolate, made while crouching under the chart table. The Captain and wardroom went on to much greater things. The Captain became Captain of the Dockyard at Johore, the 1st Lieutenant became Admiral Sir William Staveley, First Sea Lord, and the NO not only skippered the Navy's yacht to victory on the Sydney/Rio sector of the round-the-world-race but became Vice Admiral Sir Jeremy Dreyer as well.

The next day I was bussed to RAF Transport Command at Changi for a lift back to Hong Kong. We were instructed to wear long whites, proper shoes, and a cap. On boarding the aircraft, I found all the seats faced aft. The plane's quartermaster explained that the RAF's policy was maximum safety. The idea never caught on with the world's airlines and I still feel aghast at all the bare flesh exposed on a holiday flight to the Mediterranean.

The next year I took local leave again and joined HMS

List 1, The Royal Naval Reserve

DAMERHAM of the Hong Kong inshore squadron. The Hams were 105' all wooden craft built by Vospers and powered by two diesels that gave them 13 knots. They were equipped with small scale sweeping gear for both ground influence mines, and wire sweeps for moored impact mines. On the fo'csle there was a Bofors 40/60, quite a big gun for a very small ship. It had been naval policy for them to be manned with a Captain, 1st Lieutenant and Coxswain from the UK, with twelve Chinese ratings recruited in Hong Kong. The ratings were good ship-proud sailors who kept their ship very smart. But about a month before I joined things went wrong. A young CO in the squadron was bringing his small ship back from a two day courtesy visit to the neighbouring colony of Macao and was in Chinese waters crossing the Pearl River estuary. Two Chinese gunboats bore down with their guns manned and trained on him. He did not lose his cool, maintaining course and speed with his unmanned Bofors trained fore and aft but he did sound the action stations alarm. His two British shipmates appeared immediately but none of his ratings would turn to.

Nothing happened and after ten minutes the Chinese bore away, and the IMS entered Hong Kong waters, returning to a berth in TAMAR. But the crew had acted mutinously and were put under close arrest. The radio waves to Whitehall became busy and all the Chinese ratings except chefs were discharged. In Johore dockyard HMS NEWFOUNDLAND was undergoing a six month refit, something much enjoyed by her crew: it meant a little work in the forenoon and sport and picnics in the afternoon. But quite suddenly 60 or so ratings were packing their bags and being bussed to RAF Changi for a flight to Hong Kong. They were not best pleased at their loss of an idyll.

I joined DAMERHAM and reported to CO Lieutenant Chris Parry, newly arrived from the UK, which enabled me to offer my services as his NO because I had sailed a lot in Hong Kong waters. The squadron carried out a lot of local tasks, but the most important were inshore minesweeping, assisting the marine police in arresting immigrant smugglers, and showing the flag on the extremities of Hong Kong waters. In a tri-service exercise the whole squadron set off to sweep and mark the various channels between the islands to the South. Having spent all day sweeping and marking we went to anchor in Stanley Bay for the night with individual ships patrolling for two hours to try and stop local fishermen from stealing our dan buoys. The weather had got up and approaching Waglan our progress was being impeded by a large junk making expert short tacks to windward. Chris was becoming impatient but I counselled him to stay well clear knowing that any contact would result in DAMERHAM ending up as matchwood. To prove it I later took him to a junk building yard in Aberdeen where he was amazed at the size, weight and strength of pieces of timber being built into a large junk.

The Marine police owned several large launches, capable of 15 knots, but they were over-worked and so for our support role we embarked two armed Chinese police officers to show us where to look and to do the talking for us. We went to a large bay to the East where there were many large junks moving slowly at about 4 knots and with fishing lines streamed astern. On approaching one she suddenly took off. She looked to be going at 18 knots or more and we could not catch her. The smugglers were making a lot of money by smuggling refugees from China into the colony. The Hong Kong government never sent them back and in fact made Herculean efforts to build homes for them but the police wanted the smugglers. They had ordered new and faster launches but even without them sometimes they would score in the dark by using two launches, radar and R/T to seal both ends of a channel. There was a story going the rounds but not made public, that in one of the junks they seized, a minute inspection revealed a third engine on the centre line. This turned out to be a Rolls Royce Merlin engine, probably recovered from the Spitfires donated to China after WW2. Whether anything in this story is true I do not know, but given Chinese ingenuity, it could well be.

Showing the flag involved three IMS steaming right round Lantao Island to the West. In 1959 the island was almost uninhabited and without the new airport and hotel complexes of today. Hong Kong waters were defined by treaty and the limits sometimes followed the shore line, but to the West the line was straight and ran from North to South. On the Western side the waters of the Pearl River were part of China. It was possible to send small ships around the South West corner of Lantau within Hong Kong waters but it needed accurate navigation. Several years before I arrived, the squadron, then consisting of Harbour Defence Motor Launches, had been following the routine when a Chinese shore battery opened fire on the lead ship causing severe damage and casualties. The up-to-date Chinese tactic was to harass the squadron, but not to open fire with their canons. On our trip round, three gunboats duly appeared and took station quite close to us but still in Chinese waters.

Each gunboat had trained their guns on us. Our response was to keep a stiff upper lip, maintain course and speed, with our gun trained fore and aft and unmanned. Our gun's crew, clutching clips of four rounds crouched in the lee of the wheelhouse on the off side where they were out of sight, just in case the inscrutable enemy got serious. When we turned to starboard on reaching the North of Lantau, they took off back across the Pearl.

When we returned to live in the UK in 1960 I applied for further training as opportunity offered. I spent two weeks in HMS PLOVER, an antique minelayer, but we spent nearly all the time propping up the quay in Portsmouth dockyard and not going to sea, which demonstrated very well that in peace time the Navy could be very boring. The mess wine caterer obviously had plenty of time to haggle with suppliers because a tot of Plymouth gin cost only 1.5d. The stokers were kept busy because after an officer had taken a bath it was necessary to call out their duty watch to pump it out.

A year later I joined HMS VIGILANT in Plymouth and spent two busy weeks at sea with further ship handling. She was a fleet destroyer from the 30s downgraded to frigate because her weapon systems had not been updated. But she could still make over 30 knots which was ideal for training both artificers and stokers from the engineering school HMS RALEIGH. She had the typical two boiler room configuration of a destroyer, of which the first was in everyday use and the second was connected in when 30 knots was required. Making the connection required both accuracy and timing by a large engine room crew. It was part and parcel of a small ship powered by steam turbines but which changed dramatically when the Navy switched to gas turbines.

We went to sea each weekday with our classes being taught while steaming up and down in the open sea in the Western Channel with quite a lot of shipping around. The CO was Commander Peter Richardson, a very experienced sea officer who left his ship to me once we were clear of Plymouth. He told me my presence would help him clear up his paperwork since he had no watch keeper available who could be left on the bridge at high speed in the traffic outside Plymouth. It was a welcome spell and I enjoyed it.

In 1962 I was told that I would soon have to leave List 1 since my civilian employment was no longer that of a professional sailor. However I might wish to transfer to List 3, made up of the officers and ratings who manned the eleven RNR Divisions in the UK and which were in fact the old RNVR. To put a toe in the water I was invited to join HMS ST DAVID, the sea tender to South Wales Division, HMS CAMBRIA in Cardiff, for two weeks as 1st Lieutenant, and I accepted.

Throughout the 50s the East/West tension increased, with the American eagle and the Russian bear glaring at each other across the Atlantic. It was a multi threat situation with airborne nuclear weapons on both sides, a very large Red Army ready to move into West Germany, and a large and modern navy which ranged worldwide. The Russian Fleet Admiral Gorshkov was busy enlarging his fleet to include nuclear powered submarines designed and built from scratch and from first principles. The nightmare scenario was that the Red Army with air support would move into West Germany. The NATO response would have to include the movement across the Atlantic to Europe of millions of tons of war material. This would invite the attention of the Russian navy, and particularly their submarines, to be countered by the NATO navies. But there was one small area that needed attention which was mine clearance in the approaches to the NATO European ports. It was not much use to bring convoys into the Channel if they could not be berthed to discharge their cargoes and the Russians had always

My grandparents Captain Stephen and Jane Penney circa 1900.

P&O VICTORIA.
One of four Jubilee Class ships built in 1888. OCEANA was one of her sisters.

My Pa Stephen Leslie MBE and my Mama Ivy May.

With my parents and sister in Richmond, 1934.

Pangbourne, Founder's Day June 1943.
HM King George VI with HRH Princess Elizabeth, inspects.
Author's face just above HM's left shoulder.

62 years on. Founder's Day 2005.
Presenting the 1945 OP's Instructors Bugle to headmaster Dr K M Grieg.

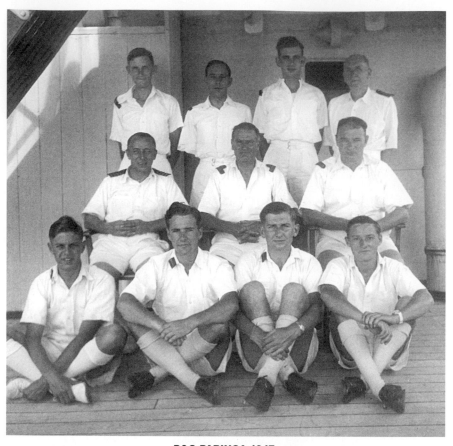

P&O PARINGA 1947.
Captain Cyril Pollitt and his officers.
Four apprentices in front row. Roger Game, Horace Biggs, author, Derrick Bolas.

Bunty.

Two brand new second mates partying with friends.
April 1948.

P&O CORFU.
Built in 1933, pictured after refitting in 1948.
Her original second (dummy) funnel was removed in 1939 on conversion
to armed merchant cruiser as HMS CORFU.

P&O CANTON.
The last of the six C class, built 1939.
Pictured in 1948 after refitting, the C class were all very popular
with the expatriate community in the Far East.

P&O MOOLTAN.
Built in Belfast in 1923 and still in service in 1952.

P&O CHUSAN.
Built in Barrow in 1950.
Pictured in Hong Kong in 1955.

St Luke's Church Torquay, 8th February 1950.
"All the nice girls - love a sailor."

With Lindley Jane age three months at Sidcup, 1954.

demonstrated competence in mine warfare.

All the NATO navies included on their fleet lists squadrons of mine countermeasure (MCM) ships, but in total they did not add up to enough to counter the threat. The Royal Navy had three squadrons each of about six ships in full commission and with one - the Fishery Protection Squadron - working with the fishermen in peacetime. In the 50s the Navy built a large number of CONISTON class coastal mine sweepers. These were composite craft of wood and aluminium construction and ideally suited to the task. A lot of them were laid up, mainly because there were not enough crews. The Admiralty decided that with proper training they could be manned by the RNR Divisions and each Division was allotted a CMS as their sea tender.

In this role, berthed usually at their Divisions all year round, they could provide both weekend training and four or five longer periods of 14 days per annum in which to participate in NATO and national exercises and operations. In meeting their NATO obligations the Navy had persuaded its NATO partners that the eleven ships could count as one squadron. Much later, when cost-effectiveness entered the scene, I learned that the cost of running the whole RNR was about the same as one RN MCM squadron. In the meantime we had to demonstrate their competence to NATO, which meant producing the ships fully manned and able to perform.

I reported to CAMBRIA, and got down to work, moving around swiftly to find what a CMS was all about. It soon became apparent why the staff of Admiral Commanding Reserves had cast a net over me. CAMBRIA was a small Division and could not man ST DAVID for the required period. The CO was Lt. Cdr Don Bairdow, an experienced officer who, in civil life, was a Marks and Spencer store manager. The only other seaman (apart from myself) was a Skipper Lieutenant from List 2 and obviously netted by ACR like me. He was a very experienced seaman, and brilliant on the sweep deck with all the wire knitting over the stern but MCM navigation in the Navy was a closed book to him and he seemed more comfortable in the Chief's mess than the wardroom. CAMBRIA provided a Lt Cdr (Weapons Electrical), a friend of the CO and another M&S manager, together with a Lieutenant (Mechanical Engineer), to complete the wardroom.

The 1st Lieutenant's main work station was the quarter deck both for minesweeping and Harbour Stations. We left the berth in a South Westerly Force 6 and proceeded towards the lock that would take us into the Bristol Channel. From the quarterdeck I got my first lesson of how a CMS behaved in a beam wind and at a low speed. My CO was in difficulty and before we got into the lock had crunched a yacht alongside the quay, and sinking it, not a very good start but we kept on going. We had an uncomfortable passage round Lands End but arrived in Portsmouth in one piece to join a training period with five other CMS. This was something that VERNON did very well, providing a staff officer to ride in each ship and knock off a lot of rough edges. I managed to hint to our staff officer that, whilst still being 1st Lieutenant and XO I should shift my station to the bridge and the Skipper Lieutenant's to the quarterdeck. He suggested it to my Captain who agreed and things went a lot better.

After ten days of quite hard work we sailed for an R&R single ship visit to Concarneau, in Brittany, a major French fisherman's port. This turned out to be very enjoyable, partly because we were made very welcome. A close knit trio of Mayor, Chief of Police, and a local businessman who seemed to own most of the town, made it their business to entertain us. They made many arrangements for the ship's company and one evening invited the wardroom to a dream-like restaurant a few miles away. We drove there in two large Citroens and on a country road the speedometer read 160 km/h, but of course there is no problem if the Chief of Police is driving himself.

There was only one blot on the landscape. It was very rare indeed for RNR crews to misbehave ashore, but our Chef got very drunk and assaulted a couple of locals. He was in fact an RN rating because for some reason the RNR was not allowed to recruit cooks. On weekends there was always a volunteer seaman or stoker from our own resources to run the galley but for longer periods the RN provided a chef. The chefs we got were not usually very good but it must be taken into account that a fortnight in a CMS would not appeal to those who aspired to Michelin stars. He appeared on board in the company of a couple of gendarmes complete with a report of the incident. Quickly consulting our books we established that assaults had to be brought before an officer of the rank of Commander which we did not have. It was quite clear that he had to be placed under close arrest but what did we do then? Close arrest requires either the cells, which we did not have, or an armed guard round the clock, which was difficult in a CMS. As a temporary measure we locked him in the tiller flat. But we could not go to sea with him there. Don Bairdow decided to send him back to Plymouth by train and ferry. So the engineer was sent to Concarneau station armed with cash for a single ticket to Calais via Paris and a warrant thereafter to Plymouth. Our friendly Chief of Police provided escorts to the station, in Paris, and at Calais Maritime. A signal to the Provost Marshall in Plymouth covered the rest.

There was just one more problem; from where would the cash come. A CMS had a £50 contingency fund so Don Bairdow drew the cash and recorded it. What he did not know then was that for six months he would be in correspondence with a civilian official in the Admiralty who would not believe a word of Don's report and demanded a fuller explanation.

I had enjoyed my time in ST DAVID and decided I could not only enjoy List 3 but could make a useful contribution to it (as long as I could keep my sense of humour).

Chapter 9. Apprentice again

After leaving CHUSAN, I first took some leave and then purchased a monthly season ticket from Sidcup to London Bridge to work as a clerk in P&O's head office. Today this is not an honoured title but it was commonplace at the time and after all there were some very important Clerks around. My first place of work was to be the Correspondence Department, the modern equivalent being the Secretary's Department. The department reported through the Company Secretary to Wilfred Mize, who had joined P&O as a clerk in September 1908 along with my Pa. The department had a very wide range of activities, many of which would be farmed out to other departments or outsourced in a company of the 21st century.

The Head of Department was Douglas Blythe, whose son Gordon I had sailed with in PARINGA. Deputy Head was Harold Duncombe, whose personal task was to be a sort of Sea Daddy to the Learners, arranging their London programmes in all the departments and monitoring their progress. He did it very well as long as they did not need him in June, when he took his holidays to be able to umpire the tennis at Wimbledon. He continued to umpire after leaving P&O and was in action when Gonzalez exploded to dispute Harold's line call and called for the referee, unheard of in those days. Next day in the press, Harold was depicted in a cartoon on court with a broken racket over his head.

Peter Sherwood was Chief Clerk, and my immediate boss, and I got on with him very well. Brian Redrup was in charge of the carriage of mails for the Post Office. There were about ten other clerks dealing with various areas, including the Company's share registrar, properties, ship's voyage instructions, marine casualties to the ships, luncheons in the ships at Tilbury, which were provided free of charge to both shareholders and pensioners, and legal matters,

Apprentice again

amongst others.

We were supported by four secretaries who would work for whoever needed their support. The department was responsible for recruiting secretaries and always selected the crème de la crème for itself. Two in particular did a lot of work for me: the first was Margaret Bell. One day I was dictating a letter to her that mentioned Darling Island, in Australia. It seems that Mr Pitman's shorthand book did not include those two words and she asked me to repeat them. I did so but they still did not click and she had to ask me again. This time I turned up the volume for the first word which was all that the rest of the staff in the open plan room heard. This was embarrassing for Margaret but greatly enjoyed by every one else. The other was Jean Childs, a newcomer sharpening up her secretarial skills, who later went to sea as woman assistant purser, and changed her surname to Constantine after meeting another P&O Matey.

Whilst I had to work in every activity area to learn what they did, I spent a lot of time with Peter Sherwood on marine casualties since his work had fallen behind and there was a large stack of current files by his desk. If there was any damage to a ship a casualty report had to be raised. The scope of reports was enormous, from collisions ending up in court to minor storm damage, and I was able to learn about the complex world of marine insurance starting with Lloyds Room just across the road. This world encompassed the business of general average, which started with the Greeks and advanced over the centuries to serve the interests of both ship owners and cargo owners very well. The principle of general average was that a voyage by a ship was an adventure and if there were problems en voyage whereby the ship made a financial sacrifice in the interest of both parties, it would be borne by both parties in shares linked to their different interests. It was quite different from particular average, which was caused by Acts of God and which was the responsibility of the relevant party and their insurers.

I think I was of quite a lot of use to Peter because I knew the answers to many of the questions without needing to refer to the

Marine and Engineer Departments or the ship. When it was necessary to refer, I knew the questions to ask. I took particular pleasure in writing a demanding and searching letter to a senior captain I personally disliked - for Peter to sign of course. Not only did I learn a great deal about marine hull insurance but Peter's stack of files slimmed down agreeably.

It was Sir Donald Anderson's idea to provide the ship luncheons and he personally took great interest in them. As far as the shareholders were concerned, he felt that the Annual Report was inadequate to explain to shareholders how the company invested their funds. Each summer we mounted two or three luncheons, catering for about 300 shareholders on each occasion, and they went very well, although it would be impossible to quantify any benefit arising. In the world of today it would probably not be the right thing to do with the stock market attracting so many short term shareholders.

The pensioners' luncheons were similar in style but the atmosphere was very different. Apart from anything else, the wine bill was obviously much higher. Organising them was quite a challenge, particularly in view of the chain of command in the office to the very top, all demanding people. But for me, the pensioners' lunches were a double whammy since my Pa was a pensioner. He used to stay the night with us in Sidcup before the lunch, and his opening words on arrival consisted of a complete cross examination about what I had arranged for him. Was there a good curry? Who were his table companions? Were they thoroughly good fellows or the other sort? But he always enjoyed himself.

The address of the P&O office was quite simply 122, Leadenhall Street, London EC3. This obscured the fact that it was really quite large both above and below ground. It had originally been a coaching house, complete with large courtyard with room to turn a coach and four. As the years rolled by, P&O purchased adjoining hereditaments on both sides and at the back. In the cellars, a bullion room was created for bullion and specie landed from ships at the weekend when the banks were closed. It was also a company rule that captains might not sleep ashore if their ship held bullion. To

Apprentice again

facilitate turning large vehicles loaded with heavy bullion, a turntable had been built in the courtyard. The building had its own water supply from deep wells in situ. Before the building was pulled down to make way for a new tower block, the courtyard provided a good car park for the Chairman's car and a couple of visitors. In the 1950s, Leadenhall Street was the Mecca of British shipping with about 90 per cent of its buildings housing ship owners. The Baltic Exchange was just around the corner in St Mary Axe. There were only a very few bankers in the street.

The Correspondence Department was in charge of the company's archives which were housed in cavernous cellars. There could be found all the voyage reports of all the ships over the years. There was also a Missing Steamers section, which I found fascinating, not least because there were three files labelled OCEANA. The files contained several letters from my Grandpa, typed with an early machine that had letters but no numerals, which had been inked in after typing. Reading these enabled me to get to know a little more about the man.

My next department was the Export Freight Department, which dealt with all the cargo shipped out from London. It was a big department, not least because the paperwork was considerable and very labour intensive. Its first task was sales to maintain contact with our customers and persuade them to use our services. The next task was to accept bookings and provide booking lists for other departments. Once cargo had been loaded, an army of clerks tackled the documentation. Shippers delivered their goods to the docks and received a mate's receipt or dock receipt. They then prepared their Bills of Lading and lodged them with the office. Clearing and signing their Bills was something they wanted done as soon as possible so that they could collect their funds from the bank at which their letter of credit had been established.

I joined a line of bill passers. Our job was to match up the dock receipts with the bills, just about the most frustrating work imaginable. For one ship there could be 2,000 bills to pass, using many more dock receipts. Each bill passer had a large "too difficult" basket which could take a long time to sort out. It was nevertheless an important task, because passing a bill for goods that had not been received left the company wide open to a claim for them. Mistakes were made of course but in those days people on both sides of the counter seemed to be able to admit to mistakes and get them sorted out. In this century it would be seen as a promising opportunity for fraud.

The next expert was the rating clerk, who marked up the bills with the applicable rate of freight and provided the figures for the shipper's freight account. Our tariff listed more than 2,000 different commodities, with some very similar to others. The pricing policy was based upon "what the trade would bear", which meant that radios carried a much higher rate than bags of cement, and bullion was ad valorem. But the rating clerk's problem can be demonstrated by his having to determine whether the goods were "steel angle", or "steel angle, galvanised", or "steel angle, galvanised and worked", all differently rated. In today's world of containers his job has disappeared, since the rate is per container.

The next team were the manifest typists using typewriters with a very long carriage to compile the freight manifests. Each page measured about 24" x 18" and had five carbon copies. These had to be ready to accompany the ships, a job that could not wait for another day.

It was logical to go next to the Import Freight Department, which did similar things in reverse. The department swapped a consignee's bill of lading for a delivery order enabling him to collect his goods from the dock company. It was still a labour-intensive activity, but on a smaller scale, mainly because imports into the UK arrived in larger size shipments than exports. The freight cost had been calculated on shipment, and nearly all freight was payable on shipment. It was of course on discharge that damage and goods missing came to light and these were dealt with by the Claims Department. With cargo ships visiting a number of ports in North West Europe during their voyages it made economic sense to both discharge and load at some of them, but this led to weekly battles between the two departments to decide on the ship's port programme. At one stage this reached hysterical proportions, resolved by appointing the line manager responsible for overall operation to decide and a truce was achieved.

The Claims Department was much more interesting intellectually. Of course there were routine simple tasks but a lot of detailed knowledge about marine insurance was required. Simple and clear-cut claims were met fairly promptly but there were others that needed time for arguing with either customers or their cargo underwriters' recovery departments. The really difficult ones were usually settled over lunch with both parties present, in batches by negotiation and horse trading. Market forces played an important part, especially for commodities such as fresh fruit from the Southern hemisphere. If a reefer ship with fresh fruit arrived at a port which had not received a similar ship for weeks there would be no claims even if there was spoilt fruit. But when three independently owned and operated ships arrived on the same day there would be an avalanche of claims.

I went next to the Passenger Department at a separate office in Cockspur Street in the West End. The customer entrance at the front led to a most elegant and lofty hall, superbly furnished. Around the walls were desks for about eight booking clerks, all of them wearing their suit jackets. Each desk had chairs in front for visitors. In the centre was a waiting area, with armchairs, sofas and tables with the latest magazines, such as the Tatler and London Illustrated News. Prospective passengers were led by a uniformed messenger to a vacant desk, or the waiting area. Today I recall it as something taken straight from P G Woodhouse's book "My Man Jeeves".

Having received details of the customer's requirements, the booking clerk completed a booking slip. This showed sailings, dates and the type of accommodation required, which could range from a First Class De-Luxe cabin with its own bathroom to a six berth Tourist Class cabin on the lowest deck. Experienced travellers to the East could also ask for the POSH treatment. This stood for "Port Out, Starboard Home", which signified that on the outward voyage they sought a cabin on the port side of the ship, in order to be in the shade on the four day easterly passage across the Indian Ocean, and vice versa on the return passage.

The messenger then carried the booking slip to the berthing section, located outside the booking hall. This was necessary because the opulence of the booking hall was not repeated outside it and the berthing section consisted of a large cupboard under the stairs, furnished with very large bookshelves to accommodate the berthing books. There was a counter for two berthing clerks in their shirtsleeves to write up the books. Even ships of the same class were not identical in their cabin layout so a berthing book for every ship had to be separately printed. A separate book for each voyage was necessary and bookings could be made two years ahead. The many books needed a lot of shelf space.

On receiving the booking slip, the berthing clerk dragged down the appropriate book(s), searching for vacant cabins that matched the customer's requirements and price. He then wrote an offer on the booking slip, while at the same time pencilling his offer into the berthing book. Another messenger carried the slip back to the booking clerk, who revealed the offer to the intending passengers. In many cases it was accepted on the spot and a cheque book was produced, in which case the berthing clerk inked in his book, sending the cheque to the cashier and details to the accounts department. If the passenger was unable to conclude there and then, needing perhaps to consult family and others, the offer was marked as open for a week or more in the berthing book (in pencil).

In the 21st century this must seem to many to be how Noah filled his ark, but it worked very well, providing a great deal of contact with real people that no longer occurs today. "Look what I got" says the modern man to his "partner", brandishing an email confirming that he has spent a quarter of his bonus on a cruise costing £60,000, without speaking to anyone, not even a telephone android.

Harold Duncombe suggested that I might be interested in joining the Chartered Institute of Transport, since the company believed it was the appropriate professional body for shipping and encouraged membership by way of a contribution towards the cost of books and examinations. I therefore joined as a student and during my year in

Apprentice again

London attended evening school, at the end of which I sat the three day examination for graduate membership and passed. Whilst shipping would always be my first choice of transport, there was a clear identification with trains, aircraft and road vehicles that has always endured.

I went to other departments which provided vital if unexciting information and completed my year, at the end of which I was appointed to the Learnership. My instructions were to proceed to the East for three years or more, starting with Hong Kong. With my small family I was to join SURAT, a cargo ship carrying twelve passengers. I had hoped that we might sail in a passenger ship where Bunty and I could enjoy ourselves after our austere life in the UK but Wilfred Mizen, feigning ignorance of my cargo officer experience, decreed that I needed to learn about cargo work, like the other learners.

For safety reasons the company refused to carry small children in cargo ships, not least because the ship's side rails had 12" spacing (passenger ships had 9"), and this was to cause us much concern during our passage. The ship did not carry a doctor either, but we coped with a two year old who appeared close to death at one moment, and bright as a button the next.

We needed to sell our house, not least to raise the wind to buy a car, which was essential equipment for the Hong Kong office. We quickly found a buyer, who turned out to be a charming Polish gentleman called Zbignew Mygrodski, and his English wife, and so we bought a brand new Ford Anglia for £360 tax free, and took it with us in SURAT.

Chapter 10. Makee Learnee Taipan

In September 1956, having parked our furniture with my sister, we exchanged the key to our house for a key to the car and set off on a round of visits to both sets of our parents, and other family members and friends. In Lymington both my parents were in good shape, and were enjoying their Hampshire surroundings. They also enjoyed the company of their first grand-daughter for a few days during our visit. We went on to Paignton to stay with Bunty's parents, who were also fit and well. By this stage they had sold the Park Hotel, and moved into an attractive cottage for their retirement. However it was not long before William Riley got a bit bored and he took on the job of managing director of the Queen's Hotel in Torquay.

Our tour of Southern England complete, we drove to Southampton to join SURAT, then completing her outward cargo and embarking her small passenger list. James Dunkley was in command so we were in good hands and he never asked me to keep a watch. Another old friend was Michael Bradford (Sammy) who was 2nd Officer, and who later went on to be Commodore. Amongst the other passengers were soldiers and their wives, and old Straits hands, except for one young man who worked in tin mining and with whom Lindley, then two and a half, fell madly in love. Keeping an eye on her when at sea was a very difficult task. Despite our vigilance she did go missing a few times, nearly giving her parents heart failure but she returned at last, reporting she had been to talk to Pete, whoever he was. To keep her occupied I scrounged some dunnage and old canvas from the ship, to create a small paddling pool which was then put to use daily at sea. It was a leisurely and routine voyage to Hong Kong, although whilst we were berthed in the old Port Swettenham we did witness the arrival of HMY BRITANNIA, with HRH Prince Philip aboard. The

Makee Learnee Taipan

passage from Singapore to Hong Kong was very rough with a North Easterly monsoon and our reception party found Bunty still dizzy from sea sickness.

The fraught political and military situation in Hong Kong at that time is described in Chapter 8 and was always present in our lives for our two and a half year's stay. Of course it affected everyone in the colony but did not seem to affect the colony's commercial and industrial development, which proceeded apace. The Hong Kong Government believed that if the Chinese army crossed the border, the Chinese population would collapse into chaos, so every European living in the colony was required to be listed for essential work, perhaps in the power station, or driving a lorry. As a RNR Lieutenant I was excluded from the list and the Commodore Hong Kong had me listed as CO of the examination vessel.

We were met on arrival and Bobbie Tagg, wife of director George Tagg, escorted Bunty and Lindley to our new home on the Peak whilst Jim Davis took me to the office to meet my new work colleagues. The first of course was the Taipan, the word used locally for the top boss of a large business, and Tim Flanagan was not only Managing Director of MacKinnon, Mackenzie and Co of Hong Kong Limited, but was also a member of the colony's Legislative Council. He was a director of China Light and Power, which provided the electricity, and a director of the Star Ferry which connected Hong Kong and Kowloon before the tunnel, and which carried more passengers each year than any other shipping company in the world. Tim was an Irishman, reputed to hate the English but it never showed to me. He was an old China hand who had been interned by the Japanese in WW2, which meant that he was a member of a very special club. He was both a friendly and amusing man. He and his wife Enid lived in the company house at the top of the Peak, a huge rambling place with a large garden, where they hosted frequent parties with great flair. I had yet to learn that an invitation to lunch on a Saturday, after a half day in the office, was to be avoided if possible, not least because the drinks went on until 1700, after which lunch was taken, resulting in the half day holiday being entirely lost. Tim's co-director was George

Tagg who did not seem to do very much, apart from being very friendly to us. Both directors left their juniors to get on with their jobs, but were always available for advice and help, though it was better to consult them before lunch. In any event, their team was very competent and needed little supervision.

The shipping manager, Eric McGregor, was in charge of all shipping operations. He and his wife Paddy lived just across from us on the Peak and were a very lonely couple who did not seem to fit in with the rest of the team. Paddy clearly enjoyed Bunty's company very much, often inviting her to meet, and accepting the unruliness of a two year old at her elegant table without demur. The Senior Assistant was Gerry Salmon, who was then line manager for the P&O passenger and cargo services and who was later to become the taipan, being awarded the style of Officer of the British Empire for his services to Hong Kong. He also managed the P&O Group's Eastern and Australian Company business, a top class cargo service between Australia and Japan. Their ships were all manned with Australian officers and Hong Kong crews. He and his wife Margaret, one of the first BOAC flight hostesses, produced a large family.

Alan Cook looked after the many British India (part of P&O) services that were employed between Japan, the Gulf, Pakistan and India, and the Knutsen Line. The latter was our only non P&O agency, the line being owned by Knut Knutsen, Old Andreas' Son, of Haugesund, Norway. It deployed five modern cargo liners between San Francisco and Fremantle in Australia. Alan had fought as a Royal Marine in WW2, and was on leave when we arrived but Jim Davis had taken over his desk for eight months. The expatriate team was completed by Malcolm Stark, who ran the passenger department, and Fred, the shore bo'sun who managed the two very smart harbour launches. Later in our stay he was relieved for leave by Bruce with whom I had sailed in ARCADIA.

Meanwhile Bunty and Lindley had been exploring our new home, which turned out to be a modern and spacious third-floor flat in a single tower. It provided two bedrooms with bathrooms, a large living and dining room, and a kitchen, off which led two small prison cells for staff. Overlooking the Peak School playing field, and other blocks of flats, we could see the chain of islands stretching for 40 miles to the South. To the North the bachelor's mess of the Hong Kong and Shanghai Bank blocked our view of Hong Kong, but it only needed about 50 steps from our entrance to see laid out the whole of the magnificent harbour. There were times, particularly in the South Westerly monsoon in the summer, when a cloud would descend on the Peak and blanket us in thick fog for up to three weeks, but at all other times we lived on top of the world.

Bobbie Tagg had provisionally engaged for us no less than three amahs, categorised by cook, wash and child. The last girl was a nice natured girl but within about 15 minutes Lindley had convinced them all that she was the boss. This was something we definitely did not want to encourage and Bobbie Tagg quietly removed her from the scene. The wash amah also soon left and in her place we recruited Chan Oi Lan, a young woman of our own age with a mind of her own but who worked very well at any house-hold task. A bit later, our cook left in preparation for yet another addition to her large family, and Chan Oi Lan became our only maid, an arrangement which suited us very well, and lasted until we left Hong Kong. The relationship went on long after that and continues to this day, and she and her husband visited us in the UK a few years ago. Our children grew faster and taller than hers and back in the UK we sent her cast-off clothes. Her eldest child, Fong, came to the UK for secretarial training in Stockport, at a time when Victoria was living in nearby Congleton, and was able to offer her a lot of support. When Fong's student visa expired and she wanted to stay in the UK, a letter from Hong Kong invited me to ask the Prime Minister to extend her visa. I had to decline, not having the right connections. Fong solved the problem for herself by marrying a Chinese UK resident but the marriage failed. This was after the arrival of three grandchildren for Chan Oi Lan. At Christmas each year Bunty still sends the three children "lucky money", a Chinese custom that involves placing bank notes in red envelopes for their New Year.

Sea Officer

The next morning I went to work in the Hong Kong office and was placed in charge of two departments: Inward Freight and Claims, each department with its own Chinese Chief Clerk and his staff. The Chief Clerks were experienced in the work of their departments and appeared completely unfazed by having yet another green expatriate assistant thrust upon them. They were both friendly and communicative and seemed anxious to put me at my ease. We acted on behalf of all the ships under the agency, not just one particular line. With my training from London I got to grips quickly with the tasks.

Hong Kong was one of the world's crossroads for shipping, encompassing every activity associated with the business and of course was a naval base for warships. Our office was always a hive of activity, with ships under our agency arriving and sailing every day. Whatever the day or hour, they were met on arrival and despatched on departure by an assistant. A great deal of transhipment was also carried out with small coasters from SE Asia arriving with consignments to go on to Europe, America and Africa by the frequent and regular long haul services available.

One of the BI ships, ITINDA, arrived with cargo for Hong Kong and later Japan, much of which was baled cotton for local mills. During her voyage the cotton had caught fire. It was extinguished at sea by the ship's company using salt water. On arrival all the damaged cargo was discharged for assessment by a local surveyor. The fire damage was an Act of God and classed as particular average whilst the water damage was classed as general average, being an act by the ship to prevent further loss. With quite a lot of damage apparent, BI declared a general average and stated a first estimated cost of the damage, expressed as a percentage of the value of both ship and cargo, such as 5 per cent. In fact, in practical terms this meant that the consignees could not be allowed to take delivery of their goods until they had put up either cash or an insurer's bond for 5 per cent of the value of their goods. The bond was the usual way to proceed, with insurers sorting it all out at a later date.

However one of ITINDA's consignees was a young and inexperienced Indian trader working in the colony who came to talk to

106

me because one of my clerks would not give him a delivery order for his (undamaged) bales of cotton unless the general average contribution was provided. Our client, who was a very presentable and well educated young man, was furious and believed that the clerk was on the lookout for a bribe. It took a very long time to explain to him the mysterious world of general average, but eventually I got sight of his insurance certificate issued by an Indian company in Bombay. A telex to them produced a guarantee next day which secured the release of his goods, and we parted good friends.

After about six months in the job I made a bad mistake on releasing cargo. Our cargoes were often discharged into the godowns of the Kowloon Wharf Company, who delivered them to consignees, or stored them free of charge for a week, and for longer if required, when they attracted storage charges. Over the months and years unclaimed goods mounted up, no charges were paid, and storage space was used. About 99 per cent of the goods were real junk, consisting of bits of steel, or heavily crushed cartons. The wharf company sent us a list, seeking our permission to sell the goods at public auction, in the hopes of raising a few dollars against their charges. I agreed, completely missing one wooden package of piece goods consigned to the Hong Kong office of a major UK trader. A couple of months later, the consignee presented an undischarged bill of lading to exchange for a delivery order. I personally believed the consignee had previously mislaid his bill, because the goods had arrived more than a year earlier, but in legal terms P&O were completely in the wrong and liable.

I reported events to George Tagg, who immediately offered his help and advice. When I called upon the consignee he was very friendly and understanding. A telex to Freddie Bond, Chief Clerk of the Export Freight Department in London produced the response that he had been in touch with his customer, who reacted very well. The wharf company cancelled their storage charges and to cap it all Tim Flanagan agreed to meet what had become a minor claim from a fund he had for such contingencies. I was clearly surrounded by a lot more friends than I deserved.

Sea Officer

A very important member of the office was Wong Chi Po, who was the office comprador. His principal task was to look after the company's cash and he recruited and appointed a team of cashiers, known locally as shroffs. He was required to furnish a large bond to the company for their integrity, so that when one absconded Chi Po made good the loss. He was also a commission salesman for the company, soliciting the Chinese business community who were our customers predominant in the local trades. He was a very able and successful business man which was particularly useful when his great love of gambling produced a loss. Gambling is of course a Chinese obsession and Chi Po would gamble on anything at any time. He was not what would be described as polished by European standards, but his lovely wife Julie was absolutely charming.

Together they lived in a large house at Magazine Gap off the road up to the Peak, and which was a mixture of Hollywood and Old China. The colonial protocol at that time meant they could not live on the Peak itself. The site of the house and its approach road had been cut into the side of the hill quite clearly at great cost and the approach road was definitely a one way track. It was a great honour for an assistant to be invited to join a dinner with about 100 of his clients but it needed to be approached with care. To start with Chi Po was the only Chinese present who could speak English. As the long meal wore on toasts were made. When one of the top guests called for two small glasses charged with neat spirit to be placed before him and me he said "Yam Sing". The correct response was to repeat his words and for both parties to drain their glasses in one gulp, upending them on the tablecloth. It was of course all about respect and not losing face. The final hurdle of the evening was to take Chi Po home. The big gates to his house at the end of his drive were closed which meant dropping off Chi Po at a side gate and driving my car backwards up the narrow road (very slowly).

Hong Kong is situated in an area subject to Tropical Revolving Storms, named typhoons when occurring in the China Sea. We lived through three of these and two were particularly fierce and frightening. At our flat on the Peak we were not exactly crowded in like the inhabitants over the hill, but it was still very unpleasant.

Makee Learnee Taipan

The windows of the flat were of galvanised steel, made by Crittals of Witham, Essex, and looked very strong. This did not stop the horizontal rain from being driven through the edges, and the French window to a small balcony bowed in alarmingly. Bunty and I had to shore it up using heavy furniture and we also had to mop up a flood of water. In the crowded tenements of Hong Kong life was sheer misery. By the time our smart harbour launches reached their registered berths in the Wanchai typhoon shelter it was full and the two crews stayed on deck for as long as it lasted, trying to fend off and avoid being damaged by other craft.

During a typhoon it was the harbour and its ships that commanded the most attention. Any ship berthed at a wharf had to leave to avoid damage to both ship and wharf. The first line of defence was the Marine Department's mooring buoys, of which there were many but not enough when it happened. These consisted of a huge block of concrete on the sea bed connected by chain cable to a 25 ton concrete block. This was connected also with chain cable to the floating heavy steel mooring buoy to which ships secured. The smaller concrete block acted as a brake on sudden strains imposed on the system by lifting off the sea bed. It was a first class system which I believe never failed. Failures did occur when a ship's cable to the buoy carried away. Once they were adrift it was all too easy for them drift downwind on to other ships unless they could use their engines to avoid a domino scenario.

In one of the typhoons there was a spectacular grounding of a ship called TJIBANJET but happily without loss of life. She was a small combined passenger and cargo ship of about 5,000 GRT, owned by the Dutch Royal Interocean Lines and operating throughout SE Asia. She was approaching Hong Kong at the same time as the typhoon and had been advised by the Marine Department that there was no typhoon buoy available for her. Her master decided he would not ride it out at sea and proceeded to anchor in the large Junk Bay just to the East of the Lyemun pass, the harbour entrance. She used two anchors but they were unable to hold her and she was dragging towards the Northern shore of the bay, so he weighed and tried to go to sea again. While abreast of

Sea Officer

Lyemun his ship was lifted bodily by the storm and flung down on the North shore of the pass, where quite miraculously she came to rest. Later, when it was all over, I paid a visit to Whampoa Dock's dry-dock to which she had been towed, and was able to inspect her bottom which was in a terrible mess. Whampoa re-built it completely.

I could never get accustomed to the poverty in Hong Kong, although the immigration figures suggested that it was much worse in China under Comrade Chairman Mao. Against the brick wall of our office building there leant a wooden shack measuring about 8' long by 6' high and 2' deep, which was a cigarette shop that I patronised. It was the only home of a couple with two small children. The construction and location were bad enough, but what never failed to upset me was the sight of a three-year-old eating an evening meal of about 90 per cent rice and the rest bits of fish from a discarded cigarette carton. The only consolation was that both children looked healthy, with beautiful clear complexions, and they were always full of smiles and chuckles.

Hong Kong offered many recreational facilities and they were all very local. I chose first to join the Royal Hong Kong Yacht Club on Kellett Island in the harbour, which was connected to Wanchai by causeway, forming a typhoon shelter for small craft. The clubhouse was a very elegant colonial building and included an excellent restaurant which Bunty and I enjoyed. I started crewing in Dragons and Redwings until I yearned for a boat of my own. I could not afford to buy a Dragon and none of the Redwings were for sale so I decided to build a boat myself. Redwings were a National Class boat designed by Uffa Fox for the Looe yacht club for offshore racing in Cornwall and they were good sea boats. At 14' long, sloop rigged and partially decked, they were just right for a crew of two. George Tagg offered an unused garage as a workshop, and I collected teak for the eleven clinker laid planks on each side and some Japanese oak for the timbers which were steam bent in a Heath Robinson steam box fed from a kettle via a hose. The mast and steel centreboard were made in a local shipyard whilst Jekyll's sails were sent from the UK and I was able to procure all other items easily in Hong Kong. There came at last the day when the boat, now bearing the name AIRSTREAM, was ready to be measured for class. The Class Measurer turned out to be the Director of Marine no less, who grubbed around happily with his section measures and passed the boat.

It was not long before I was racing my new construction and did quite well, although my teak planks were heavier than the China pine of the rest of the class in Hong Kong, which was a disadvantage when racing inside the harbour. However, the longer races outside the harbour in rough water were much more to the boat's liking and I started to do well. On leaving Hong Kong I sold AIRSTREAM to a business acquaintance who was rather chuffed that the builder's plate revealed the only boat ever built on the Peak.

AIRSTREAM was a good racing dinghy but no good for small children or family picnics, which prompted me to look for something larger. Using one of our launch coxswains as a broker, I purchased for a very modest sum an 18' small junk which had a Marine Department hawker's licence and which previously been the home of a family of six. She was beamy and comfortable, sailing well with a battened Chinese lugsail. I needed to add a small outboard engine since I did not fancy trying to use the "ulo", the local name for the single oar at the stern. There was no centreboard and no leeboards to reduce leeway, but the rudder was very large and fenestrated, which seemed to grip the water well. She was very well built, with five watertight bulkheads, although the small forward compartment was open to the sea to keep any fish catch fresh. I was so impressed with her design that I wrote a short paper about it, which was accepted by the Royal Institution of Naval Architects. She came with the name LEUNG ZSE, which we decided to keep, and was berthed at the old disused dry dock in Aberdeen where, for a very small retainer, a family kept an eye on her and bailed out the rain water when necessary. Some details of these superb local craft appear in Appendix 7.

There was no shortage of good beaches on Hong Kong island but they did get very crowded with local inhabitants on weekends. There was another problem because all small Chinese children have black hair and the sight of a child with blond hair, which was natural for a child of Lindley's age, was a real crowd stopper. A tight ring of gapers would form round her which looked threatening but was not, but Bunty and I thought it was not good for her. With LEUNG ZSE available we could go off to one of the many small and uninhabited islands where we could enjoy a sandy cove to ourselves all day. We became friends with Dougay and Kathy Dickson, whose daughter Anne was the right age for Lindley and we had some memorable picnics. It was sometimes so quiet and peaceful that we stayed until after dark and both children fell asleep in our roomy junk. Returning to Aberdeen in the dark was quite tricky, but we had the proper lights and just hoped that the many local craft we passed were not pirates. Dougay was a subaltern in the Army with no ideas about seafaring, and it took a little time to teach him that at sea the Captain's Word is Law, without any argument. By the time we were berthed in Aberdeen both he and Kathy had vowed never to accompany us again - that is, until the next weekend.

Back at work in the office, Jim Davis was packing up and attending farewell parties before setting off for the UK at the end of his learnership. One result of this was that his stewardship of the Knutsen Line desk passed to me, which meant that I became a Steamer Assistant, one rung up from Assistant. It was a task I really enjoyed, not least because I admired the Norwegian officers and their professionalism. At this time they carried out a two year stint in the Pacific, before taking leave in Norway with their families. Their deck and engine ratings were also Norwegian, being recruited at the Norwegian Seamen's Pool in San Francisco, whilst the cooks and stewards were Chinese and recruited through a crew manager in Hong Kong. The ships were well run and carried twelve passengers in addition to cargo.

Their voyages started in San Francisco and Los Angeles, where they loaded a wide range of goods including a lot of citrus fruit in their reefer compartments. They then crossed the Pacific to Manila and Hong Kong, going on to Singapore and finally Fremantle in Australia, discharging and loading concurrently. At Fremantle they loaded frozen crayfish for the USA, then returning to Singapore, Hong Kong and Japan. They left Japan fully loaded and crossed the Pacific again to discharge in Vancouver and California. They brought a steady supply of citrus fruit to Hong Kong and we loaded them with fresh Chinese vegetables in large baskets on deck for Singapore. This latter trade, which was booked by Chi Po, was a stunning example of Chinese gambling. If the ship's arrival at Singapore was timely the shippers made a fortune. If not, they lost their shirts.

The Knutsen ship ELIZABETH BAKKE achieved a timely arrival and on her next voyage was awarded a very large Joss (Good Luck) Flag by the shippers which, when flown in Hong Kong, attracted cargo like a powerful magnet. Cargo carried on deck was carried at shipper's risk without any liability to the ship. I don't know whether it would have been possible to insure fresh vegetables not under refrigeration with a very short shelf life but the custom and practice of our shippers was to look to the ship's officers to take care of their goods - which they would do anyway - and to pay them a small premium for the service. It was very Chinese thinking.

On their way back to the USA, we would book cargoes of a very wide range including both manufactured items such as cotton piece goods and agricultural products. There were manufacturers of the former in the colony but a lot more came from China to be both transhipped and accredited with a Hong Kong certificate of origin to circumvent the US entry regulations. The walnuts and groundnuts that we loaded could not have originated in Hong Kong but the problem was solved by discharging them in Vancouver, where the local Chinese community re-packaged them as bakery ingredients of Canadian origin, which were acceptable in the USA.

The nut cargoes arrived for transhipment in Hong Kong by coaster from Qingdao and Tianjin, and this cargo attracted a premium rate of freight. It seemed to me that we would be able to increase our share of this cargo if we mounted direct calls, and I put the idea to Haugesund, who were far from enthusiastic. They were eventually persuaded when we mentioned that a P&O ship had been berthed every month in these ports over the last few years without undue incident. The next step was to go and call on the shippers who were government corporations with their head offices in Beijing. I wanted to do this for another reason, because P&O had received a lot of support from North China without ever having sent a member of staff visit them.

To acquire a visa to visit China on business it was necessary to apply to the Chinese Government's travel agency in Hong Kong, a procedure that took about six weeks. The first surprise, after a couple of weeks, was that Chan Oi Lan suddenly announced that she needed to go to China to see her aunt. She would give no further explanation, and off she went despite being about six months pregnant with her first child. She returned about ten days later and our life returned to normal; but her "aunt" must have found that there was nothing wrong with me and a week later my visa was issued.

Travel to Beijing was quite a prolonged business. I took the train to the border where it was necessary to walk along the track and cross the border before boarding a Chinese train to Changzhou. This was packed with Chinese Army soldiers going on leave, with most of them singing at the top of their voices to taped music on loudspeakers. At Changzhou there was a night in a hotel, followed by a pre-dawn ride to the airport, where, if the weather was good, a flight by an Ilyshun 14 aircraft would take off for Beijing via Changsha, Wuhan and Zhengzhou. The Ilyshun carried about 40 passengers, and the two cabin attendants were walking about during landings and take-offs. To my astonishment, whilst taking off from Changsha, a British passenger was snapping away through a window at the Mig fighters that ringed the airfield perimeter and I thought we would all end up in gaol. He was from the Ministry of Works in Singapore and on his way to service the boilers in the British Embassy in Beijing! We landed at Beijing just before dark and I went on to the hotel reserved for foreigners with its big Intourist desk.

Next morning I started my programme of visits in a Morris Oxford taxi complete with Intourist minder. It was very cold in Beijing and the driver only knew of one choke position - full out.

Makee Learnee Taipan

The meetings with the export corporations followed a standard pattern. The boss could be distinguished from the others because he sat at the head of a long table and his comrade's jacket was not only high fashion Chinese blue but was made from No 2 grade cloth. (I was told that only Comrade Chairman and his team aspired to No 1 cloth.) To his immediate right was a young man from the university acting as interpreter, although I noticed that the boss appeared to correct the young man from time to time. All statements from the corporation were made in Mandarin. To his left were two political commissars who did not say a word and could be distinguished by their beige jackets of No 2 cloth. Beyond them were two clerks who knew about the business and were dressed in blue jackets of No 3 cloth. It took a long time to discuss very little on account of all the translation necessary but progress was made. The nuts corporation was really very pleased with a proposal for direct calls and promised their support, which happened from the first sailing. At the other corporations there was always politeness and courtesy with regard to the P&O business but they did have a grumble about the freight levels. I had the staff explanation ready of course, but it did not convince anybody. When the proceedings came to an end, it was quite usual for the boss to get up from table and ask me in perfect English about the state of the weather in Hong Kong, which was a good curtain for a pantomime.

The other people I made contact with all lived in my hotel and they were the government buyers from the East European countries that imported frozen foodstuffs from China. After they had purchased the goods, the reefer space required in a ship was booked not by them but by their government's freight agencies on the floor of the Baltic Exchange in London. Despite not having booking control, they were clearly important bystanders for P&O and so I hosted a small party for them in my hotel room using Chinese whisky, gin, brandy and beer acquired from the hotel. As soon as I opened the "whisky" and allowed it some air the bottle cracked from top to bottom, without actually breaking up, which demonstrated that firewater has adhesive properties. Two of the buyers were accompanied by their wives and we had a jovial evening. They were desperately pleased to see a new face, because they were shunned by the Chinese and they stayed months in Beijing living in a hotel room. There was nowhere to go out to in the evening because outside the hotel all the power was switched off at 2100.

Looking back at what went on, the first thing that strikes me is the total failure of Communism. Both Russia and the East European countries had economies based on agriculture, yet they could not feed themselves, and Moscow tried to hide its failure by demanding food from East Europe. The East European countries had to spend a fortune, not necessarily on the food, but certainly on the freight costs of moving it half way round the world. The ocean freight was payable in a hard currency and even when discharged in Hamburg the goods still had to be moved right across Europe in insulated rail wagons. I could not find out if Russia was buying food from China but if they did it would almost certainly have been moved at that time by the trans-Siberian railway.

Several months later, the London office asked me to accompany Managing Director Michael Thwaites, in his capacity as Chairman of the Far Eastern Freight Conference, on a courtesy visit to Beijing. The Conference was an old fashioned cartel of ship-owners serving the trade, setting the rates and keeping a firm grip on it. The Chinese were reluctant customers of the Conference lines, mainly because they regarded the rate structure as much too high. I joined Michael in Hong Kong and we had a fraught journey by air due to poor flying weather, which meant we spent hours in warehouse type lounges drinking tea and playing chess. Our most important contact was the redoubtable Captain Liu, who was head of Sinofracht, which was the corporation charged with chartering-in tonnage to lower the freight costs of China's exports. Despite the conflicts of interest between the two top men, Captain Liu (grey jacket, No 2 cloth) conducted meetings that were very cordial. It was a courtesy call and no specific business was discussed. We were well entertained and shown the sights of the old city. At the Temple of Heaven I took a photograph of Michael sitting just below a stone lion. Due to my appalling photographic skills it looked as if the lion was about to bite off his head but I was forgiven.

One feature of Hong Kong was the sheer efficiency of the traders and shopkeepers who supplied so many personal goods. Many traders held passes from our office to board our ships and solicit business from both passengers and crews. I think my favourites were Chang Kee and Harrison Wang. They had started in the old International Settlement in Shanghai but fled to Hong Kong in 1949 when Chairman Mao's forces were approaching the city. They arrived in Hong Kong by train with $50 between them. In pre WW2 Shanghai, Chang Kee's father had tailored suits for a large percentage of P&O's officer corps, whilst Harrison Wang's business as a dental mechanic provided dentures that my Pa claimed were the best and least expensive in the world. By 1949 Chang Kee senior felt he was too old to move house but his well trained son departed with his blessing. In Hong Kong Chang Kee was soon making good suits for his shipboard clients and extended his client list to take in the ships of the Commonwealth navies - the Royal Navy was the client of another supplier. When HMAS ANZAC and TOBRUK appeared for six months on the Far East station, Chang Kee would appoint two of his team to each ship. Working in the confined space of the tiller flat, they would not only launder all the ship's company's white suits but also tailor both uniform and civilian suits for them. On one occasion, Chang Kee appeared rather late in my office to check and deliver a suit for me. He offered apologies for being late but went on to explain the reason. HMCS ONTARIO, the training cruiser with the year's mid-shipman's class embarked had just been in Hong Kong for a week, during which time he had made 129 suits.

Harrison Wang was the ugliest man I had ever seen but he had a heart of pure gold. He measured about five feet tall and just about as wide and his visage would have passed as a gargoyle. On arrival in Hong Kong in 1949, he had been informed that he could not trade as a dental mechanic because he lacked a UK certificate for such work. He turned his hand to carved teak furniture, especially chests lined with camphor wood, and created a good business. A few years after we had returned to the UK he wrote to me asking for advice and assistance. He had been abandoned by two debtors who between them owed him quite a lot. The first I was able to deal with quite quickly. He was the CHUSAN's shop manager who left

P&O to start a high street shop and had purchased stock from Harrison Wang on credit. His high street shop failed and he then sought to return to sea as shopman. On being asked on re-engagement whether he had any debts he quickly paid off his Hong Kong debtor. The second was more difficult as he was doctor in a Blue Funnel ship who had paid for his goods with a dud cheque. I went to see my old family solicitor, John Edwards, who was an old fashioned gentleman and who told me that it would be necessary to appoint a private detective in Dublin, which would incur costs without a guarantee of success. On referring to Harrison Wang, he told me to go ahead. John Edward's private eye uncovered a trail of dud cheques but not the doctor. When this was reported to Hong Kong, Harrison Wang invited an invoice but John refused to comply, expressing the view that it was inexcusable for white doctors to fleece the natives. About six weeks later, a large packing crate for John arrived in one of our ships containing a top grade carved chest with a camphorwood lining, and he was very thrilled. It all goes to show that there are indeed nice people about if only you can find them.

During our stay in Hong Kong I did find some spare time(!) to study and improve my education. I sat for Extra Master Part A, which I passed in spite of the invigilator - the senior nautical surveyor - emptying my pencil box and shaking out my log tables for illegal cribs, as if I was a teenage apprentice. At another more relaxed examination at the university, I passed for Associate Member of the Institute of Transport.

In August 1958 Bunty provided the family with another small addition to our family when Victoria was born at Matilda Hospital on the Peak. They both came through very well but on return home Victoria developed a bad case of prickly heat in what was a very hot summer. We were in fact entitled to have a room air conditioner in our main bedroom but had not previously felt a need for one. We changed our minds and Tim Flannigan quickly approved the purchase. After one night with the machine the unsightly blisters disappeared. Victoria's birth was recorded with the Registrar and we accepted local advice to arm ourselves with several copies of her birth certificate, not knowing what might happen to the registry when the Chinese took control.

Our time in Hong Kong was coming to an end and I received instructions to proceed to Japan in March 1959 to relieve Tony Murray in Yokohama for his leave in the UK. We had enjoyed a really marvellous stay in Hong Kong, and had met many fascinating and agreeable people, but only a few had become long term friends. It has often puzzled me how we failed to meet up with Chinese people of our own age group who were upwardly mobile and later to emerge as major figures from Hong Kong such as Mr C Y Tung, who became a major ship-owner. When the Chinese government took control of the old colony, Mr Tung became its Chief Executive. (I did meet him in London years later.) He was just one of the taipans that Hong Kong produced from the 1960s onwards, most of whom became world class. We could certainly list as friends Dougay and Kathy Dickson, Chan Oi Lan and Harrison Wang but this is a small list from a very busy work and social life. Of course, P&O ships calling brought with them old shipmates and we always enjoyed entertaining them and their Norwegian counterparts. HMS CAVALIER revisited Hong Kong which was a good excuse for a party. Half the wardroom turned up as did some nurses from the hospital, which gave me the chance of taking a photograph which shows a small crowd sitting on the floor with two future admirals amongst them.

Whilst I was on good terms with the Chinese staff in the office there was one person to whom I felt very close. This was the Knutsen Chief Clerk Kwok Iu Shu. He was quite unusually a devout Christian, and had a family with two small sons. Not long before we left he presented me with a copy of the revised New Testament with a generous inscription inside. I responded with a book voucher for his two sons and suggested he might supervise their purchases. His letter of thanks included a report that he had allowed them only one cowboy book each with the remainder being devoted to English text books.

Another important person during our time in Hong Kong was Dougay Dickson. He was one of those-larger-than-life characters with a strong sense of humour. He was on his second tour in Hong Kong and was part of the Army. He had completed his national service in the Army in the UK and had been commissioned towards the end. His ambition then had been to start work in his father's business with a nice cushy job, but Dickson senior had other ideas and told him to go out and find a job. Absolutely furious, he went at great speed to the Colonial Office in London, who had been advertising vacancies in the Royal Hong Kong Police for probationary Sub Inspectors.

He signed up on the spot and a week later was afloat en route to the East, leaving behind his young bride who followed a few months later. He served out his full tour but at the end decided he preferred the Army and re-enlisted on return to the UK, only to find he had been posted to Hong Kong. Stories that he told of life in the RHKP were out of this world, particularly those about the management and organisation of the force, in which Sub Inspectors and above were then all expatriates, whilst sergeants and constables were locally recruited. The best story I remember was about a raid on a well known house of ill repute in Kowloon. It was led by a Chief Superintendent newly arrived from a Northern constabulary in the UK who was determined to stamp out vice.

As the raid progressed, Dougay was instructed to take his three constables and to clear the rooms in a hallway. After banging on the first door and shouting out "Police, open up" the door opened a little and a Chinese girl emerged clutching her robe about her and saying "No tlouble, no tlouble" and slipping away quickly. On a bed in the room there lay a very tall American serviceman clad only in a pair of Texan cowboy boots. "What's with the boots then feller" inquired Dougay, receiving a reply "Wal youse guys, stateside they warned us to look out for that Hong Kong foot".

After a number of farewell parties, we joined BI's SANTHIA for passage to Yokohama. Unfortunately I had to decline an invitation to attend a party in HMY BRITANNIA and to meet HRH Prince Philip, who was to arrive just after SANTHIA sailed. My bosses had been very indulgent, so I could not ask for another favour which would have allowed me to stay a few days longer.

Makee Learnee Taipan

SANTHIA was one of a class of four ships that traded between Calcutta and Japan, carrying cargo and a small number of passengers in three different classes. A lot of people waved us off as we sailed for Yokohama via Shanghai. On passage to Shanghai there was a christening service for Victoria, conducted by a slightly reluctant but very competent Captain Douglas Gill. As a sailor I believed that all small children should be christened with salt water and at sea, so I achieved another ambition. SANTHIA's bell was unshackled from the fo'csle and brought to Captain Gill's cabin, upended and full of sea water. It all went very well and all the correct screams to cast out the Devil were produced. After that it was champagne all round whilst a suitable certificate was typed.

The call at Shanghai was mercifully short. There was no shore leave and at all times there was a bunch of pushy guards on board. It seemed that their sole counter attraction to brusquely bossing us about was watching two small children taking a bath.

We sailed for Japan and I prepared to enter a new world. The biggest difference was that we would no longer be British citizens in a British Crown Colony, but foreigners in a sovereign state. However, there are many parallels between the British and Japanese which are sometimes overlooked. We both live on small islands with long histories and traditions. We cling to constitutional monarchies when so many others have forsaken them, and we both have excelled in the maritime and overseas trading world.

Fourteen years after the end of WW2, Japan was still recovering from that war. Many of the older citizens were still conscious of the huge loss of face that was the result of their country's total defeat at the hands of the Allies. The American eagle was now the real power in the North Pacific basin and had faced down the Communist bloc threat over a very long sea and air border. In the early 50s the Communists had tried a ground war in Korea but it led only to a truce and the partition of that country, guarded by heavily armed troops on each side. In SE Asia, insurgency was on the rise but in 1959 it was the United States Navy and Air Force that kept a fragile peace. In the 1960s the American Army became involved on the ground again in Vietnam, but it was a disaster for them.

Sea Officer

The US Navy was virtually self sustaining at sea but the USAF needed proper bases, and established several in Japan. It was unclear whether the Japanese welcomed them or not, but in any case there was little they could do about the situation since they had no real military establishment. The bases were large fortresses full of modern air power containing wholly American staff to fly and maintain the aircraft. Their staff were accompanied by their families and the bases were each a Little America, with exclusive houses, schools, shops and cinemas for their people.

Like Britain, Japan had to export and trade overseas to prosper. They first attacked the markets in Asia, of what had been their Asian Co-Prosperity Sphere, which they had failed to acquire by military force. As the young people emerged from the excellent Japanese educational establishments they soon showed their worth by helping to increase the value of their exports and extending their market world wide.

Soon after we arrived, Japanese morale received a huge boost with the marriage of Crown Prince Akihito and Princess Michiko, thus securing the position of the Chrysanthemum Throne. Their official wedding photographs show them both in traditional and Western dress to strike the right note.

I had to work on my attitude towards the people we were to live amongst. My previous attitude was largely governed by my exposure to the Japanese army in Malaya when I was sixteen and was unfriendly to say the least. They had behaved like savages and even in defeat were surly and uncooperative. Looking forward to the opportunity to gain both knowledge and experience amongst them I decided to buckle on my best suit of armour to protect me and see what happened. During the eight months of our stay, bits of my suit of armour were to fall off or rust away.

Tony Murray met us on arrival in Yokohama and took us to the New Grand Hotel where we were to stay until he and his wife Valerie left for the UK a couple of weeks later. The New Grand was amongst the first ferro-concrete buildings created after the horrendous Yokohama earthquake of the 20s. It was rather austere in appearance but comfortable enough. We were soon to learn about earthquakes. Drinking tea in bed next morning the bed-head suddenly rattled against the wall, which was unnerving to say the least. From the dining room windows overlooking the sea I was amazed to note how quickly the weather would get up. It would go from flat calm to become Force 7 a few minutes later. This characteristic was not confined to Yokohama and was probably due to the topography.

The Customs procedure was long winded and obtaining our residents' permits took four hours. We all had to be finger printed, including seven month-old Victoria. I needed to obtain a driving licence, since my UK licence was not acceptable. There was no driving test but I had to complete a paper form which asked twenty questions and provided four multi-choice answers for each. This took about 30 minutes at the most, but the time allowance was two hours and in a freezing cold examination room candidates could not leave earlier. Needless to say I failed, three times, largely because the Japanese English answers were so ambiguous. Each attempt required attendance at 0600 to get in the queue which formed in the open. It was my worst ever examination but I did eventually pass.

Tony Murray gave me a good teach-in for his job and introduced me to my office colleagues. The Managing Director for Japan was Duncan McFarlane, whose grasp of written and spoken Japanese earned him the unstinted admiration of the senior Japanese managers and officials with whom he dealt. I believe that on his own he was responsible for creating good relationships with many senior Japanese personnel. During WW2 he had avoided internment by being out of the country when the war started. He was therefore available to assist the Allies, by using his language skills to decrypt Japanese radio traffic. He went on leave at the same time as Tony and was relieved by Bobby Barrow, his No 2, who was usually stationed in Kobe. Bunty and I got on very well with both Bobby and his wife Mary.

The Yokohama office was principally a ship's husbandry office, since the focal point for sales was Tokyo, where we had a sales office managed by Dennis Faulkner. There were about 30/40 ship calls per month, so there was plenty for me to do and I took very few days off in eight months. The ships were mainly from P&O Group's cargo liner services either carrying import and export cargoes or due to spend two weeks dry-docking at the Mitsubishi repair yard nearby. For me, a new cargo type appeared, consisting of 10,000 tons in bulk of either grain or maize (sweet corn) from the United States. Grain and maize were being introduced into a Japanese diet that had previously been dominated by rice as the staple. One result was that the younger generation was starting to grow taller.

In the major passenger liner market, P&O and Orient Line pooled their passenger services to provide a new trans-Pacific service between Australia, Japan and California. The summer of 1959 saw the arrival in Yokohama of P&O HIMALAYA, to start the new service and the ship was the centre of Japanese attention for two days, and many more parties. HIMALAYA's Captain Jim Slinn was presented with a spectacular wisteria bonsai in full bloom and about 18" in diameter. The new generation of jet aircraft were making serious inroads into the passenger traffic to Australia for both P&O and Orient and the new service was a major diversification which increased passenger load factors.

I was introduced to all the Japanese staff in turn, including my driver Suzuki-san, by Kadji-san, the Japanese manager for all four of the offices in the country. When Tony Murray left on his leave, I decided to have a quiet face-to-face meeting with Kadji-san to get to know him a bit better and to make clear my own intentions. He was a small and very dapper man whose English was perfect. It turned out he had served in the Imperial Japanese Navy as a gunnery officer and it was very easy to converse with him. I apologised for my complete lack of ability in the Japanese language but promised to try hard to learn enough to get along. However, I did have to mention that I did not have the linguistic ability of my colleague Jim Davis and that he should therefore not expect quick results. At this Kadji-san's face crumpled with a mixture of amusement and embarrassment and he held open a sleeve to laugh into. "But Davis-san speaks Japanese like a woman" he said, trying hard to control his mirth. Of course Davis-san was a bachelor during his stay in Japan and had learnt much of the language talking to delightful bar girls during his lonely evenings, which explained everything. Japanese grammar is a lot easier than German grammar but to be polite you had to use irasshaimas (go out) for a superior and ikimas for an inferior person (I think). After we broke up the meeting I found that a small bit of all that armour had gone missing.

It was very important to learn some Japanese quickly. Few people spoke English and the first thing to learn was how to greet and thank people in the polite way required. In the evenings it was sometimes necessary to telephone my colleague in Kobe about shipping matters. There were no automatic switchboards and it was necessary to speak to female operators in Japanese. My language primer of course listed the numerals so I had to keep it open and search for each one of an eight digit number. On the domestic front I needed to help Bunty shop for the groceries she required. Some progress was made and some phrases still cling to my memory. In London years later I was asked by a well dressed Japanese couple, who spoke fluent English, the way to the Royal Festival Hall. It was my destination too so I accompanied them. On reaching the doors, they thanked me politely in English, but some small imp prompted me to bow slightly and say "Doi tashimasu" (don't mention it) which clearly pleased them a great deal.

Our house was one of two semi-detached houses owned by the company and originally built for the Americans. One was for use by the Tokyo Manager Dennis Faulkner and his wife, and the other for the Yokohama Assistant. The houses were quite large and comfortable by Japanese standards with three bedrooms each. They were built from timber and plaster and so did not collapse when there were earth tremors. Each had a small garden cared for by a local contractor. The gardener himself only appeared for work of great importance, such as twice replanting a weeping willow blown down by the typhoons. The day to day tasks of weeding and cutting the lawn with a pair of scissors was the province of two women who appeared every week.

We tried to find a maid without realising that the sort of housemaid we wanted did not exist in Japan. Scrubbing floors and the like was not a local habit. Whilst Bunty could easily cope with the household chores we really needed someone to look after the two children so that we could go out and participate in our social obligations. In answer to our prayers there arrived Yuki-san (Ms Snow) who was looking for part time work provided it was not heavy, and who did not mind attending during evenings when we wanted to go out. She was a delightful and gentle woman of about 40, who was completely besotted with her only son who was by then grown up. The children adored her and she clearly liked them. She also accompanied Bunty to the big stores in Tokyo for shopping expeditions. Not only did she sort out the sales staff expertly but her whole demeanour was that of a very high class ladies' maid who made Bunty feel she was royalty. Yuki-san also persuaded me remove and discard my armoured helmet.

Whilst still in Hong Kong we had booked Lindley into the American International School in Yokohama for two terms as this was where all the children of civilian expatriates went for their education. Aged five, she joined a junior school class for four hours a day. What we had not realised was that her classmates were all from mixed marriages of expatriate American fathers and Japanese mothers. Lindley's main task appeared to be to teach them all English. In general terms we did not mind this but it seemed we had to pay quite high fees for providing a teacher. Later we regretted not sending her to a Japanese state school for the two terms. To see a long crocodile of neatly dressed little girls wending their way through Yokohama's streets under the care of just two teachers was a demonstration of self discipline at its best. Their laughter and happiness proved that they were not oppressed. We thought Lindley would have reacted well to the discipline and would have benefited from learning how to write her name with a fine paint brush.

There was no shortage of food in Japan but provisioning in general was quite a difficult task. So many local items looked very attractive and tasted good but we got the impression their nutritional value was low. We had to augment them with purchases from

Makee Learnee Taipan

Hong Kong, where half my salary was paid to avoid the local high tax. We were also allowed to purchase from our ships, although it was not strictly legal. Happily my raincoat had pockets large enough to conceal some sausages, kippers and perhaps the occasional cheese.

In the office I soon learned about the skills of our local staff. My secretary Kenmotsu-san was not only a delightful girl but took dictation in English without hesitation. It was not at all surprising that she had other admirers and one day I received a letter from Hirai-san, the chief clerk for imports, which read:

"Mr Penney. I would like to take one week leave from 13th November for my marriage and taking this opportunity Miss Kenmotsu and I wish to express our hearty thanks for your beautiful and useful present with which we would like to enjoy our married life. Please give our best wishes to Mrs Penney. S Hirai"

When a Royal Navy cruiser paid a visit to Yokohama I wanted to provide hospitality. I therefore commissioned Yoshie-san, one of Bobby Barrow's secretaries, to take four officers on a whole day tour of Hakone National Park. It was a great success, judging from her multi-page report to me, which closes with a short sentence "Thank you so happy tour to Hakone".

In addition to all the ship husbandry, the Yokohama office was the local secretary of two shipping conferences, the Far Eastern Freight Conference and the Japan Persian Gulf Conference (Jappers). P&O and BI were members of both, as were the two major Japanese ship owners, Nippon Yusen Kaisha (NYK) and Osaka Shosen Kaisha (OSK). Each Conference consisted of between 15 or 20 ship owner members. One of my tasks was to assemble the carryings loaded in Japan of all the members for a monthly report to London. In the FEFC the figures revealed that P&O was bottom of the list whilst our UK owned competitors such as Blue Funnel, Glen Line, and Ben Line, together with the Japanese lines, ruled the roost. The report also revealed the growing complexity and value of Japanese exports to Europe. One of the reasons for P&O's failure was its commitment to China for refrigerated cargoes. I became determined to redress the situation but it was five years before I could be involved in a major overhaul of P&O's Far East cargo operations.

In Jappers there was a problem with an outsider attracting our customers away from us. This was not only achieved by rate cutting by the outsider but included his deployment of ships with a heavy lift capability that most of the cargo liners of the day did not have. There was a growing movement of large and heavy pieces of machinery for the Emirates' new oil industry. It was a problem for which there was no ready solution but Jappers decided that tackling the customers as a Conference would at least be a palliative. I joined two young men from NYK and OSK to make the rounds of Tokyo which took two whole days and produced almost nothing to show for it. However, it did give me a new dimension to think about, and the company of two very bright people whose English was passable even if they did not know anything about heavy lifts. The round of visits was very exhausting and not helped by gallons of green tea, but at the end of the day they were very pleased to join me in a suitable Tokyo bar.

I also made short visits to smaller ports in which a local company acted as sub-agents for us. One of these was Otaru in the Northern island of Hokkaido where we used to load machined Japanese oak for elegant wood block floors. The boss Fukuda-san, who was more Anglophile than I was, had never been seen without his thorn proof Harris tweed sports jacket. After a very cramped flight from Tokyo to Sapporo, he met me with his car and drove me to an onsen (hot springs) hotel close to Otaru. There he left me for the night and I was expertly bathed by two giggling maids, provided with dinner and put to bed on a futong on the floor. It was an unforgettable experience.

There was good sailing to be had in Yokohama and I joined the Yacht Club. The club also had a children's area with suitable swimming pools which my family found agreeable when I was racing. The club's 30 or so boats were all of one class and designated L class, after the expatriate called Laffin who designed them. They were 18' long, sloop rigged and half decked, and sailed very well in the open sea. I crewed for an American civilian owner in his boat ARTEMIS of LONGSTREAM, who offered me the boat for five months whilst he took leave. I could not find crew and appealed to Kadji-san who got straight in touch with his old university.

On Saturday afternoon there were two likely looking lads shouting out "Penney-san" and off we went. It was really quite remarkable, despite conversation being out of the question, and we still got on like a house on fire using hand signals. I think their main purpose was to learn English but they worked well and clearly enjoyed themselves. On the last downwind leg of a race, the wind got up quite dramatically and ARTEMIS was planing and creaming along but they were yelling with pleasure. This did not distract them from smartly dowsing the sails as we entered the yacht basin and before hitting anything. In another race I showed them how to overtake a competitor by pretending to go to windward, and then suddenly bear away to overtake to leeward. They were astounded but exhilarated. So much for the armour.

Another Japanese institution to be enjoyed was sumo wrestling. This is a hallowed sport which attracts the attention of the whole population when the big series takes place and every shop window has a television screen showing the current match in progress. I found it interesting because the wrestlers are superbly disciplined and at a single word from the referee just freeze in their tracks. It appears to attract a lot of money in all directions and yet to remain a clean but very real sport. A small TV screen does not really do justice to the sport and the place to watch it is at the main sumo halls. Tickets are very difficult to obtain and hideously expensive but I had the very good fortune to be given two for the Tokyo hall. Accompanied by an old shipmate, Commodore John Wacher, we found the hall and our seats on the floor. The whole atmosphere was sheer magic. In addition to the wrestlers and the referee there were two judges dressed in long colourful robes designed centuries before, who made pronouncements in the language of the same era. Each contest was quite short and ended when one wrestler was either on the floor or outside the small ring. There appeared to be three qualities that produced a win - sheer weight, perfect balance and split second timing. I was amazed when an old and very large wrestler, contesting a younger, lighter and more athletic opponent, just bulldozed him out of the ring in about two seconds.

The time had come for the Penney family to go home. We joined E&A's NELLORE for passage to Hong Kong via Shanghai and were given a traditional send-off. In command was Captain Bernie Dun who looked after us well. In WW2 Bernie's ship had been sunk by the Japanese. He was taken as a prisoner of war to Japan where he had to work as a coolie labourer in a flour mill in Yokohama, an experience he survived very well. When the ship's Chinese agents in Shanghai insisted on loading fragile cartons of fresh eggs 10 feet high Bernie looked to me to help persuade them to be a bit more practical.

Waiting for us in Hong Kong was my old friend CANTON, who would take us (and our car) to London, where we arrived right at the start of 1960. Bobby and Mary Barrow were aboard on their way for leave. There was another P&O man on board, John Crossman, a chartered secretary who had been on a short visit to the colony, and was later to become P&O Secretary. We had an uneventful but enjoyable voyage home and prepared for the winter. We were able to look back over three and a half years, which had definitely been life-enriching for us, both as individuals and as a couple. It was an experience we have never forgotten.

Chapter 11. Leadenhall Street, London

The family settled into a rented house as our temporary new home, and I reported my return to Wilfred Mizen in the P&O office. I was told that I would be appointed an assistant manager of the company after I had taken the six months' leave due to me and that my salary would be £1,500 per annum. It was unclear what my job as an assistant manager would be, but that was the nature of the company. It was not the era of clearly defined responsibilities that would arrive later with McKinsey and Co.

The most important domestic task was to find and purchase a house. Some friends had recommended the area around Virginia Water, Surrey. We found it attractive; in a semi-rural area with good access to both London and girls' schools. We also found a site of a new house to be built, which we helped to design, and we concluded a verbal deal with the builder vendor for £4,750. Unhappily this simple intention fell apart in its execution and we ended up with a home that was completely different from our original plans.

The lease for our initial renting came to an end and we started looking for another rental for six months whilst building work proceeded. By a piece of good fortune an office colleague and ex P&O learner, Walter Kerr, lived in the area. His wife's parents, the Caswells, had purchased a two-acre orchard on which to build their retirement home. The orchard was part of a property of seven acres called Highclere, on the East Drive of the Wentworth Estate, and which had been built in 1929. Highclere also comprised a partly converted three car garage with chauffeur's flat over, which the Caswells had rented whilst their new house was built. The Caswells' builder was nearing completion whilst our own was doing little and had learned how to gazump up the price. We inquired of the owners about renting the garage and I was invited to meet them one evening after work. When I was about to depart for a visit to Highclere, Bunty dropped a bombshell by suggesting that we should attempt to buy the garage instead of renting it, and then sent me on my way.

Highclere was owned by Mr and Mrs Agar-Robartes. He was from the bluest of British blood and his wife Peggy was a dynamic American divorcee. She referred to him as "The Baron", which was a glimpse towards the future, because when his elder brother died he inherited the viscountcy of Clifden. Sitting in their handsome drawing room, dressed (black tie) for their dinner, I was made welcome and we started to discuss a tenancy. I then dared to broach the idea of a sale. They were surprised at first but soon agreed to a sale at £4,100.

At this time, P&O, like so many older British companies at the time, provided their established staff with mortgage funds at 2.5 per cent interest, which was a great benefit when the market rate was 5 per cent or more. By the time this desirable benefit was withdrawn I had cleared my loan. Highclere Cottage has been enlarged and improved over the more than 40 years we've lived there and it has been a wonderful home. It is now owned by Lindley and her husband Andrew but we still enjoy it.

With six months leave on hand we were able to take time to visit our families and UK friends. Both sets of parents were still in good health and comfortable, but it was not long before this would change.

In Leadenhall Street Sir Donald Anderson was now chairman and Lord Simon was deputy chairman of the company. The P&O Group owned many companies, both shipping and shipping related. There was a clutch of cargo liner companies with long histories and traditions such as BI, Strick, Nourse, New Zealand Shipping, and E&A. Another important company was Orient Line, which operated seven large passenger ships to Australia. All these companies had a complete Board and management structure and were almost autonomous, although the times were changing and new ship acquisitions had to have main Board approval. In human terms it was difficult to introduce rationalisation of the structure as the shipping scene changed.

P&O had two managing directors, Michael Thwaites and Sir Andrew Crichton, but most of their energies were directed towards the P&O Fleet and not the other near-autonomous companies. They were as alike as chalk and cheese, and their mutual antipathy was clearly apparent to all those who worked for them. There was always much debate amongst the junior managers as to why this situation was allowed to continue and why the Chairman tolerated it. However Sir Donald, who did not suffer fools gladly, appeared to accept the situation. Michael appeared to be roughly in charge of what is now classified as the production process, but he clung to many other things as well and especially the chair of the powerful Far Eastern Freight Conference, which was a prestigious post. He knew a great deal about the technical and commercial aspects of liner shipping. He came over as a difficult and grumpy person with little sense of humour but my sea service had taught me how to deal with such people.

Andrew was quite different. He did have a sense of humour and was always rushing about although it was usually not clear what he was up to. He appeared to be in charge of freight marketing and sales but there were times when it seemed that he did not know anything about shipping at all. This was a complete smokescreen because behind it lay a sharp sense of exactly what was going on, both for the company and himself. He was Chairman of the Dock Labour Board at a time when the unions were at their most militant, and this was without doubt an horrendous task. It did, however, bring him an accolade for his work when he became a Knight Bachelor.

On the passenger marketing side Malcolm Millar was the Director in charge. He was a much respected man who inspired all those who worked for him and his early death came as a shock.

At the first level below the board were a band of senior managers. They were very experienced in their departments but regarded them as sacrosanct private empires. My own belief was that the two MDs were not managing them properly and a few heads needed banging together. It was madness when the Marine Superintendent found it necessary to stop a ship for a fortnight to carry out hull repairs, only to find out a week later that the Engineer Superintendent had to stop the same ship again for engine room repairs. The longstanding war between the two freight departments about discharging and loading itineraries should never have started, let alone drag on for months.

Below all this was a group of younger and well trained managers who really did not know what they were supposed to be doing apart from bystanding and grumbling at their inactivity. There were small chores handed out but they did not amount to a manager's job. Studying how our two MDs set about furthering their careers it seemed to me that the best policy was to grab what you could and hang on to it for dear life. Michael Thwaites regarded me as his PA, although he abhorred that particular handle. He was a very hard taskmaster but taught me a great deal, particularly in the world of the written word. I learned how to read and understand long legal contracts and how to minute accurately protracted and complicated meetings.

In the early 1960s there were two happenings of great significance, and neither of them went well. The first was the full merger of the passenger business of Orient Lines and P&O. The second was the acquisition of the two new large passenger ships, CANBERRA and ORIANA, P&O. The latter, built by the Orient team with Vickers in Barrow, was a success apart from a lack of higher class cabins with their own facilities, for which the demand in the market place was growing apace. CANBERRA, built by a P&O team at Harlands in Belfast, was a technical disaster.

When a merger is created between two large companies in the same business there are usually opportunities for substantial cost savings and streamlining, but this just did not happen. To start with the whole board of Orient transferred straight to the P&O board. There were obvious good family reasons for this because the close knit Scottish clans of Anderson and Geddes predominated. At the next level of ship superintendents and their ship's officers, there was no merger at all and the company ended up with two of everything.

Leadenhall Street, London

Shedding manpower is never an easy or welcome task but it can be achieved with patience and caring attitudes and without resorting to one-line emails. For this merger, it appeared no one was prepared to grasp a nettle.

In the end, CANBERRA turned out to be a very successful ship, both in the eyes of her customers and commercially. She also distinguished herself as a troopship by venturing twice into San Carlos Water in the Falklands, a place where others feared to tread. Her Captain, Dennis Scott-Masson, was also a Captain RNR and, whilst his ship had no weapons of substance, he could at least understand how the Royal Navy worked, and how to prepare and conduct his great ship in a war. Admiral Woodward described the ship as a "floating bonfire waiting to be lit", which was perhaps a realistic risk assessment but does not highlight the ship's achievements. At the end of her life, when the TV showed her being broken up on a beach near Karachi, I certainly joined the mourners.

When building a new design of ship it is absolutely basic to get two things one hundred percent right from the start - the hull and machinery. These priorities are the province of the naval architect and superintendent engineer working with their opposite numbers in the shipbuilders. CANBERRA started life with both priorities seriously wrong. The hull was too heavy and trimmed so much by the stern such that her draft aft was too deep to berth at all the ports in her itinerary. The trim was corrected by putting 250 tons of cement in her small forward hold, at the cost of adding yet more weight to drag around the world for the rest of her life.

Her main propulsion machinery was steam turbo electric. It was selected because, prior to WW2, P&O had chosen this type of propulsion for three ships, which were judged to be successful. But CANBERRA was much larger and the turbo electric machinery had barely advanced since 1931. The big AC drive motors soon showed large cracks and it was touch and go whether the DTI would agree to issue a Passenger Certificate for her maiden voyage. Her boilers produced steam at much higher pressures and temperatures than before. There were serious steam leaks, and the furnaces were starved of air. She was supposed to be able to fill double bottom tanks with fuel or salt water as required for stability but the separators were not up to the job. The boiler tubes became encrusted with vanadium and all had to be replaced. Her auxiliary power was AC, which in a ship was a new idea. P&O's experienced electrical staff all had a DC background and found it difficult to cope. She was soon to experience a total electrical failure of which there are details below. There was a long and expensive programme of refurbishment with which I assisted Michael Thwaites, who was in charge.

P&O had a wealth of experienced people to provide the skills required for a successful acquisition but did not manage them well, or even at all. There was no director or senior manager in sole charge of the project because the company was so informally organised. It was clear that the Naval Architect needed some visionary assistance with the ship's internal layout and it was available from a young NA, David West. In the end he provided a splendid layout that attracted much favourable attention. It was very difficult for him because the NA clearly resented him, and he had little authority. It was just the same with the machinery. Thomas Walter Bunyan was a brilliant inventor and fault analyst, who somehow appeared and joined the engineering team without the proper authority. The Superintendent Engineer, who had years of ship engineering experience to draw upon, virtually refused to talk to him. It was all down to the senior management to sort this out and demand team work, but they shied away from it. However I believe the board eventually hoisted in the message because the next big ship acquisition went like a dream and was extraordinarily successful.

We learned from experience that it took just one small human misjudgement to reduce CANBERRA to a hulk without power or lights adrift with a full complement of passengers. Fortunately this occurred in the Mediterranean in fair weather, and STRATHEDEN was not far away.

For her auxiliary power, the ship depended on four steam turbo alternators each of 1200 kVA and her sea load was carried easily on three. At about 0200 one night the electrician on watch noticed that one machine was motoring and was powered by the other two. This was in no way a danger to anything, but the electrician believed the motoring alternator would overspeed and destroy itself. He went to disconnect it from the switchboard but neither switch would open (they were both gummed up with condensate from steam leaks). Instead of calling his chief, he decided urgent action was needed and proceeded to open the isolating switch which lay inside the switchboard behind a bolted plate on which was inscribed in big red letters "DANGER. Do not open when switchboard on load". He unbolted the plate and reached inside for the knife type isolating switch and pulled it open. In so doing he pulled out an arc from the machines generating about 2000 kVA. It was amazing that he lived to tell the tale. The ship lost all power and great chunks of the switchboard melted. Emergency power was provided by the two diesel generators in the fo'csle, but did not last long.

CANBERRA was towed to Malta where the unhappy passengers were disembarked and transferred onto chartered flights to their destinations. She spent a few weeks in Malta making temporary repairs in order to enable her to steam under her own power to Harlands in Belfast for permanent repairs. I accompanied Michael Thwaites to Belfast for an inquiry board which established these facts. The young electrician had to go of course, but he was a straightforward person who neither lied nor tried to cover up when he gave evidence.

It was about this time that my parents badly needed some assistance. Quite suddenly my Pa was struck down by a severe stroke and was taken off to Southampton General Hospital. They attended him very well but whilst he did not lose his mobility or his usual cheerful behaviour, he completely lost his speech and the ability to read. After about six weeks he returned to his home where my Mama did her best to look after him. But before that, my Mama needed immediate financial assistance from me. She was not a careful spender and my Pa's bank account, into which his pension was paid, was in his sole name.

I covered my Mama on a weekly basis and my solicitor John Edwards provided me with the paperwork to take a power of attorney on my Pa's account. Unfortunately he could not sign and execute it so we were back to square one. After a few weeks I made an appointment to call on his banker at the Piccadilly branch of a high street bank to see what could be arranged. I explained the situation to an assistant manager who was totally unhelpful and who claimed there was nothing he could do. I am not quick tempered as a rule but this was a time for a bust-up. He slunk out of his office to be replaced by the manager. The whole tone of my visit changed quickly and I promptly got help. He invited me to open an account in my own name without a deposit of funds, and draw upon it as necessary. As long as my overdraft did not exceed the funds in my Pa's account, there would be no interest charged. At the time most banks had not introduced arrangement fees. In the end I managed to bludgeon two doctors to attest that the scribble on the power of attorney was my Pa's signature (it wasn't) and we put finances on an even keel.

It was time for frequent visits to Lymington to see both my parents and to be supportive but it turned out to be very difficult. My Pa was always trying to tell me something but just could not get it out. After ten or fifteen minutes Bunty and I could sense his growing frustration and we needed to leave. Having driven for two hours to reach Lymington we felt we were inadequate in our support, but there was little we could do. I did suggest to my Mama that they both came to live closer to us but she would not entertain the idea. Unfortunately, the strain of looking after my Pa and her own declining health was too much for her and she died suddenly a few months later. My sister Shirley and I set about all the tasks that were necessary and arranged for my Pa to be looked after in a local nursing home pro tem. We soon arranged for him to transfer to a caring home much closer to us so it was easy to arrange a weekly visit to keep in touch. He was always cheerful and pleased to see me, particularly when I was accompanied by Bunty and two little girls but for the rest of his life he tried to tell me something without success.

Back in P&O, the group of ex-Learners were starting to take over various tasks. Peter Parry became associated with the passenger ships, and Sandy Stirling from Orient became manager of the West

Leadenhall Street, London

End booking office. Keith Reynolds was making a name for himself in the freight sales area. Jim Davis was also working in the passenger ship world but more importantly established a Public Relations function which was much needed. Walter Kerr was assisting with the Indian trade cargo services and becoming involved with sea staff personnel management, for which he was well suited. A trend of upward movement was visible, but only Peter Parry from the group ever reached the P&O board.

For my part, Michael Thwaites delegated an increasing number of tasks to me. One was that of "Ship Knacker", which amounted to ship sales when their time had come. We sold CARTHAGE and CORFU to a Japanese ship breaker who took delivery in London, transferred them to Japanese colours, and steamed them to Japan with MARU after their names. To replace them in the Hong Kong service we purchased BAUDOUINVILLE and JADOTVILLE from Compagnie Maritime Belge. Their passenger traffic to the Congo had fallen flat on its face, and after being re-named CATHAY and CHITRAL, they were exactly the right size. There were the passenger ships from the 1930s to sell, mostly for scrap. I did keep ORION out of a dull scrap market for four months by chartering her out to a German hotelier. As a hotel ship in Hamburg for the Planten und Blumen exhibition, she both earned some hire money and gave the scrap market time to improve. We sought offers for STRATHMORE and STRATHEDEN and were surprised when a young Greek ship owner named John Latsis made an offer for them as "runners", at more than double the scrap price. He undertook not to trade them against us since his market was the Haj traffic from Libya to Jeddah. He asked for deferred terms by way of interest bearing debentures. At first a lot of board eyebrows were raised but Michael Thwaites decided to go ahead. Every payment was made on the dot. Not only that, but I got to take mementos from STRATHMORE to St. James Palace for the Queen Mother.

Another task was to join P&O Research and Development Ltd as company secretary. This wholly owned subsidiary had been set up to exploit the inventive genius of Tom Bunyan. The board consisted of Michael Thwaites in the chair with Harry Mitchell and Peter Parry as directors. My handle was quite wrong since I was really the commercial manager and my main task was to deal with the patents and licences stemming from them, something that was not Tom's scene. The company did succeed with products that generated a good long term income. They included stern shaft bearings lubricated with oil instead of water, hydraulically tightened nuts for large nut applications and interference fitted propellers that needed no stress inducing keyways. These may sound like mind-numbing gadgetry but were in fact major advances in stern gear engineering. It was Tom's other ideas that were a bit far-fetched. In his own garage he had built an internal combustion engine which used wobble plates instead of cylinders and pistons, and he was convinced it would take over the market. The idea of approaching British Leyland with a few millions of P&O funds for a joint venture was a pipe dream but one that Tom carried with him to his grave.

Our home was proving a great success and we turned our attention to schooling for girls. Lindley had started in a local infant school but had outgrown it. After research, we selected The Lady Eleanor Holles School in Hampton for her. This had been founded and endowed a couple of centuries before by the sixth daughter of the Earl of Newcastle, and had a well earned reputation of helping girls to succeed. The Head was Miss Garwood-Scott, who was a for-midable person dedicated to her task. Lindley joined the junior school and we managed to find the fees. At 11 she moved up to the senior school and was awarded a full scholarship by Surrey County Council, which meant there were no fees for seven years. This was very good news for her parents. She did very well and achieved the required results for university entrance.

Victoria first started at the local church school but did not make much progress. She had great difficulty with reading and we were worried about how we could help her. It used to be thought that a child that could not read was just dim-witted. She was bright and very numerate but the simple reading primers were too babyish for her intellect. On holiday on a beach in Languedoc we met a couple with whom we became long term friends, and we heard a new word for the first time - dyslexia. The husband, Glyn Morgan, is now a well established artist, and his teacher wife Jean was a specialist in remedial teaching. She conducted a simple experiment by making a hole in a large piece of paper and invited Victoria to look at her through the hole with one eye. Victoria used her left eye. Jean had noted that she was right-handed and explained that she was cross lateral, or dyslexic, and needed specialist teaching.

We transferred her to Hurst Lodge in Sunningdale, where the emphasis on academic subjects was minimal and more on how to prepare for a good life. There was also a teacher who specialised in teaching dyslexics. Victoria commuted by train each day, which was in contrast to many of her classmates who arrived in a chauffeur driven Rolls. One of her juniors was Sarah Ferguson before she became Duchess of York. Victoria generally enjoyed herself at this school and Bunty and I also spent a lot of time nearly every day helping her to read to us. She was completely fascinated with all the newly discovered creatures found in the Galapagos by Darwin and Fitzroy and so well described by Alan Moorehead in his book Darwin and the Beagle. The book has particularly clear type which was helpful and is also so well illustrated. She did in fact master the problem in time, proving this by being a successful salesperson for the new fangled word processors that were appearing on the market.

In the passenger shipping world I became involved with the modernisation of the seven large ships bearing both P&O and Orient names built between 1950 and 1958. They all had been designed and built for the passenger liner trades and were now deployed on extended cruise type operations. They all needed up-dating and the major task was to provide air conditioning throughout each ship. This entailed taking each ship out of service for three months in turn and placing the work with Vosper Thorneycroft in Southampton. A complete new machinery space was created in No 3 hold for all the refrigerating machinery. At the same time other improvements were made, particularly better first class cabins, which were provided with en-suite facilities. The passenger market was changing fairly quickly to a cruise operation and the customers were looking for better accommodation. The programme went well and was completed on time and on budget. At the end of their repair period each ship was inclined to ascertain their new stability characteristic. With one ship, IBERIA, we inclined her before work started and found out what many people had felt for years; her original stability book was incorrect, and her stability was over-stated.

In 1966 there was a major review of our Far Eastern Freight Service, which deployed eight S class cargo liners with a sea speed of 17/18 knots, plus a few other slower ships. The board wanted to continue to participate in the trade and order new tonnage, but the financial results were far from encouraging. The return on capital employed (ROCE) was only five percent. Looking very closely at the trade, our lack of success was a typical chicken and egg situation. We could not attract the highly rated Japanese export cargo on which our competitors were making hay because our transit times were poor. Poor transit times were the result of voyages that were much too long. They ignored the clockwork timing necessary for the end of month rush of Japanese exports. This we could not change because it was the way the trade worked. Japanese exporters were mostly paid by letter of credit valid to the last day of a particular month. A ship loading in Japan might, under Conference rules, issue bills of lading dated for the previous month provided she had embarked a harbour pilot before 2359 on the last day of the month. The cargo was loaded in the first few days of the next month and bills issued for the previous month. The P&O ships were not programmed for this discipline and their round voyages were often up to 160 days long. A first priority was to shorten our round voyage times, and match them to calendar months.

Whilst the sales abilities of our offices in the UK and the Far East were good, there was a very grey area in the near Continent area, and particularly in Germany. Here we were represented by a P&O Group company called The General Steam Navigation Co Ltd, whose head office in London managed a large fleet of small coasters. They had always done a good job for us as port agents but the times were changing and they did not have the reach to cover the Ruhr. Securing customer support had always been associated with soliciting the shippers of cargoes, but this was changing in many cases to the importers who wanted to control the shipping. We needed to have a change of sales agent in such an important export and import market.

We looked at a potential operating pattern in the context of acquiring new ships. Our competitors were ordering new ships with a service speed of 21 knots. This was achieved with a single screw slow diesel for propulsion that was becoming the norm and we would need to adopt it if we were to compete. One of the things that came with the speed was a much larger hull size, with about one million cubic feet bale capacity. This capacity would stow about 20,000 measurement tons of break bulk cargo, an increase of about 65 percent on our existing S Class ships. To fill this we would need a strict monthly service and top class sales. There was a lot of debate about whether we should acquire four ships on 120 day round voyages or three ships on 91 days. The obvious attractions of reducing the capital required for a monthly service, at a time when containerisation was looming had to be weighed against being able to handle so much cargo in such a short time. In the end we decided it was feasible with the newer cargo handling gear available and a paper was prepared for the board.

I had been appointed a general manager of P&O Lines, which was more a rank than a job title, but in practice I was the operating manager for the Far East cargo services with the line manager reporting to me. I went to Hong Kong for a week of discussions with the steamer Assistants from Japan, Hong Kong and Singapore to get their thoughts on what we were planning. They were all constructive and excited about the future, especially those from Japan.

It was time to put together a ship acquisition team in London. It was led by Ford Geddes as the board member. Whilst he had not been associated with building cargo liners in Orient Line, he had headed the team acquiring passenger ships and they had turned out well. He knew how to deal with shipbuilders. David McKee from Orient would be our Naval Architect, and John Tuke, who had joined recently from Shell Tankers, would be responsible for all engineering as Technical Director.

An old shipmate, Chief Engineer Bernard Hill, would lead our team in the shipyard, assisted by Chief Officer David Hannah for hull matters. I was given two tasks; the first was to design the layout of the holds and hatches together with the cranage; the second was to be the co-ordinator of the shipbuilding contract. It was a big team and there were others with additional skills needed for navigational, radio and catering equipment.

For the first task I was able to get John Wacher to help me for a couple of months. The central point of our many debates was how to maximise the vertical element in lifting cargo into and out of the ship and minimise the lateral element. Lateral movement wasted a lot of time and increased cargo damage. Ideally the ship should be like an open boat but this was impracticable in a large ship because the decks provide longitudinal strength for what is sometimes called the ship box girder. And of course the sea has to be kept out. The solution we adopted was to design three hatches abreast at the four biggest holds to make the ship as "open" as possible. All the hatches throughout the ship would be hydraulically powered to save a lot of time when opening and closing.

The adoption of an "open" ship that maximised vertical movement would mean that there would be little fixed "shelf" space, which cargo officers held dear. It took a lot of skill to load a ship at six ports for discharge at a further six ports, and they relied on "shelf" space for this. We would need to retrain them to think entirely in terms of vertical slots - like a container ship of course. John also moved a few bulkheads a foot or two to ensure compartments were equal in size where possible. When selecting cranage we ruled out guyed derricks and old fashioned union purchase which was both slow and limited to lifts of a ton and a half. In their place we designed in hydraulic cranes, some of five tons and others with a heavier lift. In stowing a ship for a six load/six discharge ports voyage it was inevitable that the tonnages in each hatch would not be equal. By positioning each crane so that it could plumb two hatches it enabled the cargo officer to concentrate four cranes in one hatch when need be. The huge benefits of this work were soon to become apparent.

The pre-requisite to a proper shipbuilding contract was a specification on which builders could base an offer. This specification was strictly a statement of what we wanted the ship "To Do". In the past the company stated what they wanted the ship "To Be". This included specified sub-contractors' equipment that we knew and trusted. In many cases in the past the company had ordered such items directly themselves, which often brought not only higher prices but delayed delivery of the ship. The "To Do" concept did not exclude the company from pointing a shipbuilder towards trusted sub contractors but it left the shipbuilder free to negotiate price and terms with the sub contractor. Apart from such mundane items as cups and saucers etc, <u>everything else</u> would be supplied by one contractor - the shipbuilder. The "To Do" statement would concentrate on things like speed, capacity, cargo handling capacity, stability, trim, fuel consumption and a few others. Each of the "To Do" characteristics would be a warranty of the contract with financial penalties for non performance.

Over the past 40 years I have seen many instances of these principles being ignored, both for complete new ships and other acquisitions with complex engineering systems. The result has always been a costly and inefficient acquisition. I witnessed (but was not involved in) one ship acquisition where the owners decided to purchase the complete electrical equipment themselves from a leading European supplier. They decided to sub-contract the switchboards to a company that had never supplied the marine industry. When the switchboards arrived at a Far East shipbuilder they were too high to fit into a ship's tween deck, and had to be re-built. The only happy person in the end was the shipbuilder.

A request for quotation for three new cargo liners was sent initially to about twenty shipbuilders, but only three showed real interest. One was a UK shipyard, the second was a Dutch shipyard and the third was from Japan. During negotiations that went on for three months, it was clear that Mitsui in Tamano, Japan, were leading the race in both technical and financial matters. The team was concerned about whether the board would agree to build in Japan, but Sir Donald put his seal of approval for the first ever P&O ship to be built in Japan. In 1965 a deal was done subject to contract.

Prior to this we had grown accustomed to the efficiency of Mitsui's managing director and senior technical team, but it was now time for their commercial team to join the party. This was led by a very able manager with two colleagues. We spent a total of 34 hours round the table, with solicitors for both sides present. After a great deal of work a very comprehensive form of contract emerged, which provided both sides with a crystal clear picture of what they had to do. The contract was signed and there were no disputes arising from it. When the first ship was nearly ready for delivery, Mitsui's MD appeared to report that a trim problem had arisen that breached the trim warranty. He then laid out some small hull changes needed to correct it, for Mitsui's account. All of our preferred sub contractors were included and not one of them delivered late, something almost unheard of in Europe. The three ships were all delivered to time and on budget with no "extras".

It was of course the exclusive right of the Chairman to select names for the ships. Sir Donald decided to revive the Strath prefix that had been so successful in the 1930s and was obviously close to his Scottish heart. STRATHARDLE, STRATHBRORA and STRATHCONON were chosen. He was not an "old Far East hand" himself and so had not lived amongst the Chinese and Japanese. Had he done so he would have realised that STRATHARDLE would be called STLATHARDLE in Hong Kong, and STRATHARDARU in Japan. But of course it did not matter since the Far East customers were drawn to the service, not the Highland names.

Whilst the ships were being built Keith Reynolds set about producing the right sales organisation in Germany for the new and upgraded service. To head it he appointed Wolfgang Buschorn, who soon demonstrated his grip of the market and identified all the top importers and exporters. Jim Davis disappeared to Japan for two months to assist the Tokyo and Osaka offices in soliciting the important exporters whose business we needed to capture.

On leaving Tamano, STRATHARDLE covered the Japanese ports for the end month position, and then went on to Hong Kong and Singapore, which she left completely full of cargo. Her first discharge port was Rotterdam where she discharged about 4,500 measurement tons of cargo "to mark" in 29 running hours. Of course, Rotterdam worked round the clock which helped, but there were only two of the expensive night gangs. The consignees were well pleased to retrieve their goods "to mark" since this saved them time when they otherwise would have had to scout around for missing packages. The ship's vertical stows made it much easier to keep packages to their mark.

Just after the ship's arrival in Europe, Michael Thwaites stormed into my small office waving a single sheet of paper. It was the management accountant's preliminary voyage account for STRATHARDLE. He told me it was a load of rubbish and that I was to go straightaway and see Monty Poiney, the accountant, and get it sorted out. I looked at it quickly to read the bottom line and found that it was an absolutely delicious 23 per cent ROCE. It was not a case of a maiden voyage bonanza either, since all three ships consistently returned 20 per cent or better throughout their lives in P&O.

I sat down with Monty for an hour or so and we checked every figure twice but could find no mistakes. On my return Michael was sitting at his desk head down and studying some papers. I put the account on his desk and reported that it was correct. He never looked up but just grunted. It was typical of the man. Had I been in his shoes I would have danced on my desk and summoned everyone in the team to a slap-up black tie dinner at the Café Royal, in the best Nelsonian tradition.

It was not just the financial results that mattered. The success of the new service and its ships boosted the morale of the cargo ship officers who now saw themselves as "Cocks of the Fleet". Everyone in both the overseas and London offices was elated, and my old dream from Yokohama office days had come true. The other liner companies in the P&O Group, even BI, were looking at us with respect, and wanted details of how it was achieved. Whilst Blue Funnel were not part of P&O, we were moving closer to them when it became clear that we would have to take on containerisation together. Quite unexpectedly I received an invitation for lunch on board Blue Funnel's new PRIAM. I was received most handsomely and shown round a splendid new cargo liner by able and enthusiastic ship's officers. But PRIAM had only twin - not triple - hatches and so was not as "open" as the Straths. She could not handle cargo as fast as we could. This was borne out by the fact that Blue Funnel deployed four ships on 120 day round voyages. In terms of annual gross revenue we only needed three ships to their four to achieve the same revenue.

When the Suez Canal closed for another war, we had a dilemma on our hands. If our ships had to steam around the Cape on their voyages both to and from the East, we would have to abandon 91 day round voyages. After much heart searching we decided to route the ships out via the Cape and home from Japan via Panama. This was achievable within 91 days but it entailed discharging and loading concurrently from Singapore to Kobe. But the Straths had demonstrated their ability to stow vertically and could cope. This bold move succeeded brilliantly, not least because our competitors who stuck to the Cape route both ways had to increase their voyage times and have less space to offer overall.

The board clearly believed I needed more education and booked a place for me at the newly created London Business School. I handed over my desk to Bob Lamb who had been part of the operations team in Singapore and who needed all of five minutes for the handover.

It was about this time that my Pa succumbed to another heart attack. One day he was there as usual, cheerful but unable to speak, and a couple of days later he had "weighed and proceeded". But I had been able to keep in touch with him on a near weekly basis for quite a long time. His carers were very decent people who always treated him with kindness. I did take him out from time to have a lunch or go shopping for new clothing. After his cremation we took his ashes to a memorial garden in Christchurch on a spot next to the ashes of my Mama.

I went to The London Business School, which was a British initiative modelled on the business schools of the USA. As a temporary measure the school was set up in a vacant building in Northumberland Avenue with accommodation in the Regents Park Hotel. Its principal activity was to offer two year courses for a Master's Degree in Business Administration, but it also offered courses of shorter duration. These included courses for senior financial people and younger managers typically in their 30s. With about 30 classmates I joined Executive Development Course No 2 for a three month course. My classmates came from a wide range of well known British companies and were middle managers from all the business disciplines. The companies included such names as ICI, British Airways, Unilever and Vickers Barrow. The disciplines included marketing, production, finance, personnel and general management.

It was an extremely intensive course. After a long day filled with lectures and syndicate work there was another lecture just before dinner. After dinner there were at least three case histories to read so as to be in position to discuss them on the next day. We were allowed out on Saturday afternoons but needed to take books or case studies for weekend study. After the first week I duly went home for a night and spent the time wandering about our house like a dazed zombie, almost oblivious to my family. It wore off with time of course. Most of my classmates applied themselves to the course diligently, but a couple treated the whole thing as a holiday from real work.

A lot of my own time was directed towards marketing, finance and general management. The marketing professor had previously been a director of Mars (Bars). There were many occasions when he displayed his skills, but there was one small case that seemed to enshrine them all. A salesman for Rolls Royce Cars called on a customer and spent an hour extolling the technical virtues of his product. At the end of his pitch he at last revealed a very high price based on cash with order. He left without an order. He was followed by another salesman who asked the customer what kind of sticky toffee bar he would like to buy for 6d, with thirty days free credit. This salesman left with an order.

The finance studies really helped me. A lot of the work was way above my head but I did learn how to read a balance sheet. The importance of quick ratios of current assets and liabilities was highlighted. It was not a skill I really needed in P&O but was later to come in very handy for my own small limited company. On a higher level I was not of much use to my syndicate, one of whose members was fortunately a chartered accountant. At a time when a cash flow statement was not a statutory requirement for the accounts of major companies, our syndicate was tasked to produce one. We were given the accounts of Marks and Spencer from which to derive the statement. After a great deal of work the CA did lead us to an answer, but other syndicates produced quite different answers, and we were not told who was right.

There was a great deal of time spent on general management cases. This involved carefully reading a case history and analysing it to suggest the road a company should take to become more profitable. I did take in the importance of improving profitability and perhaps that was my real lesson learned. Forty years later it looks as if this may have gone too far, because profiteering is all the rage. The only thing that matters in business is how much money can be taken out. Fraudulent activities are almost smiled upon and many business leaders should be ashamed but are not.

A few classmates arranged visits for the whole class to their own businesses which was a break from the lecture room, although I found stationary chemical plants a bit boring. Not to be upstaged I arranged a visit to a passenger ship in Tilbury and every classmate attended. It turned out that one of them, Jim Glasgow from Vickers in Barrow had built her. The ship put on a splendid dinner which was a great help, and P&O's new PR Department provided all the right sort of assistance. This included smart and lightweight vinyl document cases which contained a lot of company and sales information for each guest. The cases were dark blue with the new P&O Logo in gold in one corner. Unfortunately the design studio had problems with the logo and most of my classmates pulled my leg by claiming it read "El Al".

EDP 2 broke up just before Christmas 1967 and P&O asked me to re-appear in the New Year. There was a new job awaiting me which was to turn out well, but heralded a period when my P&O career went distinctly pear-shaped.

Chapter 12. List 3, The Royal Naval Reserve

The choice of which RNR Division to join was usually left to individual officers.   For most it hinged on being a division reasonably close to work and home, since each week there were one or two drill nights, with a few drill weekends as well.   The latter involved going to sea in the tender from Friday evening to Sunday afternoon.   My nearest division was in fact London Division, then based in HMS PRESIDENT, moored to the Thames Embankment. I duly made a call on their Training Commander but was not encouraged to join because they had a lot more officers than they needed.   This meant that a billet in the sea tender was difficult to obtain for weekends and almost impossible for a two week training period.   The Division's tender was in fact berthed in Southampton to be nearer the open sea.

The next nearest division was Solent Division in HMS WESSEX, at 50 Berth in Southampton.   This was a "stone frigate", having started life as a British Airways terminal for their flying boats of the 1930s. It was not a very smart building and often looked as if was about to slide into Southampton Water, but it was serviceable enough and provided a quay for berthing two CMS and an IMS.   Attending a drill night on a weekday involved a 60 mile drive after work in London but this did not seem unduly onerous.

I arranged to call on the Commander and XO John Clarke, and was warmly received.   John had joined the RNVR in WW2 and had spent a lot of time at sea. Before settling down to be a solicitor, he had also spent a couple of years in the Merchant Marine and certainly knew what seafaring was all about.   On qualifying as a solicitor, he joined his Pa's practice in Basingstoke and soon was both the senior partner and Coroner for NW Hampshire. He was a major figure, always bashing on to life's next obstacle.   He was pleased to see an extra pair of watch keeping hands, but warned me

152

that service in the RNR did not bring great riches (as if I did not know). He took me to call on the Division's Captain, Tommy Tucker, who had followed his active WW2 career by becoming General Manager of Huntley and Palmer's (Biscuits) in Reading. John also introduced me to the Training Commander, John Elgar DSC, another solicitor and Coroner for South Hampshire. I shipped my half stripe as Lieutenant Commander and joined.

In The Royal Navy its officers were all of one corps. They tended to look upon RNR Divisions as parochial and with the same family social structure as regiments of the Army. Of course this was both true and quite different from their own corps, but it was dictated by reasons of geography. A few years later when I was a squadron CO of six divisional sea tenders, there was the usual mix of over-manned and under-manned tenders as we assembled for an operation. I made some re-appointments and was nearly bowled over by a storm of protests. The threat of sending them back immediately to their divisions produced a calm, but for a couple of days there was much sucking of teeth. This family type organisation also had quite a lot of bearing on the question of promotion to higher rank.

Within the division, I was tasked to take charge of the Commissions and Warrants (CW) class. The majority of RNR recruits for all branches were entered as junior rates. Direct officer entry was limited to degree engineers, doctors and dentists. Recruits initially joined the New Entry class, where they spent about six months before becoming ordinary seaman or their departmental equivalents. It was the job of the New Entry officer to spot young men and women who were intelligent, well educated and showed OLQ (Officer Like Qualities) and to recommend them for the CW class. Thus I had a small class who could absorb lots of new information and were prepared to do some homework as well. There was also one golden rule - they had to go to sea with me. This made sure they could live in a crowded mess deck and enabled me to see how they behaved in bad weather, or when things started to go wrong. Their time in the CW class was typically a year, after which they presented themselves at an interview board chaired by the Captain. Success brought a commission as midshipman or acting sub-

Sea Officer

Lieutenant.

As regards seafaring in the tender, John Clarke invited me to join him as NO for an Easter weekend trip, comprising minesweeping in the Channel and a visit to a Dutch port, with two other CMS in company. One of his purposes was to assess me at sea and I think I passed his test. We had a useful training session but had to return against a Westerly gale. It certainly proved that a CMS was a good sea boat, but John insisted on proceeding at 14 knots, which was very uncomfortable. The CMS, then named HMS WARSASH, pitched very heavily into the sea and the forward half came right out of the water. This produced a sea-sickness factor of about 75 per cent of the ship's company including me. Motion sickness is never a matter for contempt or ridicule; it can affect human ability and vigilance quite seriously. There is no way of changing the weather but there are ways of mitigating its effects with a little careful planning.

I learned a great deal about the characteristics of a CMS, both in respect of ship handling and mine clearance ability. The first-of-class HMS CONISTON was completed in the early 1950s. In all about 80 were built. They were originally named after small towns and villages in the UK with the suffix of "ton". Whilst attached to the RNR Divisions as sea tenders, they were given other names reflecting their divisional associations. They were built in wood planking on aluminium frames to reduce their magnetic signature and given high and long forecastles to keep them dry in bad weather. Their sweep gear consisted of serrated and armed sweep wires to sweep moored contact mines, and towed magnetic and acoustic sweeps to detonate influence mines on the sea bed. These were all worked by way of powered winch drums on the quarterdeck. For AA defence they carried a Bofors 40/60 on the fo'csle and a twin Oerlikon 20mm abaft the funnel. Their complement was about 30 but in the RNR role was higher.

The ships were diesel powered and twin screw. In WW2 wooden fast patrol boats were powered by petrol engines and a whole squadron was lost by fire whilst alongside their base at Walcheren. The Admiralty rightly decided that wooden craft and petrol were

OCL's ENCOUNTER BAY. The UK's first large cellular container ship, 1968.

Signing MORETON BAY's guest book. The author, CFL Chairman Ford Geddes MBE, Captain Michael Ryan OBE, CFL Director Robert Huskisson.

The Container Fleets team. From the back: Alec Stevens, Graeme Dunlop;
Stan Mole, Peter Clark, Ken Blackett, Geoff Millings;
Temp, Sheila, Charlie Brownson, Derek Smith, Paul Ogden, the author.

Loaded with loot at my farewell party. With Bunty, Paul Ogden and Derrick Smith.

P&O Managing Director Sandy Marshall (right) presents Eagle's three sailors to the secretary of Lloyds to receive their brave conduct medals.

Victoria assisting at the Marine Trades Show in London, 1991.

Powered by Sunware marine solar modules, 100Wp Survival capsule for two Greenpeace members for six weeks on Rockall in the North Atlantic.

The Strait of Hormuz. 440 Wp solar generator powering Racal Hyperfix system.

Jock Wishart relaxing in Barbados after finishing eleventh in the two handed rowing race from Tenerife, 1993. 110 Wp of solar modules powered his water maker, lights and GPS receiver.

Netherhow Cleugh, Scotland. 210 Wp solar generator for British Gas to power cathodic protection system for their underground natural gas pipework.

"By the right, dress."
Milford Haven's solar powered buoys lined up ashore for inspection.

The Ecos Centre Ballymena, Northern Ireland.
12 kWp grid connected solar generator.

Trans-Australia solar powered car race, 1994.
Built by a private competitor in his garage.

Private house in Whitwick, Leicestershire. 2 kWp grid connected generator. The first four bottom row modules and roof straps secured through the tiles to the rafters.

The completed array. The owner grinned broadly when his meter showed his house was feeding the grid.

not good bed mates and asked English Electric to develop a high powered diesel, which appeared in due course as the Deltic engine. It would take time and so the Tons were designed with two conventional in-line Mirrlees diesels, which produced about 14 knots. A third diesel provided the power for the magnetic loop sweep. When the Deltic engines appeared their power/weight ratio was about three times better than the older diesels. It had been hoped to achieve a speed of 16 knots with the Deltics but they suffered piston seizures and were downgraded to provide 15 knots. The new engines were much smaller and lighter. They not only provided a spacious engine room but also reduced the ship's displacement to the extent that their freeboard increased. The ships were sometimes likened to corks bobbing about and they moved sideways easily in a beam wind. Under these conditions the high fo'csle was rather like a large genoa jib-sail and at slow speed it was difficult to hold the ship up into the wind. These difficulties could be mitigated by various means and the twin rudders were excellent at slow speeds.

The TON class was a great success as a whole for the Royal Navy. Their roles covered a lot more than just minesweeping. They were used for coastal patrols in Cyprus, and counter insurgency patrols in Malaysia. They were suitable for fishery protection around our own coast and were later converted to mine hunters when that new technique emerged. They made trans-ocean passages that rather belied the coastal image. They were also invaluable in providing early command experience for young officers in the Navy; as demonstrated by a certain Lieutenant HRH Prince Charles, who became an early "driver". They were ideal for foreign visits to quite small ports to show the flag and make friends. Ships of this size and type became the norm for the European NATO navies and it was not long before shipbuilders were producing similar hulls in Glass Reinforced Plastic, sometimes known as fibreglass.

Some time later I joined WARSASH again for a two week training period with John Elgar as my CO. We steamed North to Invergordon in the Cromarty Forth and there joined the other ten CMS sea tenders for a week of intensive exercises as an enlarged squadron. Our Admiral Commanding Reserves and all of his staff were present. They came to sea with us each day to correct mistakes and poor procedures and to improve our efficiency. The Cromarty area is a very scenic place with lots of wild country and a tiny population. Just outside the Forth there are miles of open sea with few if any ships, so there is plenty of space for exercises. I was asked to berth the ship alongside Invergordon jetty in a strong beam wind. It was a tight fit but we secured without damage. Afterwards I talked to the staff NO, who had looked concerned during the berthing, and told him I would have preferred to let go the weather anchor off the berth to act as a brake on the bow. It was not a practice he had ever heard of and was not "in the book".

Our exercise programme complete, we sailed in horrendous weather for a squadron courtesy visit to Hull. The Westerly was still blowing hard as we steamed up the Humber, but at least there was no seaway and chef was quick to provide lunch, or "dinner" for the sailors after their tots of rum. Abreast of the old town there was a little used fishing vessel dock, which was to be the squadron berth for the visit. It comprised a small entry basin out of the tideway, and a lock into the dock proper. Getting eleven CMS into the dock was a difficult task with the strong wind but somehow nobody suffered a collision or other accident. As NO, I was there to assist my CO with the task, and I became aware that he was finding it difficult. In a small entry basin he was using far too many engine movements and too much power. His exasperation started to infect the coxswain and two telegraph men in the wheelhouse below, who were losing track of what they were doing. At the time there were two other CMS in the basin behaving in much the same way. I later learned that it was quite usual behaviour for people getting used to handling a small but powerful ship, and until they learned to approach the task slowly and calmly, and to use their twin rudders as well.

I offered to take the con and was told to carry on. With everything stopped the first task was to calm the coxswain and his team. A few quiet words and a small leg pull got them back on their feet. We moved slowly and safely into the dock, turned short round and secured to the quay. My CO was so appreciative that he asked me to take over the ship handling for the remaining week. My own confidence rose as we left Hull and crossed the North Sea to Ijmuiden, steaming up the North Sea Canal to Amsterdam. By the time we returned to Southampton, I felt that I had been driving a CMS all my life.

ACR accompanied us on the visit, flying his flag in an MCM support ship equipped with saluting guns. It was possible to fire gun salutes with a Bofors but it was difficult to get it right. Off Ijmuiden, ACR saluted the Dutch nation with 21 guns and the shore battery returned a salute of 13 guns to his flag. It was quite a high level official visit and we were entertained by the Royal Netherlands Navy in great style. Their officers' mess provided a rijstaffel lunch which was new to me. I learned it was the Dutch East Indies/ Indonesian answer to curry, and very good it was too.

It was time to start studying for the Command Examination. This was based on a slightly scaled down version of the Royal Navy's examination. A large part was devoted to navigation, pilotage and ship handling, but there were oral examinations for gunnery, mechanical and electrical engineering, and supply. In the workshops of HMS SULTAN in Gosport I was confronted by a Deltic and instructed to start it. Chief ERA Red Harris in WESSEX had trained me for this, using a cartridge start, and the engine fired at the first attempt. The written papers were both long and complex but past memories of star sights took me through.

What did upset me was that I failed my first attempt in the oral pilotage examination. The examiner was a long course N† from HMS DRYAD, the navigation school. He told me that my methods lacked precision and relied too much on eye-balling. Thinking about it later, I believed his mind was on Devonport and Plymouth whereas mine was on the outer Thames estuary. In the latter there are no shore marks on which to take fixes even when the visibility is good and eye-balling the buoys is the only way to proceed. This analysis tended to be confirmed when I learned a bit later from another examiner that his predecessor had in fact put a carrier on the beach in Plymouth Sound. (This examiner passed me.) The ship handling part took place in WARSASH in Southampton docks one evening and was conducted by Solent Division's RN staff officer. There were several berthings and un-berthings, which all passed muster. I sensed that the ship's company were all getting thirsty when I was directed for another berthing. This involved making two complete turns to berth stem to the tide. I berthed stern to the tide, which all went well and we returned to WESSEX. I was told that I had passed and asked where I had learned the stern to tide technique. When I revealed it was from the pilots in Keppel Harbour in Singapore long ago, staff officer was surprised, since it was not naval practice. One final hurdle remained; I needed the Captain of the Division to approve me for military command, and this he duly did. My own short definition of military command is quite simply to know when to pull the trigger, and when not to pull it.

One of the results of my new certificate was a new respect for volunteer reservists who had no seafaring background and passed the examination. Each division contained young men from many other walks of life who had joined as ordinary seaman (OD). They all shared the same ambition of becoming the CO of one of Her Majesty's Ships. It took a long time and considerable application to move successfully through all the necessary steps, but they got there. At a very small cost to the nation they were a significant addition to available naval manpower and two world wars had proved they were up to the job.

After WW2, the divisions recruited women, who were offered the choices of three jobs for which they could train. Communicators who manned signal stations and wireless offices; supply staff who took over Naval Stores and general administration duties; or degaussing teams of the WRNR who were exclusively responsible for manning the shore end of the degaussing stations. This long name stood for rather antique wooden huts on a shoreline close to a degaussing range on the sea bed offshore. The huts were fitted with equally antique electrical equipment to measure the magnetic signature of a ship as she steamed slowly over the range. The signature revealed a strange picture which allowed the DG officer to adjust the signature to zero by changing the settings on the ship's own DG coils. It all sounds weird and even mundane, but it must be remembered that the magnetic mine was a most potent and efficient weapon. Queen Alexandra's Royal Naval Nursing Corps also contained reservists who were free to join a division. As the 20th century moved to a close women were allowed to go to sea and to be seamen. The officers exchanged their blue cuff lace for gold and took on the rank structure of their male counterparts. I was one of those sad to see this last change because the old rank structure was a huge compliment from the Navy to the Merchant Service.

Apart from all the training, Solent Division provided an active social life for all ranks. The wardroom staged formal mess dinners, particularly for Trafalgar Night. There were other parties, dinners and dances, all well supported by non-reservist wives. In the wardroom's collection of table silver, there was a small oak coffin. This contained a sub lieutenant's cuff lace of a gold stripe in the "wavy" design of the old RNVR. At dinner, an officer approached the Commander as President of the mess and sought his permission "to uncover the wavy stripe" so that the top table could inspect it. Both the Chief and Petty Officer's mess and the junior rate's mess also staged their own functions to a high standard.

Before going away to sea on my own as CO, John Clarke invited me to be his squadron NO for an important operation named CABLEWAY in the North Sea. The North Sea is quite a big place in which to lay mines and many British influence mines had been laid by both fast patrol boats and aircraft off the German and Dutch coasts. There was no accurate record of their exact positions, partly because the small ships and aircraft could not fix their positions accurately, and partly because they were at times under heavy fire from Schnellboots and flak ships. At the close of WW2 the Navy swept channels to provide access to all the ports which were designated NEMEDRI routes and marked them with proper navigational buoys. The area was too vast to clear completely and after nearly twenty years it was thought that any mines still on the sea bed would be inert. The mines had been fitted with 12 volt Exide lead acid batteries to power their detection and firing circuits and the manufacturer's stated shelf life was six years. However, from time to time a German Navy diving team would recover a British ground mine, disarm it and then find the battery was not quite dead.

In the early 60s, Anglo-German landline telephone traffic was growing by leaps and bounds and new capacity was needed. The two governments agreed to provide a new cable and the preferred path for this in the North Sea lay across about 40 miles of un-swept water. The Germans undertook to mark the new channel with proper buoys five miles apart and the Royal Navy would provide small dan buoys every mile and carry out the sweeping task. The Navy's 1st Mine Countermeasure Squadron (MCMS1) of six CMS would be supported by the 10th MCMS, with six CMS from the RNR Divisions forming MCMS 10. The operation took about ten days in all with the whole long channel receiving at least two passes by the CMS using their magnetic and acoustic sweeps. The mines had been fitted with ship count mechanisms which ignored the signal from the first ship passing overhead and then detonated on the second or subsequent signals. It was an anti-sweep device designed to sink the second ship, on the assumption that a major ship target would be preceded by a less valuable minesweeper. Minesweepers were clearly dispensable. No mines were detonated and the channel was declared clear for the new telephone cable.

The CO of MCMS1 was Commander Paul Greening, Royal Navy, with whom I had been a classmate at Pangbourne in the early 1940s. He was later to hoist his flag as a rear admiral and become Flag Officer Royal Yachts. Some time later he appeared on my television screen at Windsor Castle checking the arrangements with his boss for a large state dinner in his new capacity as Comptroller of Her Majesty's Household.

For the second week MCMS 10 was joined by HMS KILMOREY, the sea tender to Ulster Division in HMS CAROLINE in Belfast. Whilst preparing for her first sweep, she succeeded in getting her large magnetic loop sweep around one propeller. She had to return to our forward base in Den Helder on just the other engine alone for diving assistance to clear the propeller and repair the sweep. On her return to the swept area all the other ships were carefully recovering their sweep gear in the dark, having already completed the sweeping task. . KILMOREY was instructed to recover the 26 dan buoys, before continuing to Hamburg for an eagerly awaited R&R visit. Admiralty Pattern dan buoys were simple and inexpensive temporary markers, consisting of a 12 foot stave with a steel flotation collar and a small sinker to hold them upright. They were secured to the sea bed by a large concrete sinker attached to a mooring wire, and at the top of the staves were fitted with a distinguishing flag and radar reflector. Recovering dan buoys in the dark, with the wind across the tide, is quite a tricky operation, especially prone to a wire round a propeller. On the tactical primary voice net an Ulster accent announced "Am about to recover buoy Alfa". Two minutes later there were two bangs as if from a small calibre weapon. About twenty minutes later there was another announcement "Am about to recover buoy Bravo", followed by more shots. And so on. It is usually called the luck of the Irish.

In the summer of 1965, I was at last able to go to sea in command. There was no billet in WARSASH available but we borrowed HMS ISIS from London Division for a week. Although ISIS was a Ham class IMS like DAMERHAM in Hong Kong, she carried no sweep gear and was just used for seamanship training for new sub lieutenants and ratings. It was particularly useful for me to take sailors from my CW class to sea and have the opportunity to train them. Our week took us to Enkhuizen on the Ijselmeer via Ijmuiden and the North Sea Canal. About 400 years earlier Enkhuizen had been a major seaport when the House of Orange had been struggling to free Holland from its Spanish master King Philip II of Spain. Just off the port Dutch ships had overcome their Spanish opponents, an event never forgotten in Enkhuizen. Our small voyage proved instructive; one sub lieutenant learned how to secure anchors for sea following one letting itself go in mid Channel, and I learned how to handle a ship with controllable pitch propellers.

Later I took WARSASH to sea for a weekend of minesweeping practice followed by a short call at Dieppe. I was piped ashore for an official call on Dieppe's Mayor and the British Consul took me in his car to the Mairie. It was late on a Saturday afternoon and Monsieur was very busy with civil marriages. We sat in his Salle D'Attente together with an excited young couple already dressed for their church service that would follow the civil service in the

Mairie. The door to the mayoral parlour opened and out flounced another gorgeous creature in a white wedding dress, towing a new husband dressed in "le smoking". Monsieur was full of entente cordiale, shaking my hand and producing a bottle of cognac and three glasses from his desk. It was a short and very congenial visit which ended when he returned the bottle to its discreet storage, and the impatient couple were summoned before his presence.

In May 1966 I again took WARSASH to sea to participate in a NATO exercise called WOODEN WALLS, and an official visit to Sweden. WOODEN WALLS was a joint MCM and NCS (Naval Control of Shipping) exercise in the Southern North Sea conducted by COMBENECHAN, the NATO title for Commander Belgium Nederland Channel. He was also CinC Nore in the Royal Navy and flew his flag in Chatham. Two MCM squadrons were involved. The Navy's MCMS1, consisting of six CMS based at Harwich, and the RNR's MCMS10 of five CMS at Lowestoft. NCS teams in both ports and at their Chatham headquarters were mustered. Live minefields (with reduced explosive charges) had been laid off East Anglia. The task for a week was to locate the minefields, sweep and mark channels through them and then guide merchant ships into the ports.

HMS WARSASH, and HMS CURZON from Sussex Division in Shoreham, arrived at Lowestoft earlier than the three CMS from the North. One of these was HMS MONTROSE from Tay Division at Dundee, whose CO Commander Stewart was MCM10 for the period, and whose civilian task was to manage his family's jute mill in Dundee. In company were HMS KILLIECRANKIE from Forth Division in Edinburgh, and HMS NORTHUMBRIA from TYNE Division in Newcastle. There was no opportunity for a squadron COs' meeting before starting operations so we assembled at sea to get on with the task. After 24 hours without locating any mines the weather deteriorated to the point where sweep gear was being damaged and the squadron retired to anchor in Caister Roads. Without sweeps streamed, a CMS is very manoeuvrable but the situation changes substantially when towing sweeps stretching 1,000 feet astern. Any turn has to be made very slowly and carefully especially when using the magnetic and acoustic sweeps which were prone to damage. Manoeuvring to turn 180° needs to take into account both consorts and commercial ships, not all of whom are warned off by the minesweeping shapes and lights. Bad weather aggravates the problem so, to reduce the stress on a ship's company, minesweeping sorties were usually restricted to about 48 hours.

At anchor there was a chance to call on the boss by way of WARSASH's small motor cutter and I climbed aboard MONTROSE. Without a squadron meeting before operations I had got various things wrong and was duly pointed in the right direction. With the business of the squadron now quite clear a bottle of best single malt was produced and we shared a glass (or two). Bob Stewart's mill transformed raw jute into gunny cloth for all the best carpets and flour sacks and I recalled discharging bales of jute from KARMALA in Dundee. It turned out that he had spent time in Bengal and was fluent in Hindi. We resolved to use Hindi for strictly private voice signals on the minesweeping net. This must have confounded both consorts in the squadron as well as other eavesdroppers such as the Royal Navy and the Russians. When I got up to leave I found that it was dark and the wind was rising. My coxswain appeared and we went to look at the cutter to find the painter was on the point of being chafed away. We secured the cutter, but I decided to stay put and MONTROSE hoisted the cutter inboard for the night and offered us berths. WARSASH looked comfortable in another anchor berth nearby but I needed to speak to my 1st Lieutenant on the net to tell him of my decision. Arthur Wolstenholme was a good XO but was not qualified for command and sounded apprehensive. Much later I cheered him up with a postal order for one day's command pay of 5s 0d.

We resumed our interrupted sortie the next day, and managed to detonate a combined magnetic/acoustic mine. There followed a day in harbour when CinC Home Fleet Admiral Sir John Frewen paid a visit to the squadron in Lowestoft. Our second sortie lasted a full 48 hours, with all five ships working well. We detonated more mines and were able to report that the channel was clear. The NCS team brought in a couple of merchant ships and there were no more muffled bangs. For the second sortie I was joined by a very large

Sea Officer

Captain R Neth N, whose NATO job it was to appraise a new CO. Sitting in the tiny CO's cabin with a glass he went through his check list and announced that I was fit for the job. He then slapped my leg heavily as a mark of approval. At first I thought he had broken my leg.

The next day about twenty officers from the squadron, and the MCM and NCS teams, boarded a naval bus and spent four hours reaching Chatham via the Blackwall Tunnel. We attended the "wash-up" to learn that it had gone well and that COMBENECHAN was well pleased. The only black cloud on the horizon was another four hour journey back to Lowestoft. Once into East Anglia it was clear that everyone was tired, hungry and very thirsty, but our driver from Ipswich knew the ropes. He took us to Hintlesham Hall, just outside Ipswich, where a marvellous dinner at one large table was provided without delay.

In the morning the squadron sailed for Sweden via the Kiel Canal in perfect weather for a change. This was a new experience for me and left me wondering how in the past great battleship squadrons had made the passage. In Kiel Bay MCM10 detached WARSAH and CURZON to proceed to Halmstadt as Div 2, whilst MONTROSE, KILLIECRANKIE and NORTHUMBRIA, as Div 1, headed for Mälmo. We sailed North through the Great Belt and about 0130 I was called to the bridge by the OOW who told me he was lost. We appeared to be surrounded by shore lights but the critical buoys were missing. Div 2 was stopped until we could positively identify lights and fix our position and were able to proceed. Five hours later we anchored in Halmstadt Bay in really thick fog until two pilots appeared, when we used radar to find the harbour entrance and crept in. A military band was playing on the quay inside which we could hear but not see, which at least provided a new helm order "Steer towards the music".

Halmstadt is the capital of Halland Province. Our visit was clearly an important occasion because, on arrival, there were four visitors to call on the ships. The first was the provincial Governor, followed by the First Vice Chairman of the City Council and the COs of the Halland Regiment and Air Regiment. It took CURZON and me all morning to return each call in a car provided by the Royal Navy's attaché from Stockholm.

Our hosts had taken a great deal of trouble to ensure that both ship's companies would be looked after for every minute of our three day stay. We took on the Halland Regiment at football and drew the match. We also took them on in a shooting match which we won. There was a lot of fraternising and mess parties between both senior rates and junior rates with their opposite numbers in the two regiments. The two wardrooms provided a cocktail party on the arrival evening and had to use both foc'sles to cope with the numbers. I had previously been in touch with Mr P D Sobart, Her British Majesty's Consul General in Göteborg, about the arrangements he required and in reply he wrote that a party for about 30 would suffice. In the event he appeared with a list of 70 guests, and that did not count the gatecrashers. He also asked for a small lunch party for eight guests on the second day. The small galley in a CMS is not up to Ritz standards, beside the fact that the wardroom was designed to seat six maximum, not ten. We managed, and the ship's company fell over themselves to assist. A lady guest expressed surprise that we carried such a large catering staff, but I did not let on to her that all but one were seamen or stokers. On the second evening, the Halland Regiment were our hosts and staged a tattoo at 2100, inviting both complete ship's companies. Prior to this, six officers sat down to dinner in the Regiments' officers' mess. Wives were also present, and Mr Stobart advised us that Swedish military etiquette forbade toasts to the Colonel's lady (she must not appear plastered) but other diners were fair game. CURZON and I were not told about the tattoo until 2100, and on a fine and twilit evening we were ushered to the parade ground to find the whole regiment fallen in with band and torchbearers. Also fallen in were our ship's companies. At the end of a countermarching display the Colonel invited CURZON and me to join him in taking the salute as the regiment marched past.

It was a really stunning occasion. It impressed not just our officers but the ship's companies were cock-a-hoop too. There were yet more parties on the third day; one given by the Governor in his palace, and another for about 40 children, including six crippled youngsters, given by our chief and petty officers in the ships.

The next day we sailed for home at 0800 and I decided to go North of the Skaw to reduce the navigational workload after so much social activity. It was the wrong decision because the North Sea was back to form with a force 8 gale ahead for 12 hours. The next week saw the arrival of several very nice letters of thanks from our Swedish hosts, and I had of course already written mine.

I was to make a number of seagoing trips in the sea tender, for MCM operations, exercises, and foreign visits. They were all of interest and provided job satisfaction but WOODEN WALLS was probably a highlight. Its excitement did not stop it from being two naval tasks well performed for the Royal Navy and even the taxpayers could smile.

At the end of 1967 I was promoted to the rank of Commander and had to wear a "brass hat" with its peak decorated with gold lace, which was usually referred to as "scrambled egg". This put me No. 4 in the divisional pecking order. Tommy Tucker had retired as Captain to be succeeded by John Clarke. John Elgar became XO and Commander David McCarraher became Training Commander. David was a capable seaman but poor eyesight prevented him from being a seaman officer, and he was a specialist communicator. His naval career started in WW2 when he was appointed to the signal branch as a decoder. He had many naval connections and after the war became a solicitor. His elder brother became Chaplain of the Fleet whilst David and his younger brother Malcolm were partners in McCarrahers in Southampton. In the Navy the family were seen to have a firm grip on matters when naval marriages fell apart. The Chaplain looked after the spiritual side whilst his two younger brothers sorted out the nitty-gritty, such as money and property.

I relinquished my divisional task as CW Officer and became Sea Training Officer under the scrutiny of three lawyers.

In 1968 there was another major mine clearance operation in the North Sea called NEW BROOM. The NEMEDRI Dutch Coastal Route was a swept channel three miles wide which needed widening to ten miles to cope with the increase in shipping. The operation was conducted by the Admiral Netherlands at Den Helder, the R Neth N's main base, and 66 minesweepers participated. The navies of the Netherlands, Great Britain, Belgium, Norway and France took part. The inclusion of France was a big surprise because France was not a NATO member under the rule of General de Gaulle, but they sent three efficient squadrons. The Royal Navy sent a total of 21 CMS and I found myself as MCM10 with 6 CMS. The Royal Navy's contingent was under the command of Captain MCM in HMS ABDIEL, a new support ship, and our forward base was at the German island of Borkum on the river Ems.

MCMS10 were worked very hard for twelve days in rough conditions and there was no time for a foreign visit apart from two days in Den Helder. We did succeed in sweeping a lot of the widened channel and Captain MCM was appreciative of our efforts. In WARSASH we were accompanied by a Dutch Hydrographer who spent his time watching our echo sounder and pinpointing unmarked wrecks. It was the first time since WW2 that there had been a chance to locate wrecks originating in the war and we found quite a few. No mines were detonated but naval diving teams did locate some and found they were all inert. The task overall was hindered by merchant ships crossing the un-swept water. They had obviously made up their own minds about the risks. The operation had been widely publicised to both the shipping and fishing communities, and all ships were asked to stay clear. There was a sizeable Danish fishing vessel anchored in the middle of the water to be swept who refused to move off. The area was the province of a Royal Navy squadron adjacent to us. Listening to voice traffic on the net one night I heard one CO instruct his consort using the brevity code to recover influence sweeps and stream the wire sweeps with explosive cutters used for moored mines. About 45 minutes later both ships reported they were ready to sweep in wire. The leader then just said "Tally-ho" and the fisherman lost his anchor and fishing gear. He left.

It was fascinating to see how the French participated. Prior to the operation, when all the minesweepers had assembled in Den Helder on the occasion of the official birthday of Queen Juliana, the Admiral Netherlands held a briefing in the naval cinema. More than 200 officers attended and the briefing was conducted in English by the Admiral and his staff. To one side sat the three captains, Dutch, British and French, who were task group commanders. At one point the French capitaine de vaisseau, speaking in French, asked a technical question which the adroit Dutch staff answered in English. It was all part of General de Gaulle's national policy of course. Earlier in the day, at a party marking the official birthday, this officer had talked to me in perfect English. At sea in the danger area the British and French areas abutted off Ameland and it was sometimes tricky when the groups encountered each other when turning at the edge of their respective areas. Happily there were no disastrous Anglo/French marriages of sweeps.

When we left Den Helder to proceed to Borkum, Captain MCM in ABDIEL led 15 CMS in close formation at 15 knots out of harbour to impress everyone. Rounding the fairway buoy WARSASH heeled over and an unsecured glass detached itself from a temporary resting place and smashed when it hit the deck. Electrical Officer Tom Bowling was in the shower nearby at the time, and to steady himself moved one foot and trod heavily on the shards, producing a great deal of blood. On the bridge I asked ABDIEL for permission to talk on another channel to the squadron doctor in another ship. Medical advice was provided and 1st Lieutenant Richard Hill set about bandaging. With the patient sitting comfortably I reported to ABDIEL that all was well and I had closed down my other channel. ABDIEL must have been monitoring both channels because the immediate response was "Officers must learn to drink with their hands". Point taken.

There were many other times when I was at sea in command of WARSASH, and MCM10 as the squadron commander. These were mostly routine, but there was always the satisfaction of helping young landsmen to become seamen and to obtain watch keeping and command certificates. One exception was a week's visit to Greenwich in October 1971 for the first Naval Sales Exhibition. This was staged by MOD(Navy) to support the British companies in the defence industry who sought to sell their products to overseas navies. HMS WARSASH had been replaced by HMS SOLENT, which was an updated CMS, and offered a very welcome enclosed bridge. We joined the Leander class frigate EURALYUS, the fast patrol boat BRAVE BORDERER and the Royal Fleet Auxiliary GREEN ROVER, all berthed on Greenwich Pier, before the days of water buses. My Grandpa smiled down on my pilotage as I brought SOLENT through the South Edinburgh channel in the Thames estuary and up the river to Greenwich. The other three ships were already berthed, leaving the inside downstream berth for SOLENT. Approaching Greenwich, a Thames waterman came aboard and offered to take over as pilot. I told him he was welcome aboard but I would berth the ship in view of my seafaring ancestry. The ebb was still running strongly and of course I had to conform to EURALYUS berthed bows out. I had no intention of waiting three hours for low water to berth stem to tide, so I berthed stern to the ebb. My waterman was deeply shocked, but all went well.

The exhibition was adjudged a great success by the industry and was to be repeated annually in Portsmouth. We were very busy with foreign visitors in all four ships and watched with admiration as a naval Harrier jet landed on GREEN ROVER's tiny helicopter deck. On the first day there was a big reception for visitors in the wardroom of the Royal Naval College. Admiral Sir Michael LeFanu, First Sea Lord, was principal host. Dressed in a smart lounge suit he gave a short speech of welcome to the guests. When he had finished he opened wide both sides of his jacket to reveal a lining of the Union Jack, and he just said, "Gentlemen, buy British". It was his impish sense of humour and love of practical jokes that brought him great respect at all levels but underneath was a very competent First Sea Lord. He was often referred to as "Dry Ginger" which referred firstly to his ending the issue of rum in the Navy and secondly his hair colouring. During the exhibition the whole Admiralty Board and their wives embarked in BRAVE BORDERER for an official visit to the Palace of Westminster. Lady Lefanu had been crippled as a young women but always accompanied him on great occasions. In a BRAVE class patrol boat the only access below was via a vertical steel ladder, which she avoided by having several admirals lower her in a boatswain's chair. This mode of access was a change for Sir Michael who usually carried her up gangways single-handed.

In WESSEX, John Elgar was not selected to succeed John Clarke as Captain, and decided to retire. David McCarraher became XO and I took over as Training Commander. This meant I was responsible for all training in the Division and involved in all the disciplines. It was an interesting job because all the trainees were keen to work and study. I was also able to keep my hand in at sea since at this stage my war appointment was "SOLENT in command and as MCM10". In the next few months John Clarke also retired and in 1969 David McCarraher was promoted to Captain, and took command of Solent Division. I was appointed as his XO. My war appointment did not change, and I still went to sea, but my seafaring days were coming to an end.

The Division worked very well and met most of its set objectives. The heads of the different departments were competent and needed little supervision. We had several doctors and a dentist, and while there was little work for them within the division, for their annual training most of them took over the job of an opposite number in the Navy when they were required for a training course or taking leave. The MOD(N) identified a new requirement for the Royal Marine Commandos. When deployed on NATO's flanks from Norway to Turkey, the Royals needed field hospitals for which there was no spare medical manpower. The Navy's Surgeon General called for RNR volunteers to fill the gaps. One of WESSEX's younger doctors put up his hand and was asked to call on the Surgeon General in London. His interview went satisfactorily but for the next bit he had been set up. On re-entering the Surgeon General's outer officer a Sergeant of Marines, all bustle and business-like, announced he would introduce him to the gear he would need. Laid out on a table was a complete set of clothing required for someone parachuting into the Arctic including thick woollen stockings. The doctor, whose normal lifestyle was that of GP in a quiet Hampshire village, at first fell for it, until outbreaks of laughter made him realise what was happening.

List 3, The Royal Naval Reserve

As Commander, one of my duties was to be President of the wardroom mess and to take charge of any official occasions such as mess dinners and particularly the annual Trafalgar Night Dinner in October. In the traditional way of the Navy, the Captain was not a member of the mess but for any special occasion he was always invited as a guest. On one occasion I managed to net Admiral of the Fleet Lord Mountbatten as our principal guest. This was a coup because he was in great demand by far more important organisations than an RNR Division as principal guest and speaker. Whilst no longer in an appointment, as an Admiral of the Fleet he was still a serving officer and he managed to speak at dinner functions three or four times a week. Throughout his visit he behaved as just another naval officer without a suggestion of aloofness or of his high rank. He certainly had the frequent speech business sorted out. In his pocket he had about 30 ordinary post cards each with about three sentences typed on them in very large print. During dinner he discreetly sorted them for a small selection appropriate to the occasion. WESSEX definitely got the Churchill and Malta cards and a few more. I was later to meet the Admiral of the Fleet at a dinner in New York.

Three years sped by very quickly and soon it was David McCarraher's time to retire as Captain. Very suitably he was appointed in his last year as Honorary Naval Aide de Camp to Her Majesty the Queen. David clearly enjoyed the royal connection because when he was no longer ADC he was selected as one of a few solicitors who were appointed judges and so had to appear before his sovereign in buckled shoes to receive his new appointment

In June 1972 I was promoted to Captain RNR and in October relieved David McCarraher as CO of WESSEX. This was a great prize and much appreciated although sadly it meant the end of my seafaring days in the Royal Navy. There were no sea billets in the Navy for Captains RNR since quite rightly the decreasing number of sea billets were reserved for the Navy's career officers. Whilst they were of use in minor war vessels RNR officers did not have the background to command large warships. For a wartime appointment I was invited to re-train as a Naval Control of Shipping (NCS) officer.

My three years in command were leisurely and untroubled and I did not really have enough to do to justify my appointment. The Division ran very well and in each of the three years we were in the top three divisions competing for the Mountbatten Trophy. This was awarded on the performance of all a division's total activities afloat and ashore. About 90 per cent of the Division could be mobilised for war service in 24 hours with both officers and ratings on their way to their wartime appointments. This was demonstrated in South Wales Division when a faulty signal from Whitehall resulted in full mobilisation because the "for exercise" prefix had been omitted from the signal. Each year every division had to hold a mobilisation exercise and without the prefix our Taffy colleagues just assumed it was the real thing and rushed home to collect all their sea gear. RNR divisions not only mobilised their own sailors but were also used as assembly centres for ratings of the Royal Fleet Reserve required in a national emergency.

Once a year ACR held a Flag and Commanding Officer's Meeting which was a major management tool for the Reserves as a whole. The meeting covered the full scope of activities and took up a whole day. In addition to ACR's own RN staff, the meeting was attended by the Commodore RNR, the eleven COs of divisions and the nine "Tribal Chiefs" who were specialist advisers to ACR for their non-seaman specialisation, such as engineer or communicator.

The objectives of Solent Division were clearly set out for me, and the other divisions were similarly tasked, although the numbers varied a bit according to locality. The first was to provide five complete CMS crews (except for chef), one for the sea tender and four for ships laid up in reserve. The second was to provide a team of NCS officers to man the Southampton port headquarters which were in Wessex. The third was to provide three WRNR teams for the degaussing teams, and there was a doctor for the Marines. For the individual officers and ratings who held wartime appointments elsewhere the division acted as a base and an ongoing point of contact.

List 3, The Royal Naval Reserve

With my own RNR future becoming involved in the world of NCS I thought it was time to find out how it all worked. The NCS bible is a document entitled Convoy. Its opening sentence explains what it is about. "The North Atlantic Treaty Organisation is entirely dependent for its existence upon the merchant ships which unite one member nation with another in the exchange of food, raw materials and troops". The convoy concept is to assemble merchant ships in a group and escort them with a few warships for a voyage. It does not guarantee there will be no losses, but has shown clearly over 800 years of our history that losses are minimised. Allowing merchant ships to proceed independently, except in some special cases, has always led to a very high loss rate. After 100 years of global dominance the Royal Navy entered WW1 in 1914 and soon showed that it had forgotten a lot of things from its successful past. One of them was the convoy concept, which was finally re-introduced in 1917, by which time the loss rate to enemy submarines had become horrific. So horrific in fact our citizens had to queue for two hours daily to buy a pound of potatoes. The Royal Navy did not repeat the mistake in WW2 and quickly adopted convoys. By the end of the war the NCS corps was large, but in peace time they soon became a low priority.

There was one officer, Lieutenant Commander Cliff Kindell, Royal Navy, who kept the flame burning in the Navy almost single handedly. He manned up all the posts in NCS exercises, encouraged NCS officers to meet fairly regularly as the "Friday-nighters" and sought out new recruits. On the NCS List there were a number of ex List 1 officers who were either too old or too senior to expect seagoing billets in the Navy but their time in both the Navy and the Merchant Service provided the skills and experience required for NCS. In the event of a full scale conflict between NATO and the Eastern Bloc, all the NATO merchant ships would come under NCS control and there would be hundreds of convoys to organise. The worldwide NCS manpower requirement would be considerable. In addition to UK and NATO ports, just about every port in the world would need NCS officers to provide instructions to NATO merchant ships as to how and where they were to proceed safely. Ships bound from the South East Asia for the UK might first have to go round the Cape to a convoy assembly point in the Cap Verde Islands to await an escort back to Europe.

New recruits to the NCS List came from every walk of life and few of them had any knowledge or experience of the maritime business. But their enthusiasm and volunteer spirit warranted respect and they needed to be trained for their jobs. An NCS Introduction course was offered in HMS VERNON in Portsmouth and provided two weeks of desk work in the business of organising convoys worldwide and particularly how to deal professionally with the masters of ships. It was intensive work for them to take in the business of ocean passages, distances and ship speeds, time zones and naval communications.

I took the course and began to learn what NCS was all about. With the growth of the NCS List the RNR Divisions opened an NCS department to provide a focal point for them. In WESSEX there were soon 40 officers and the head of department was Commander Paul Ogden, an ex List 1 officer, who was also a P&O colleague. He was later to leave the division on promotion to captain and appointment as ACR's tribal chief.

After digesting what I had learnt it occurred to me that the young officers entering the NCS List deserved to be more formally trained to make the best of themselves and to recognise their contribution. I discussed this with Rear Admiral Hugo (Hard Over) Hollins, then ACR, and was asked to work in his office to prepare a report and recommendations. The report laid out a schedule of all the training required to climb the NCS ladder. One of the first tasks required from a new officer in an NCS exercise or operation was that of Boarding Officer. This entailed climbing aboard via a gangway or pilot ladder, or being winched down from a helicopter, and coming face to face with a shipmaster to give him both oral and written instructions. This was a frequent process requiring many boarding officers and was a key factor in the whole business. In the past when I was CO of WARSASH the squadron took part in an NCS exercise. The CMS took on the part of merchant ships in line, closing the NCS ship and receiving on board a Boarding Officer carrying instructions for the "Master". On completion WARSASH moved away, steamed a big circle and rejoined the queue of CMS for another boarding. It was all just a little boring for us so I decided to liven up our next turn. I told my ship's company they must not be heard speaking English to each other on our next turn, exchanged our white ensign for a Tango flag (near enough a tricolour), hid my uniform jacket and put on a beret. One AB who could manage a few words of French joined me on the bridge. When the Boarding Officer arrived I spoke to him only in French, and snarled a few words at my AB. The new Boarding Officer was clearly put out. He tried to hand me written orders but I glanced at the envelope with an address in English and just said "Je ne comprends pas Monsieur". He left without giving me my "orders". Not very entente cordiale.

The Navy produced good training courses and exercises for NCS officers but was not in a position to teach them what merchant ships were all about. I proposed to ACR that Solent Division should set up in the division a Merchant Navy Acquaint Course of 14 days. The idea was approved and a syllabus of lectures and visits was established with an examination at the end. It threw a lot of work at the WESSEX's Staff Officer, Lieutenant Commander Ken Gamson, who became the Course Officer, but he took it all in his stride. The first class of about 20 NCS officers were shown how merchant ships of different types operated in the busy port of Southampton. The NCS officers boarded ships, arriving with the pilots, and saw berthing operations, and how merchant ship masters and officers did their job. They were introduced to the tanker terminal at Fawley, the berths for rollon/rolloff ferries, the general break bulk quays and sheds, and the new container terminal. They met the port authority, HM Customs and the Port Health Officers. They sailed in a ferry to Le Havre and back, returning with some duty free goods. At the course wash-up on their last day they were enthusiastic about what they had learned and the examination results were encouraging. ACR's staff were pleased with the results and the course was repeated for several years.

Whilst I was no longer a member of the wardroom mess they always invited me as a guest for important occasions. There were also a number of outside naval and social occasions to be enjoyed.

These included calls on flag officers, receiving foreign visitors and attending civic functions held by the City of Southampton. Bunty and I attended the commissioning ceremony for HMS AMAZON, the first of a new class of Type 21 light frigates built in Vosper Thorneycroft's Southampton shipyard. The guest of honour was HRH Princess Anne, then Mrs Mark Philips.

There were many official guests and AMAZON's new ship's company brought wives and families to witness the ceremony. As an efficient organisation they thought of everything and provided every guest with a page of hints on how to treat a royal guest. The hints included the correct form of address. On first being spoken to it was "Your Royal Highness" and thereafter Ma'm, with the "a" as in "apple" and not as in "marmalade". It was our first ship christening ceremony and very enjoyable. AMAZON's most junior rating cut the christening cake with his captain's sword. Thereafter the CO conducted the royal visitor on a tour of his new command. He was clearly concerned about sheathing his sword when it was sticky with fruit cake, but a handkerchief was quickly produced.

There was one particular benefit provided unofficially to the Captain which does not appear in The Queen's Regulations and Admiralty Instructions. For official occasions Wren drivers were available - not only available, but very keen to spend a day without pay doing the job. There was always an MOD pool car and driver if needed but it did not measure up to my own car with a Wren driver from the Division. A likely girl drove us to the AMAZON commissioning and took everything in her stride. This was a remarkable achievement because I later learned she was not a regular driver and had no driving licence, but clearly she was endowed with the RNR spirit. When later I went with my family to Buckingham Palace another Wren drove us, spending the night before as our house guest.

It was not just the wardroom that provided a good social life since the Chief and Petty Officer's mess was also active. This contained men and women who were both fully trained for the Navy and who had demonstrated leadership qualities. Some of them had civilian jobs of an importance that belied their lack of a commission. At

Christmas each year they provided a dinner attended by both mess members and their wives. Bunty and I were invited by custom and practice and greatly enjoyed the occasion. I of course had to sing for my supper and had to think hard what to say. An elaborate "Well done, chaps" was a bit boring with so many ladies present and something else was required. I decided to select two or three of my hosts for a little gentle leg pulling by showing that I knew something about their habits and quirks. Bunty and I then set them down by a verse or two in limerick five line meter. Judging by the mirth displayed by their shipmates at some slightly red faces this was a good approach. The wives were not quite sure what it all meant until they consulted their husbands but of course laughter is highly infectious. We repeated the exercise later and when it was fun to distinguish some anxious faces when I got to my feet.

In February 1975 I received a letter from the First Sea Lord, Admiral Sir Edward Ashmore, appointing me for a year as a Naval Aide-de-Camp to Her Majesty the Queen. This came as a complete surprise, especially since my predecessor David had been similarly honoured. There followed the arrival of an aiguillette with instructions on when it should be worn. Later in the year in the Queen's Birthday Honours List I was awarded the style of OBE, and with my family attended an investiture at the Palace. It was certainly a day for all of us to remember, not least because the recipient's families were all so well looked after.

My time as Captain of WESSEX came to an end on 8 October 1975, when at Captain's Divisions I handed over to Richard Hill, and was given a handsome mounted clock and barometer by the Division. During the previous week, at my last meeting with my Heads of Departments we reviewed the arrangements for the handover. It was my opportunity to thank them all personally for running the division so efficiently for three years without a cloud on the horizon. But I very nearly had spoken too soon.

After that evening when members of the ship's company were leaving to go home a teenage junior rating was assaulted by a more mature rating in the car park. Details only emerged over the week-end when the junior's parents got in touch. Early on the Monday morning Staff Officer Ken Gamson asked me as a matter of urgency to visit WESSEX as soon as possible. On the wardroom bar he had laid out half a dozen books of reference.

He reported events that led him to believe that a Court Martial was inevitable at which I would have to be a witness for the prosecution. There were a number of telephone conversations with the Judge Advocate's office in London before events took a strange turn. A drill night lasted from 1930 to 2115, during which all in WESSEX were subject to the Naval Discipline Act. But the assault took place at 2145, outside the drill hours, and was a matter for the civil police. When the miscreant came aboard for the next drill night two CID officers nabbed him as he entered WESSEX.

At Captain's Divisions, I handed over to a beaming Richard Hill and "went ashore". After a further six months, when my ADC appointment came to an end, I was placed on the retired list. This marked the end of nearly twenty five years as an RNR Officer. Another world war had been avoided, and along with thousands of other citizen-soldiers we were entitled to say "Sleep England, I watch".

Chapter 13. The Box Business

The implications of containerisation were so wide-reaching that the old-established British liner companies had to think very hard about how they could tackle it and remain in the business. There was a huge demand for new capital, not just for ships, but for containers, ship terminals and inland terminals as well. These new style assets also called for skills that did not exist in the old liner companies. The logical way ahead was for old competitors to combine their trades into new consortia, and this began to happen worldwide. Four British liner companies: P&O, Ocean (Blue Funnel), Shaw Savill and Furness Withy created Overseas Containers Limited (OCL). OCL decided to tackle the Europe/Australasia trade first, followed by the Europe/Far East trade. The OCL board consisted of directors from the shareholders together with a managing director from outside. Sir Andrew Crichton became Chairman and Major General Prior-Palmer joined as MD. The General had distinguished himself in Normandy by leading his barely buoyant tanks on to the beach, which must have been a feat that prepared him for anything.

The OCL board realised fully that its new company had to cope with many innovations and should not have to be concerned with ship acquisition and management. For the Australasian trade, it was decided that Ocean should take on the acquisition of six ships, known later as the ENCOUNTER BAY class, and P&O should manage them. Marshall Meek, Ocean's Naval Architect and Willie Faulkner, Superintendent Engineer, set about designing and acquiring six ships from shipyards in Germany and the UK. The longitudinal strength factor of these very "open" ships was at the time completely new territory for naval architects. After some service it was found that additional strengthening of the upper deck was necessary but the basic design provided a bonus of increased capacity.

Sea Officer

I was appointed to lead the ship management team, together with Paul Ogden and Stan Mole. Paul had been a Master in the New Zealand Shipping Company, and then Assistant Marine Superintendent. Stan was a P&O Engineer and then Assistant Superintendent Engineer. We were given plenty of time to prepare, and whilst working out of our other jobs we started to meet to discuss in detail how we intended to proceed. The first decision was how to organise along the functional areas of Operations Manager (Paul) and Technical Manager (Stan), and to abandon the old functions of Marine and Engineer. This meant that the operations manager would relinquish hull maintenance, which would be absorbed by the technical manager. It was not a new idea and was to become the norm for the future. It had long been the norm outside the UK and particularly with Scandinavian ship owners. The two managers would between them decide the appropriate manning scale and senior sea appointments, with a personnel manager to administrate all the seafarers. Within ships chief engineers would undertake total ship maintenance.

We needed to establish a small office staff to assist us and this was slowly built up. Graeme Dunlop, who had just completed his time as a P&O Learner joined to take on the sea personnel function. He soon knew all of the sea staff and got on with them well. This probably helped him when later he became Chairman of P&O Ferries and a P&O director. Derek Smith assumed the accounting function, and Lynne Kirkham joined as my secretary. Paul took on Geoff Millings in charge of catering. Stan took on Alex Stevens for mechanical engineering, Ken Blackett for electrical engineering and Charlie Brownson for hull maintenance.

In financial terms, most ship management activities are a pure cost centre, and in OCL the ship management was just one of many cost centres. Within the ship management we identified the cost heads that added up to our total cost, such as operations (pilots, tugs, berthing, communications etc), fuel, manning, maintenance and our own administration costs. Having established our total cost, we were able to identify for ourselves and OCL a cost for each container we had the capacity to carry, either by voyage, or annually. This we originally called a COCO (Cost of Container

The Box Business

Opportunity) but later became known as a Slot Cost.

Although we were part of P&O, we felt we needed a distinct identity as a point of reference, particularly for the seafarers we would recruit, since our operations would be quite different from what they had been used to in the past. A first shot produced the Container Ship Division, but this did not sound very inspiring so P&O formed a new limited company called Container Fleets Limited, which proved a good name for a start-up and was used until OCL took the ship management task into their own house. The directors were Ford Geddes (Chairman), Robert Huskisson, Harry Beazley and me. Nearly forty years on the name has disappeared but it is still remembered with affection by the officers who joined in the early years. I still get friendly letters from retired officers who relate that joining CFL was the turning point in their seafaring career. We must have got something right.

It took a long time to finalise the decision on how to man the ships. One important decision had been taken by OCL's shareholders and this was that we would employ British seamen. This may have been partly to appease the UK's National Union of Seamen, who could read the writing on the wall. The six ENCOUNTER BAY class ships would carry roughly the same amount of cargo by sea as twenty existing cargo liners. These break-bulk ships had ship's companies of 50 or more seafarers, suggesting a manning establishment of 1,250 seafarers when their paid leave was taken into account. Whilst we had not finalised our manning numbers it looked as if our equivalent establishment would be about 250. This staggering economy of scale would hasten the decline of the Merchant Service.

Some of OCL's shareholders believed that the container ship's officers should be supplied on a rotational basis from their own officer corps, but we stuck out for a dedicated corps for CFL. We believed that in the early days only this could cope with the necessary changes in the way ship's officers carried out their jobs. The officers were recruited from all four of the liner companies on a voluntary basis. All applicants were interviewed carefully and given a clear picture of what we expected them to do. Most were excited with our plans but a few decided not to transfer. One pressing problem concerned the chief officers, who would no longer be responsible for cargo work or the maintenance and appearance of their ships. Break-bulk cargo skills acquired over years from apprenticeship onwards were redundant because the container stowage would be carried out by the container terminal staff (using chief officers no longer at sea). Appearance would be the province of the Chief Engineer and new paint techniques were designed to last for ever. (They didn't.)

We decided the change of circumstances should be reflected by removing the rank of Chief Officer and re-titling it 1st Officer. This was not a happy move but it was important that the individuals faced facts. There was an addition to the 1st Officer's responsibilities by way of making him the ship's personnel officer for all hands. The plans we had for our ratings would require pro-active personnel management in the ships. Chief engineers needed to acquire additional skills to deal with the ship's massive steelwork and were assisted in this by Charlie Brownson, a hull inspector on the technical manager's staff in the UK. (They also acquired healthy tans after more than a century confined below.)

New Zealand Shipping was always manned with British ratings on a casual voyage basis, so Paul had lots of experience with them. New Zealand Shipping had always managed their ships very well and the casual status did not prevent them from having a following of good ratings who were a core for any crew. With a small crew aboard a large and complex new ship, we were determined to ensure that officers and ratings worked well together and valued each other.

We decided to adopt a general purpose crew. This would remove the established seamen and firemen/greaser categories, and the general purpose ratings would watch keep and work wherever needed in the ship to make the most of a small crew. We set down a table of the skills and experience required for each grade of our new "Seamen", which stretched from teenage newcomers to experienced petty officers. For the teenagers, it started with being able to keep themselves and their clothes clean. A Deck PO, whose skills ranged from the traditional seaman's work to those required for a Home Trade Mate, was required to be a useful assistant to the officer of the watch on a busy bridge. The catering ratings were not really needed for seamen's duties but were trained to participate on a small scale to make them feel part of a team.

It was clear that we should engage our ratings on contracts of employment on the same lines as the officers, and particularly with a monthly salary paid into their bank accounts. On this basis we set out to recruit our ratings in exactly the same way as we recruited the officers. If they wanted to join and appeared suitable, they either joined the payroll immediately or on a date ahead.

For the officers we set up a salary scale which was approved by their union. For the ratings, we set out to do the same but the task was more complex and we had to negotiate with the National Union of Seamen. The National pay scale agreed for ratings was based on a 40 hour week, with overtime. Realistically a ship cannot be worked on a 40 hour week, and the basic pay was insufficient to attract good ratings. This led to a scramble for overtime and as such it was often abused. We decided that at sea on long passages the ships could be worked on a 48 hour week. Arriving and leaving port would on average add four more hours a week, so we consolidated the pay on 52 hours per week, accepting that this basis would mean that in some weeks the ratings would be overpaid and in others overtime would have to be paid. In practice it worked very well, not least because many of our sailors did not wish to work very long hours unless there was a special reason. The monthly overtime bill for each ship had to be reported by radio or telex to the office, so that individual bank accounts could be credited, but the amounts were tiny when the ships were new.

We negotiated with the NUS Head Office in London and they were intrigued with the general purpose manning concept and the staff status that came with it. They made no exorbitant claims and were co-operative. Sir Ronald Swayne, director of OCL and Ocean, suggested we meet John Prescott, whom he said was "a very modern man". At that time John Prescott, who had been a seafarer with Cunard, had just come down from university after finishing his degree course. He had been sponsored and supported for this by the NUS, and had just taken up his seat in the House of Commons. Whilst he was not involved in NUS negotiations, he kept in touch with what was going on. He was very interested in our experiment.

The effects of the staff status were very marked in the way that our ratings saw their job. When they joined, few possessed bank accounts. To provide for their families they relied on allotment notes that paid out every month when they were at sea. In the past when they were at sea and needed cash for themselves they had to ask for an advance of wages (which was at the discretion of the Master). In CFL, the 1st Officer cashed their cheques weekly and airmailed the cheques back to the office. In an age when branch managers enjoyed some authority, Barclays in Tilbury provided instant accounts for last minute newcomers and accepted standing orders for families. Despite the prophets of doom, dud cheques just did not appear.

In the industry as a whole it was becoming the practice for captains and senior officers to be accompanied by their wives for a voyage each year. With first class accommodation available in the ships, we extended this practice for junior officers and, after a pause, for ratings. This raised a few eyebrows, and attracted the attention of the more scurrilous press, but it worked well. For the first time in their lives some wives were able to witness how their husbands spent their lives at sea, and their presence raised the tone for all. A minor expense was the issuing of sewing machines to each ship, so that wives could demonstrate their seamstress skills for all hands. My own conviction that we were on the right track arrived when I boarded one ship inbound for Antwerp with the Scheldt pilot at Vlissingen on a bitterly cold winter night. Half way up the river and on the bridge wing with the captain I was dimly aware that on the long foredeck stretching ahead there was a small bundle of clothing bearing a tray of steaming mugs moving forward slowly. This was a sailor's wife providing some small comfort for the foc'sle party at anchor stations.

We opened discussions with the DTI's nautical and engineer surveyors about our proposed general purpose manning scale

The Box Business

because they oversaw the statutory manning scales. Under these, the sheer size of the ships called for more Able Seamen than we thought necessary with general purpose manning. At first they were reluctant to concede, but we showed them the minutiae of our plans and in the end they agreed a reduction. We promised them an opportunity of taking a short passage in a ship to witness events once we were up and running, and they responded affirmatively.

This duly took place in DISCOVERY BAY during a homeward voyage when she called at Las Palmas for bunkers. Off Capetown Captain John Cosker received our instructions to embark the two surveyors and to show them how the manning worked. They boarded in the anchorage at Las Palmas one afternoon and were invited to the bridge to witness the ship weighing and proceeding to sea. Later that evening at dinner they were a little surprised that the steward serving them was last seen on the wheel at Harbour Stations.

In the morning the two surveyors reported to John Cosker's cabin and each was allotted a seaman to conduct them on a tour. In the course of two hours the Nautical Surveyor was shown everything on deck and in the holds, what it was for, and how it worked. In the machinery spaces the Engineer Surveyor was treated similarly. On completion they returned to the Captain's cabin for a discussion and a glass, and the two seamen were sent for their meal. The Nautical Surveyor opened the batting to say how interesting he found the ship, and how impressive he found the Able Seaman who had escorted him. He had not realised that ABs could be so know-ledgeable. He was further astonished when told that the AB's background was that of a Fireman/Greaser. The Engineer Surveyor's report and reactions were similar. He could not believe his escort's background was that of an AB. It just went to show that training can help people believe in themselves.

The watch keeping load at sea was a major manning factor. The workload on the bridge and in the engine room varied widely from intense to relaxed, depending on the ship's position. We did consider carefully whether it might be possible to have a single officer in both positions without a rating when in a relaxed state across the great oceans but rejected it in favour of an officer and a rating on watch in both places at all times. Unlike an electric railway train, ships were not really amenable to the "dead man's handle" solution. Taking into account the ship's company who are not on watch and the colossal value of the ship, her containers and cargo, there was not a case for taking risks. The ships were powered by a single screw steam turbine and large boilers. The huge engine room also contained the electrical and refrigerating machinery, although all their controls were concentrated in a compact control room. During a steady state night watch there were opportunities for minor maintenance but there were too many risks for one person to be working on his own.

We ended up with a complement of 32 in total, which at the time seemed very daring, but in general worked well. However, with experience, we did have to add an additional steward to provide an acceptable state of cleanliness in the large accommodation block designed by Marshall Meek. This included separate cabins with shower/heads facilities for about 40 people, together with two mess rooms and two communal lounges. Forty years on our efforts look puny, with EMMA MAERSK carrying about three times as many containers with a ship's company of fourteen.

OCL's container team made a major study of container types to decide which design to adopt. There were three types in existence and early use: steel, aluminium and GRP (Glass Reinforced Plastic, or Fibreglass). This was a dedicated task for OCL, but CFL were interested in any fire hazards. In Liverpool the Bootle Fire Brigade staged a demonstration of the vulnerability of aluminium and GRP, both of which were made to burn fiercely under certain conditions. There was a further serious hazard with the polyurethane insulation used to line the refrigerated containers.

Under the right conditions of heat, air and polyurethane fragments, this material would also burn fiercely. OCL decided that steel was the only contender, and that the high maintenance cost would have to be accepted. Their decision was validated by another un-staged incident in a Hamburg shipyard. A BAY class was being fitted out after launch and a UK sub-contractor was insulating one hold with polyurethane foam. They had brought their materials with them in an aluminium container which the shipyard had craned on to the top of the open hatch for close access. Below, in the hold, their workmen were trimming the polyurethane foam to fit the ship's side so there were off-cuts, fragments and dust. It was believed that a portable light fitting fell into the debris and broke, providing a short circuit heat source that created a nasty fire which resulted in fatalities. These could have been many more, but for the fact that most of the workforce were ashore for lunch. The heat was intense enough to reach the aluminium container located across the open hatch above and this burned as well. In CFL, we made a careful note to be on the lookout should steelwork in an insulated space need attention.

One major management tool was created, to lay down our Fleet Orders, and our acronym for them was CONFLORDS. 1st Officer Peter Clarke joined the office for a few months to act as editor, drawing together the skills and experience of all of us in the office. Our concept was that all six ships, which were identical physically, should be conducted identically by their crews. One compelling reason for this was that we intended to relieve them for home leave frequently and did not want to take up days for handovers. Individual masters and chiefs would not be allowed to set up their own modus operandi. However, with contentious matters, they were asked to define with their peers an opus operandi, if necessary on a simple majority vote basis. CONFLORDS (sometimes called Cornflakes) became a must-read and well thumbed volume. When Peter eventually laid down his pen we sent the orders to solicitors for approval in legal terms, and they had no improvements to offer. It is interesting to reflect that CONFLORDS were produced several years before BS 5450/ISO3000/ISO9000 (Quality Standards) became fashionable. Later when BS5450 appeared, I attended a one day DTI conference to introduce the idea in the UK, and for a moment wondered whether I should set up shop as a QA consultant.

ENCOUNTER BAY was delivered, manned and ready to load containers. Despite protracted and continuing negotiations, and a custom built container ship terminal ready at Tilbury, no agreement had been reached with London's dockers. Without an agreement they refused to work the ships, and it would take several months to achieve agreement. On the near Continent there was a willingness to work container ships and both Antwerp and Rotterdam already had berths, the huge quayside cranes, and the necessary quayside mechanised equipment.

OCL selected Antwerp for the short term, moving to Rotterdam when European Container Terminals completed the extension of their facilities. CFL could of course present ships at any suitable berth, but the fledgling OCL was faced with the problem of assembling the loaded containers at Antwerp. This not only took time but added enormously to the costs. The containers were moved to East Coast ports such as Felixstowe and Harwich and then on to Antwerp via another Belgian port in a small short-sea ship.

OCL's Tilbury Terminal Manager, Martin Pudden, had to assemble his team in Antwerp. The stowage of the containers in the ship was entirely his job, without any input from the ship's officers. This meant providing suitable stowage for containers filled with refrigerated, chilled and hazardous goods, and recording the weight and height in the stack of every container individually. The addition of the weights and heights provided the "moment" (from momentum) of the total cargo. To this one figure the ship's 1st Officer could then add the "moments" of the ship herself, her bunkers, fresh water, ballast and ship's stores to ascertain the stability factors from the ship's stability book. If the final calculation showed less stability than desirable this could be adjusted by filling salt water ballast tanks.

Captain Michael Champneys, who had forsaken passenger ship command to join CFL, was all ready to sail on time but had not received the essential cargo "moment" from the terminal team. As the calculation was nearly ready the terminal suggested the ship should proceed across the impounded dock and enter the lock leading to the river Scheldt. A car would bring the paperwork to the lock. Michael Champneys and I discussed this and decided not to proceed until the paperwork was produced. Once in the lock the only way out was into the river, and if the paperwork was not delivered it would mean venturing into the most dangerous river in

The Box Business

North West Europe without knowledge of the ship's stability. I apologised to Martin but any delay meant we had missed a tide. It was a small teething problem not helped by the fact that all Martin's carefully laid plans had been made for the Tilbury terminal. To have coped at all for the first time in another terminal with containers appearing from everywhere was little short of miraculous. With the ship under way at last I reported to the General in London, but it was not a festive occasion.

In the ships we had discussed arrangements for the use of the lounges and bars. At that time it was appropriate to have separate areas for officers and ratings. We wanted to delegate responsibility for the orderly conduct of their bar to elected bar committees. But at the back of our minds was the fear that what started as a couple of social drinks could so easily deteriorate into drunken behaviour. Bar committees were instructed that this would not be tolerated and that they should regulate matters. In the last resort, Masters would order the bars closed if they considered good discipline was at risk. We encouraged the two messes to intermingle from time to time but only on the basis of strict invitation. Whilst the two mess rooms were separate, we insisted that both had identical crockery and tablecloths. Work clothes were forbidden in the messes and at table all hands had to be clean and properly dressed. It did not take long for these rules to be observed and respected.

As ships returned to Europe from their maiden voyages we held three meetings with them on arrival. The first was a minuted voyage meeting at which we discussed with the captain and chief engineer all the business matters arising during the voyage, including what had gone wrong and what had gone right. This feedback showed that we were on the right course but small changes were necessary. The next meeting was with the officers to establish their views on what we had arranged. The final meeting was with the ratings who had quite a lot to say, although it was presented in a fairly orderly way, and was mostly about blowing off some steam. When things had settled down crew meetings each voyage were discontinued unless either the managers or the crew asked for one.

Sea Officer

For both officers and ratings occasional meetings were held in our offices to provide them with company information and to hear their views on anything they wanted to raise. It was quite a lot of fun to watch a seaman politely putting quite difficult questions to Director Jeffrey Sterling about international pay rates for seafarers. In one ship arriving from her maiden voyage an officer got up at the end of the meeting and commended us for providing such good ratings. At the end of the rating's meeting later a seaman got up and commended us for providing such good officers. We had won.

Another example of the right spirit emerged when MORETON BAY's high pressure turbine epicyclic gear failed when the ship was at sea in the shipping lane off South Africa. To get under way again it was necessary to remove the gear train, isolate the HP turbine and operate on the low pressure turbine only. This was quite a massive task, needing every pair of hands available and all sorts of assembly work with very heavy chunks of metal. Captain Michael Heron took over the bridge for the night with a cadet on lookout, two red lights to indicate the ship could not manoeuvre, and a deck chair to doze in. The three bridge officers went to the engine room to assist their colleagues and by dawn the ship was steaming well again, but at a reduced speed.

At the end of a year's operation the chairman of P&O told me that I was needed for another new task, so I handed over my desk to Paul Ogden. The OCL board expressed their satisfaction with the way CFL had performed, and presented me with a beautifully bound copy of the Memoirs of Rear Admiral Sir William Symonds, Kt, Surveyor of the Navy 1832/47, printed in 1858. My bookmark is a newspaper cutting from the day our old coinage was removed and the headline reads quite simply, "Last Day for Pennies".

CFL provided a farewell party for me and to my intense surprise presented me with a collection of Lalique glass from staff afloat and ashore, consisting of a pair of carp, and four champagne flutes. It is my most treasured collectable.

Chapter 14. Last Days in P&O

In 1970 Chairman Sir Donald Anderson made two important announcements. The first was that he would retire in 1971, and the second was to appoint the management consultants McKinsey and Company to make recommendations for the re-organisation of P&O along clearly defined lines, to meet the challenge ahead.

He had originally designated Michael Thwaites to succeed him. He had great regard for Michael's abilities as a shipping manager, and Michael had several years of experience on the board of P&O, a publicly owned company. He was a strong-minded character, who would not bend his knee easily, and had an insight that enabled him to distinguish would-be crooks from several miles away. Unhappily, a year before he was due to become chairman he suffered a bad stroke. He succumbed to another stroke shortly thereafter. Sir Donald's next choice was his cousin Ford Geddes, who followed him on his retirement. Whilst Ford was experienced in the shipping business, his principal board experience was with Orient Line, which after 1960 was not a publicly owned company.

The appointment of McKinsey was viewed with apprehension by a large number of senior managers in the Group, particularly the directors of companies, many of whom were running similar liner services to different parts of the world. McKinsey's recommendations were along classical lines of one company with one board of directors, five operating divisions and three staff divisions. The operating divisions, each headed by a main board director, comprised Passenger Division, Bulk Shipping Division (tankers and bulk carriers), General Cargo Division (cargo liners being replaced by OCL's container ships), European and Air Transport Division (ferries, road or air transport companies), and General Holdings Division (any operation not included above). The five staff divisions were Finance, Personnel, Planning, Technical Services and Foreign Affairs. It was not McKinsey's task to sort out the huge personnel problems that would arise in the new organisation. Whilst there was a large surplus of managers with shipping experience, there was also a shortage of senior staff with the new skills. The latter would have to be recruited from outside, whilst many of the former had to leave.

One major figure emerged from the board. In addition to being head of Bulk Shipping, A B (Sandy) Marshall became the senior executive director, responsible for all maritime operations except Passenger and General Cargo Divisions. Sandy had created and managed the new bulk shipping operations, starting with Trident Tankers, ever since these were seen as the future of the P&O Group. P&O and Ocean also agreed jointly to create Panocean, a specialist company for medium sized parcel tankers. The cargo liners being phased out had mostly been fitted with cargo oil deep tanks of about 200/500 tons to carry the mainly edible oils that moved from SE Asia to Europe. It was not clear at this stage whether OCL could cope with carrying these in containers. In addition to which, the chemical industry was looking for tanks in which to move their new products. Many of these, which were hazardous and/or poisonous, required very careful handling. Sandy invited me to join him on Panocean's small board, and particularly to assist in ship management. Panocean appointed Peter Smith from Trident Tankers as their fleet manager. Whilst Peter was very experienced in the carriage of petroleum products, I did give him some assistance in the edible oils area, having written P&O's handbook for their carriage. In view of the hazards, he was concerned about providing really competent ratings for his ships, and wanted to hoist in the benefits of CFL-type training and general purpose working. It did not take long to give him the advice and assistance he needed, after which there was little for me to do.

Chairman Ford Geddes told me I was to be appointed to join the new Planning Division, reporting to a newly recruited planning director. At first sight this appeared exciting, but it did not turn out that way. In January 1972 the chairman recruited Clifford Nancarrow to the board as planning director, tasked with producing a five year strategic plan for P&O. Two group managers were appointed to assist him, David Greenslade, an extremely able and experienced accountant, newly recruited from outside, and me. I had wrongly believed that my role would be as part of a team to plan major shipping investments, for which I had the right background and track record. With the exception of Bulk Shipping, where Euan Geddes was at work on a new project for which he was ideally suited, the other divisions had no interest in major plans. General Cargo had been told their activity was to be phased out, since no more cargo liners would be acquired. This did eventually happen but they continued to be very profitable for a number of years. Passenger Division, saddled with a fleet of passenger ships of the wrong type, were struggling to reduce losses and not making much progress. The European Division contained a huge number of separate businesses, some profitable and some loss-making, with many just breaking even.

By mid-1972 it became clear that P&O's overall position was poor, and there was press speculation that it was a takeover target. The planning director had not had time to learn much about the business, and this was his first major board appointment, but there was little I could do to assist him

When the blow arrived it came from inside the company. It transpired that Chairman Ford Geddes and the non-executive directors, without the knowledge of the executive directors, had been plotting a 50/50 merger with Bovis, then a modest civil engineering, property and house building company. Many saw it as a reverse takeover, with Bovis' chairman Frank Sanderson becoming managing director of the merged companies. If a large tranche of P&O senior managers did not understand the financial implications of the merger, they readily understood what a new managing director was all about, and were horrified. One non-executive director not in the plot was the 3rd Earl Inchcape, who then made a public bid for P&O with his company Inchcape plc. This was a substantial trading company which he had built up following WW2. Whilst his grandfather the 1st Earl had been P&O Chairman, Inchcape plc only had limited shipping interests.

Also horrified was executive director Sandy Marshall, who was of

193

course senior shipping director and who, with great energy, led the opposition to the proposed merger. The outcome was that the P&O board split. After several very tense weeks, Ford Geddes and his deputy Chairman resigned and a new board was formed with Earl Kenneth Inchcape as non-executive Chairman and Sandy Marshall as the sole managing director. There was turmoil in the senior management as individuals backed one side or the other, and life in general was unpleasant to say the least. Whilst my boss Clifford Nancarrow joined Sandy Marshall and the other dissidents, I flatly refused to take sides and was berated by both sides. One reason for this was that I was privy in the planning division to a lot of sensitive data, particularly the values of more than 170 owned ships. Their asset value was a central factor in P&O's total asset value and thereby the P&O share price. I refused to divulge the figures to anyone except directors, and took a great deal of stick.

Whilst the battle raged on there was very little for me to do (and not much for my boss either) and I had a chat with personnel director Frank Thomasson who suggested I might move into the ferry section of the European Division. I was appointed general manager of Normandy and Southern Ferries in Southampton, which operated roll-on/roll-off ferries for both passengers and freight vehicles from Southampton to Le-Havre and Lisbon. It reported to John Turner, in Liverpool, the director and general Manager of ferry services. These included ferry services across the Irish Sea to Ulster from both Liverpool and the Clyde, and from the North of Scotland to the Orkney and Shetland Islands. There was also a joint service in North Sea Ferries from Hull to Rotterdam.

At Southampton there were two quite separate services. Normandy Ferries was a 50/50 joint service with Societé Anonyme de Gerance et D'Armement (SAGA), owned by the Rothschild banking group. Two identical ships, DRAGON (British) and LÉOPARD (French), provided two round voyages to Le-Havre every day. Southern Ferries operated a much larger ferry EAGLE to Lisbon every four days in the summer peak holiday period, and a weekly service to Lisbon and Tangier for the rest of the year.

The 70s saw a considerable growth in the ferry business to the

Continent, as more and more holidaymakers took their cars to France, Spain and Portugal. The growth was most significant at Dover, where there were frequent services all day provided by British Rail, French Rail (SNCF) and Townsend. Crossings took less than two hours, as compared with seven hours between Southampton and Le Havre, and not surprisingly fares for both vehicles and passengers were much less.

DRAGON and LÉOPARD were both solid and reliable ships, built to a proven design in a French shipyard. They both needed two weeks in the winter for annual dry-docking and repairs but apart from this they made a return voyage every day. Their vehicle deck catered for both freight vehicles and passenger cars. Unlike more modern ferries, they had no bow door to the vehicle deck and the freight vehicles had to be backed into the vehicle deck very carefully. Freight trailers without a motive unit were pushed in and towed out by quay tractors called dock tug masters. In the passenger role, the vehicle deck could accommodate about 200 cars and the passenger capacity was 600. On most trips there was a mix of freight and passenger vehicles. On the upper decks were a restaurant, shop, cafeteria and public lounges, together with overnight cabins.

EAGLE had also been built at Chantiers D'Atlantique in France, but she was very unreliable. Her main engines were a prototype SEMT/Pielstick diesel design, and were forever breaking down. One of the root causes was the linguist limitations of both the supervisors and ship's staff, who didn't speak French, and the shipyard foremen and workers, who didn't speak English. It was in sharp contrast to the German shipyards where all the "meisters" (foremen) spoke English very well. EAGLE was basically a passenger ferry for longer voyages, with all passengers berthed in small cabins, each with its own shower/heads cubicle. In the summer, most of the vehicle deck was required for passenger cars, but freight vehicles also were carried when space was available.

Neither operation was really profitable, and in sum was typically running at something just above break even. There was always a dilemma between passenger and freight traffic. Passenger ships are always expensive to operate because their certification is much more stringent than cargo ships. The returns from passenger cars are markedly higher than freight vehicles when the vehicle deck space used is taken into consideration. But the annual traffic pattern is such that there are only about six summer weeks when the passenger ships make excellent profits. For the rest of the year they carry mainly freight vehicles and make losses.

The administrative structure for Normandy Ferries was large and operated on both sides of the Channel. There was a supervisory board of two directors in Paris, and two in Liverpool which met every three months. Paris was also the base for the French general manager, Michel Meheut, with the French offices for sales, operations and administration at the terminal in Le Havre. In Southampton my office was in the town, with the terminal staff housed separately in the Old Docks area. With two general managers in charge there was plenty of scope for Anglo-French friction, but fortunately Michel Meheut and I got on very well. We quickly agreed a language rule for our staffs whereby we spoke only in the other language and wrote in our own. At joint meetings it meant that nobody was verbose.

We studied the lack of profitability of the two services, which revealed there were several areas that dragged down the whole. The first perhaps was the high level of dues paid to the port authorities for the use of their Ro/Ro berths, particularly at Southampton. They were roughly double the dues paid by our competitors using Dover. There was nothing I could do about this, short of moving the whole operation to another port, which was not on the cards. It could have been very helpful to run DRAGON and LÉOPARD three tines per day (instead of two) on summer weekends to increase ship utilisation at high earning periods, but without bow doors or more sea speed it would have been very tight. It would have needed the agreement of both the National Union of Seamen and its equivalent in France which would have been expensive or even impossible.

Another possibility appeared in the acquisition of another more modern passenger ferry with a bow door for faster port turnarounds, and mounting a service to North Spain. There was already a service to Bilbao provided by Swedish Lloyd using the ferry PATRICIA on four day round voyages, which we could see was well patronised.

We undertook a study of the traffic to Northern Spain, which pointed to an opportunity to challenge PATRICIA, and increase our carryings and revenue without increasing our overhead. We got approval from the board to purchase a second-hand Baltic ferry called PETER PAN, which we re-named PANTHER. As PETER PAN, she had been owned by TT Line and had been operated on three crossings a day between Travemunde and Trelleborg. Well-built in Germany, she had a capacity for about 200 cars and was fitted with both bow and stern doors. We found that we could programme her for two voyages a week to Santander (Pasajes) throughout the year with an additional return crossing to Le Havre for the all important Friday evenings in mid-summer. Our initial traffic and earnings were above expectations, but the whole Southampton operation was undermined by technical failures and the militancy of our crews. It was not helped by OPEC's tripling of oil prices, since high speed ferries are thirsty.

Apart from the technical managers, the other managers in Southampton were able and enthusiastic about their jobs. When we hit problems with machinery breakdowns or crews going on strike they would work all hours during both the week and weekends to look after angry passengers. They were also supported by senior clerks who shared their spirit. This was particularly helpful at a time when the trade unions were on the march and the local branch of the clerical union was pursuing the younger staff. This union was seen off. It was the sea staff and their Superintendents who worried me greatly. The ships were classed as short and near sea traders, for which the certification of masters and mates was at a lower level than that required for deep sea ships.

The "Home Trade" certification was generally intended for much smaller and slower ships, but the rules had not been brought up to date with the appearance of larger and faster vehicular ferries. In fact, we did have some good Home Trade masters and mates, as well as officers with full certificates. One disappointing aspect of short sea sailors was that the almost daily grind of their work produced a "nine to five" attitude which does not sit comfortably with ship management. There was an aura of sloppiness and disinterest that was unprofessional, to say the least. What was even more worrying was a reluctance or even refusal to rectify matters when they were pointed out.

These failings often bore heavily on safety aspects for both ship and machinery. Witnessing the departure of EAGLE one Saturday, I was horrified to see that she was twelve inches overladen when she heeled over and her Plimsoll mark emerged from the water. Neither the marine superintendent nor her Master seemed to give a damn, and I was told I did not know what I was talking about. On her return a few days later I ordered a deadweight survey to see how we could lighten her. I gave written instructions that she was not to go to sea overladen again. This prompted the marine superintendent to cancel the next freight trailer bookings, much to the dismay of freight manager Bill Jones. The deadweight survey provided the evidence for a very simple answer. On return to Southampton each trip, the standing practice was to replenish both fuel and fresh water to capacity. However, she only needed about 60 per cent fuel for the voyage, which included a two day steaming margin. There were emergency re-fuelling ports all along her route. In Lisbon fresh water was readily available and was in fact cheaper than Southampton. Bill Jones was mollified, and the marine superintendent had to go.

Another incident occurred in DRAGON in Southampton Water approaching the docks when the AB at the wheel put the helm the wrong way. DRAGON's crew were difficult at best and the offender was particularly militant. It was a golden opportunity to discipline him by relieving him at the wheel instantly. The master did nothing and when I asked him why, was told that the offender was the only AB on the bridge. When I asked further why the master had not put the chief officer, who was on the bridge, in his place, I was told that officers were not there to steer ships. All mates can steer since it is a seaman's basic task. In Norwegian ships the chief officer is still called first steerman, a practice that goes back to the Viking longboats.

Last Days in P&O

The engineering fraternity were no better. In EAGLE's engine room the pipework supplying very hot oil to the diesels was fractured and the pipe insulation was soaked in oil. Other ferries had experienced serious engine room fires, but in EAGLE no one seemed to care about dangerous conditions. In another ship, after heavy rain, I found a large puddle of water in the vehicle deck and it was clear that the scuppers were blocked. There was not a big problem with rain but if it became necessary to use the fire drenching system on a vehicle deck full of petrol driven cars it could lead to the ship capsizing. A number of ferries have been lost over the years as a result of water in the vehicle deck and the resulting loss of life has been dreadful. On another occasion the ship could not keep to her programme in the busy summer season. She appeared to have lost speed, which was confirmed by a lower fuel consumption. On making inquiries I was told that the cylinder pressure gauge had shown she was at full power. It later transpired that this was incorrect because the gauge had not been calibrated properly and was showing the pressure to be higher than was in fact the case.

These were just some examples of the lack of professional ability displayed by some staff afloat and ashore which prompted me to look around for some competent assistance. After discussions with my boss, I arranged for Alex Stevens, who had demonstrated his qualities in CFL, to transfer to Southampton as fleet manager. It was a very demanding task for him. Not only were there deep rooted technical problems, but the ratings were becoming more and more militant as each month went by.

Each of the three ship's crews had different agreements, and soon saw there were opportunities to make trouble by leapfrogging another crew for better conditions. Whilst I had enjoyed good relationships with the Union head office in London, the local official was a quite different matter. To start with he was a serious alcoholic, and would appear in our office unshaven and unwashed. At one point he was sacked by his head office, but he had powerful friends on the Union's executive and was re-instated. We held a meeting with the crew of DRAGON to see if they might be willing to engage on monthly contract terms with their wages, overtime and payments for lashing the freight vehicles all consolidated. (The lashing payments were classed officially as docker's work.) A seaman got up and made it clear that consolidation was unwelcome and he wanted pound notes in his hand every Friday. No one else spoke.

At the height of the summer, the crew of PANTHER refused to sail on a Saturday without an improvement to their package. Alex Stevens got them to sail by promising a meeting with the NUS official on the next Monday, at which an improvement was offered and accepted by the NUS. On their return on Tuesday, the crew refused to accept it and again refused to sail. They eventually sailed when two of their number stayed ashore for the next voyage to assist the NUS to negotiate. A new agreement was reached, but when the ship returned on Friday the crew rejected it. In the meantime, the two other crews were watching events and sharpening their pencils.

The only way out of this dilemma I could see was to lay up all three ships and sign off the crews whilst we prepared new agreements and then recruited new crews from scratch. This was unacceptable to my boss in Liverpool, which I believe was largely on account of the French connection.

Some years later when Margaret Thatcher had been in No.10 for a time, and when Jeffrey Sterling was in the P&O Chair, a similar situation arose. Dover was a hotbed of militancy and sloppiness, the latter borne out by the loss of the SPIRIT OF FREE ENTERPRISE in Zeebrugge, when many passengers and crew drowned. It was essential to have more effective crew agreements in place to meet competition from the Channel Tunnel and to justify investment in bigger ships. Despite long negotiations the Union refused to budge. At Dover, Graeme Dunlop stopped all the ships and paid off the crews. Recruits were sought for a new agreement and enough volunteers appeared to enable a ferry to be sailed on the third day. It was not long before all the ships were back at sea and fully crewed. There were some fairly horrendous scenes in Dover and the new crews had to be bussed with security protection to join their ships, but there were no fatalities. It started a whole new era in the Dover ferry business, with clean well crewed ships and P&O made good profits.

Labour relations in the UK were generally in bad shape around the time of the so called "winter of our discontent", and two other areas affected the ferry operation adversely. The first was Southampton's dock labour. From being a port handling only break-bulk cargoes, Southampton had moved on to Ro/Ro traffic and containers, which required quite different skills to that of sheer physical strength. The two new modes were also better rewarded for dockers, and their Union demanded job rotation. One result was that about every three months a new docker gang had to be trained to drive the tug masters to discharge and load our trailers. At one point, the dockers claimed it was also their work to back the large self-drive lorries into the vehicle deck. With a novice driver, this could take a very long time, and the British drivers used peaceful means to persuade the dockers that they should just sit in the cab with the driver. But the French drivers were a different matter. Most of our French haulier customers were from quite modest family firms and the drivers were personally responsible to Monsieur le Patron for their vehicles. There were some spectacular punch-ups before the dockers abandoned their quest.

The second area was the ship repairers. In fact, in Southampton we were well served by Vosper Thornycroft whose workforce was well controlled. With EAGLE withdrawing from service for two weeks, we were hell-bent on a busy refit to put right the ship's many problems, but it needed a lot of overtime to accomplish. Vospers could offer it where necessary. Prior to booking the ship repairer, I was leant upon heavily by London to send the ship to Silley Cox's yard in Falmouth, which was P&O owned. The Falmouth yard's workforce to a man were owners of bed and breakfast homes for holidaymakers and were widely reported never to work overtime. From London came assurances of overtime, reinforced by the Falmouth managers when Alex Stevens visited them to discuss the work programme. EAGLE arrived bright and early for an 0800 start and work commenced, but at 1700 all the workforce went home. I checked quickly with Vospers that they could accept EAGLE and instructed Alex to sail her back to Southampton but of course we had lost two days. Next day I had to stand fast for a tremendous rocket from the P&O board member responsible for the shipyard who accused me of disloyalty.

On her next voyage EAGLE was quite badly storm damaged when her newly serviced stabilisers failed, but there were also examples of raw courage which lightened an otherwise dismal day. Outward bound to Lisbon and off Ushant in very heavy weather, a bridge window stove in and Captain Renshaw's face was cut by the shards of glass. He was not badly hurt in fact, just unable to see anything through all the blood, but he wisely decided not to let his passengers see him. At about this time the stabilisers failed and the ship started to roll heavily in addition to pitching. One result was that objects on the vehicle deck started to move. The trailers were all secured to the deck with chain lashings but the cars were secured only by way of their handbrakes and being put in low gear, which was the normal practice. In the rush to complete the refit, some drums of paint had been left in the vehicle deck and some of these had ruptured, providing a slippery deck. Into this turmoil EAGLE's boatswain and two ABs appeared with ropes and proceeded to lash anything that could move. It was very dangerous work, but they succeeded in rendering the vehicle deck secure. On discharge in Lisbon one family saloon was found to be the right length and height, but its width was roughly the same as its engine block, which gives an idea of what was happening.

The incident was noteworthy in my view, and I reported it "up the line". The board decided to recommend the three sailors to the Committee of Lloyds for the award of Lloyds Medals for gallantry at sea. In due course the sailors were accompanied by Sandy Marshall when they were presented with their medals by the Secretary of Lloyds.

But other things were moving on, and John Turner (Senior) retired and Ian Churcher became the General Manager of all P&O Ferry services. Ian had started North Sea Ferries from scratch, with two ships running a nightly service between Rotterdam and Hull. It was a high quality service that grew with two new larger ships and a Hull/Zeebrugge nightly service, but it was not very profitable and there were those in the finance department who sought to close it down. Ian's first action at Southampton was to remove EAGLE from service and lay her up prior to sale. PANTHER was chartered out to a Baltic operator for a time before replacing an old ship in the Aberdeen/Lerwick service in Scotland. It was a good decision but left me without a job, whilst Michel Meheut became the one general manager for Normandy Ferries.

I next returned to London to carry out a survey of the general cargo services to the Arabian Gulf and Red Sea. General Cargo Division, which was expected to be phased out as containerisation was adopted, provided very substantial profits at a time when other Divisions and OCL provided little or nothing. The newly rich countries of Arabia were buying on a huge scale and the ports could not cope with the traffic which was all in the break bulk mode.

There were congestion delays at every port, some extending to 100 days. Ship-owners had to respond with freight congestion charges to compensate for the time their ships were idle. Their customers were unhappy at the freight increase and tripled transit times. The Division's profitability arose because they were despatching ten or more sailings a month to the area from most other parts of the world, coupled with the skills of the Gulf co-ordinator in Gray Mackenzie's (P&O) office in Bahrain and the local cargo superintendents at Gulf ports. The team in the Gulf shuffled ships around like a pack of cards, hastened discharge, and transhipped cargo from one ship to another. The end result was that whilst all the sailings were prolonged, the total delays were far less than provided for in the congestion charges.

To overcome the long transit times, I suggested that an interim trailer service was mounted for high value goods across the Channel to Greece and then continued by ferry to Beirut. There was little enthusiasm for this largely because the Division did not know how to operate trailers, and P&O Ferrymasters, whose business was unit load trailers, did not wish to extend into Arabia. Having visited the Gulf, Red Sea and Beirut I could not blame them. There was still a very noisy war going on in the Lebanon. At last there were signs of investing in container ports in the area, led by Sheik Rashid of

Dubai, and soon to be followed by adjacent countries. So no further action was contemplated.

At this stage in the proceedings I fully expected to be sacked, since this was becoming an almost daily occurrence. My old chum Jim Davis in Passenger Division had been sacked by Peter Parry, Head of the Division. Some time later Peter Parry was sacked by Sandy Marshall, who replaced him with Harry Spanton. It looked for some time as if Harry would become P&O's MD but he died early. There was clearly a huge rift between Sandy Marshall and Chairman Lord Inchcape, and in due course Sandy was sacked. I would have been in good company.

But this was not to be the case. To my surprise I was invited to join General Cargo Division (GCD), which was largely staffed by BI people who were well known for hating anyone from the old P&O. I was asked to take up the appointment of P&O Owner's Representative in New York for a year or two, principally to oversee the new service in break bulk mode from the USA's East Coast to the Gulf. Despite the dreadful ambiance, and regressing to break-bulk after container and Ro/Ro modes, the position sounded challenging.

The service had been running for nearly a year and was intended to capitalise on the Division's great strength on the ground in the Gulf. In the USA, the Tilston Roberts Corporation was appointed as general agents to secure business from American customers, and John Turner (Junior) was appointed as Owner's Representative.

The Owner's Representative lived and worked in the USA, using a treaty trader's Visa which precluded him from actually concluding any business - this was the task of the general agents. John Turner had made a good start on supporting Tilston Roberts and making friends with customers, but it had been based on GCD's policy of buying the business with cash bribes. Whilst this goes on all over the world in just about every business including shipping, in the USA it was strictly illegal.

The head of GCD set out for me what the job entailed. I would spend a few weeks working in the lines department in London to

Last Days in P&O

learn their operating rules and visit New York for a few days for familiarisation purposes before taking up the post. GCD would provide a furnished house in which to live, together with an overseas allowance and a leased car. Air passages for Bunty and me would be provided. The usual annual leave for overseas staff of one month in the UK would apply. Whilst concentrating on GCD's USA/Gulf service, I was to assist any other P&O Division should they require help.

My family was not enthusiastic about joining me full time. After gaining her BA degree, my daughter Lindley had joined the Secretary's Department of Eastern Electricity in Wherstead near Ipswich, and had married recently. Victoria was aged just 18 and had started to work as a secretary in a major computer company in London, which she enjoyed. Neither Bunty nor I liked the idea of her living in a shared flat in London whilst we were a long way away in New York. So we decided to adopt a plan whereby Bunty and Victoria would cross the Atlantic for visits from time to time and we made air bookings for such a fortnight at Christmas. Lindley and her new husband would make a visit later.

I went for a meeting with my new boss and it did not take long for GCD's management style to appear. His opening statement was that my annual leave in the job would be three weeks. He was clearly trying to make trouble but I said nothing. After all, it was a year away. He then went on to talk about my imminent short visit to New York. Elsewhere in P&O, I had been used to a regime where necessary overseas visits had been made without any fuss. In GCD they were a very special bonus awarded only in special cases by a boss demonstrating his power. The reason, without doubt, was that a trip yielded opportunities in regard to expense accounts. My boss then instructed me in detail on how to arrange to bring back a "box of chocolates" for my wife. Again I said nothing. It was a clear indication of how GCD worked; anyone could be bought or sold at any time.

In New York I first went to stay at the New York Yacht Club for a few days until John and Liz Turner vacated the rented family house in South Orange, New Jersey, and passed the leased car on to me. It was a convenient and friendly pied-a-terre even if I did have to pass a firmly anchored America Cup daily. John soon introduced me to the staff of Tilston Roberts, both in the North and the Gulf, a number of customers, and local friends in South Orange.

Ed Tilston managed the North from his office in New York. His company had other shipowner clients, of which the most important was Lloyd Brasilio, Brazil's national line. He had spent many years in shipping in Brazil and Argentina and was familiar with their style of business as well as being fluent in Portuguese and Spanish. He invited me for lunch and left me with a poor impression, mainly because he appeared not to know anything about P&O's business or customers. He seemed mainly involved in trying to broker a sale of US battle tanks to a Middle East country which did not sound right at all. He was supported in New York by his President Dan Mihailovich of Serbian origin, Arthur Renehan, an ex mariner, and George Smyth, as P&O Line managers. Caputo senior was his sales manager and dealt in the brown envelopes whilst his nephew Mike worked with Arthur Renehan. Tereza Mangino, a bubbly girl of Italian extraction became my secretary.

Everything was quite different in the South. With his office in New Orleans, Harold Roberts managed the Gulf offices. Not only was he a very experienced shipping man, his personal demeanour was of an archetypical southern Gentleman that any Hollywood director would cast on the spot. He was ably supported by Danny Culpepper in Houston.

There was a great deal for me to learn about the business, but about two months after my arrival the axe fell. I was away in California for a few days assessing the potential business in that vast and productive state when, in my daily check-in call with Tereza, she said "We have been hit boss, the FBI are all over the place, and they want to see you as soon as you are back". It was the start of a major FBI operation that encompassed just about every shipping agency, and owner's representative, as well as other waterfront activities. The next week two very large men appeared in my small office, their tight fitting suits bulging from their weapons, and asked me lots of questions about money and payments. I could only tell them the truth. They told me I would be hearing from the District Attorney.

It was time to get some help. The Turners had become friends with Peter and Anne Rhatican in South Orange. At this stage Peter was only a makee-learnee lawyer but he had a lot of well qualified colleagues, including one who was experienced in anti-trust legislation, which was what the situation required. I contacted William and he offered to represent me but asked for $10,000 up front. It was time to report to my boss and seek authority for funds but he refused to take a telephone call from me. The Head of GCD was absent on sick leave after a stroke so I sent an ordinary telex to GCD (which I knew would go through P&O's telex centre) and was told I might engage legal assistance. On 24th January 1977 the District Attorney summoned me to appear before a Grand Jury two weeks later. William managed to arrange for a stay of execution but the summons has never been withdrawn. A Grand Jury is a pre-liminary to a trial but it is a daunting procedure, since a defendant has to appear, without any counsel, before 23 citizens to be questioned by the District Attorney. A commitment for trial results in the defendant leaving the courtroom handcuffed to seek bail.

It took about three years for matters to be concluded and P&O agreed to a fine imposed by the Federal Maritime Commission (FMC). In the meantime the European and Japanese governments protested vigorously to Washington in respect of all their shipping nationals based in the USA. The commercial department of the British Embassy was particularly supportive and advised me that there was a senior man from the DTI about to make a visit. They suggested I should meet him and struggled to make a date in his busy schedule. This was finally arranged at a bar in Newark Airport late in the day. This very senior civil servant duly appeared and was accompanied by a comely and flirtatious junior officer from his department. They appeared completely engrossed in amorous conversation with their eyes locked together so firmly that there was no chance for me to speak. Their flight was eventually called, whereupon this wretched man, clasping the hand of his beloved, turned to me to say that he thought my position was one of considerable personal peril.

Of course, in the business the brown envelopes were stopped dead and we were despatching sailings less than half full. I had always believed it was possible to run top class liner shipping for customers who would pay without being bribed and certainly the Strath class service proved it. We had to compete against top class and well established lines like Wilhelmsen of Norway and Nedlloyd of Nederland. Their sailings went like clockwork and their ships were fast and very large, offering stowage and cranage to handle containers, Ro/Ro and break-bulk cargo. All GCD could provide was chartered-in two decker ships, which were slow, invariably arrived late, and could only handle small break-bulk cargo.

Under FMC rules, shipping lines were free to set their own freight rates as long as they published them and did not offer secret rebates. It was the major "project cargoes" that attracted my attention. American construction companies, mostly based in California, were very busy building major projects in the Middle East, such as oil refineries and gas plants, military establishments and infrastructure, and hospitals and universities. We started to go for them on a published "project rate" basis and before I left New York we had started to succeed, at least to the extent of breaking even instead of making losses. Despite the dreadful ships, our own sales concentration in California and the post sales performance from GCD's Gulf staff bore fruit. One major project was the Fluor Corporation's huge gas plant at Isfahan in Iran, which we loaded in the US Gulf and discharged at Khorramshah.

Fluor's traffic manager Robert Noon became a personal friend because we did what we said we would do. Before he left his office in Khorramshah each evening, when a ship was in the course of discharge, GCD's superintendent Jimmy Linton telexed Robert with the status quo of his cargo. In California this was received about 0800 as Robert opened his office so that he could immediately update his materials management colleagues. Apparently this had never happened before in Fluor's experience. I even got invited to lunch by the Fluor vice president! Robert was not a member of the brown envelope brigade, but we did have some memorable dinners with our wives, although quite a few of them were in Robert and Marie Noon's beach apartment.

Last Days in P&O

Not long after arriving in New York I was joined by Captain David Colley, a GCD superintendent. David had been a BI master, and had spent four years as a superintendent in the Gulf. He soon got to work in the USA, supervising the stowage of export cargoes, improving despatch and challenging stevedore invoices. As a lifelong bachelor David was expected by GCD to live only in hotels throughout his tenure. Not only was this expensive but it was soulless to say the least. After yet another row with my boss I did manage to get a modest flat for him in South Orange which certainly improved his well-being. He also turned out to be a good salesperson, not least on account of his Gulf experience, and when I left he took over my desk. His other major achievement was to instruct one of San Francisco's top chefs on how to prepare and cook perfect Yorkshire pudding to accompany the beef.

After a year in the job things were beginning to settle down and there were no further nasty missives from the DA. Victoria decided she would like to spend time in New York, as long as she could work and not sit around. Tereza had left for a better job and was succeeded by Linda Martinez, daughter of an immigrant Spanish longshoreman. I asked Linda to visit the Immigration Department and explore the work permit position. After three fruitless visits Linda gave up and I decided to pay them a visit myself. I was seen by a young woman from an ethnic group who was friendly and helpful but clearly struggling with the Department's large manual. I found out that technically, as a resident on my treaty trader visa, she could only work in the cultural area of the arts and museums, etc. But the friendly officer clearly wanted to be accommodating and provided a photocopy of some pages from her manual. These were an enigma because two important pages about treaty trader status in the middle were missing. I began to get the impression that the friendly officer was barely literate. Obligingly she undertook to provide a letter to me to show to prospective employers that said Victoria could work, and inviting employers to get in touch with her if they were in doubt.

Armed with this important document Bunty and Victoria arrived for a six month stay. Victoria soon found work as a receptionist in a legal firm but in fact her time was mostly spent re-drafting the documents of the junior lawyers so that they were in proper English. She moved on soon after to an IT company that was perfecting a word processor for the legal industry and had to learn how to use the machine and demonstrate it to prospective clients. It turned out to be the start of a long and successful career in the IT business.

It was during this time that Sandy Marshall paid a visit to the USA on behalf of the UK Chamber of Shipping, principally to canvas support from the American government. He asked me to arrange a dinner party for senior guests from the NY area which was held at the Yacht Club and went off very well. Bunty was badly held up in the transport system so I had to send Victoria, who worked close by to me, in a taxi to act as Sandy's hostess, which she did very well. CANBERRA was also visiting NY and Sandy, with a lot of help from the Embassy in Washington, had arranged a splendid dinner on board for 200 guests, who were either senators or congressmen. At the appointed hour only about 100 had turned up, so Sandy asked me to man the gangway to receive latecomers. After an hour only one appeared. But I did talk to a number of CANBERRA's passengers returning to the ship and found there was a great deal of customer satisfaction amongst them. I did miss dinner entirely but consoled myself with the thought that a quartermaster in black tie was probably a first for Captain Dennis Scott-Masson and Staff Captain Ian Gibb.

Another visitor was no less than Admiral of the Fleet Lord Mount-batten, who came as principal guest at a dinner of the English Speaking Union. Rear Admiral Michael Burgoyne, who was Naval Attaché in Washington, had originally intended to support his AF but a last minute appearance of his Minister in Washington meant he had to stand fast. He sent his secretary in lieu and asked me for support. Bunty and I were duly announced and from six feet away the AF caught sight of my miniature medal ribbons, amongst them the Burma Star. "And where were you with me in Burma then Penney?" he boomed. It was a fantastic dinner and never to be forgotten. The secretary and his wife were seated a table marked Daughters of the American Revolution. These all looked so ferocious that Bunty was worried that they might eat the RN couple.

Last Days in P&O

In my spare time I did manage to get in a fair amount of sailing. In New York there were weekend tournaments between the serving and retired RN officers which were great parties. I also sailed in Los Angeles and New Orleans.

My two year spell came to an end, and I was told that I was to head the Flower Project back in London. The P&O business in the USA was in a much better shape than when I joined it. I had learned a great deal about the world's most powerful country, which was regaining its military self-respect after the debacle of Vietnam. I had also gained a number of new friends and business contacts.

The Flower Project was quite simply a P&O design for an offshore protection vessel (OPV), which took its name from the FLOWER class corvettes mass produced in WW2 from a commercial whale-catcher design. They were sometimes called "the cheap and nasties", which prompted Winston Churchill with his customary oratory to say that although they were cheap the enemy would find them nasty. About 100 were built and they gave valuable service escorting convoys and persuading U boats to stay submerged (as long as the sailors could survive the sea-sickness).

The McKinsey re-organisation resulted in the creation of a stand-alone technical department for P&O. Its purpose was to manage the acquisition of ships from shipyards, troubleshoot technical problems, engage in research and development and provide safety training for crews. When working with clients outside P&O, it traded as Three Quays Marine Services (TQMS) and was managed by directors Douglas Kerr and John Tuke. The creation of the Flower design was seen as a diversification to utilise the skills of its staff at a time when little new tonnage was being ordered by P&O and others.

The world's nations were becoming aware of the wealth available in the oceans and seas around their coasts and in the seabeds below the water. They wanted to extend the existing 12 mile territorial waters already defined to a new 200 mile economic enterprise zone (EEZ) in which they individually controlled both fishing and offshore mining, the latter with particular reference to oil. The zone limit was a major extension to the territorial waters and would often need ocean-going ships to police economic activity. Such ships would be managed by governmental bodies, such as a navy or ministry. The Flower design clearly met the criteria for sea-keeping and other areas, and could be lightly armed, as well as providing a hangar and platform for carrying a small helicopter. This could increase the ship's search and inspection resource dramatically.

TQMS had discussions with a number of people involved who greeted the concept with enthusiasm, as did the P&O board. The board recognised that P&O had no track record in selling ship designs and, that if the concept took off, it would be necessary to seek shipbuilding partners in order to offer a finished product. They selected Bremer Vulkan AG Schiffbau und Maschinenfabrik (BV) in Bremen and Thyssen Noord See Werk (TNSW) in Emden. Both these shipbuilders were well known to P&O, having supplied them with substantial new tonnage over several years. They were also facing a declining market for commercial ships and were actively looking for naval and quasi-naval work.

It was put to me that to launch Flower would require a three year period. I would work in P&O Group Marketing with Rowland Escombe, a P&O director, as my P&O boss and report to a Flower committee comprising TQMS, BV and TNSW. Rowland was both a good boss and an old friend. His family company had been P&O brokers and travel agents since 1918 until P&O bought them out and he was a close friend of Chairman Lord Inchcape. I accompanied John Tuke on a visit to Germany to meet Andreas Harder of BV and Herr Woolman of TNSW and join my first Flower meeting.

I was to spend seven months actively trying to find a market for Flower, and had many senior level meetings in 13 overseas countries, using contacts provided for me or which I found myself. I also used old RNR contacts in the UK who were in the business, to learn more about how naval shipbuilders achieved sales of their products.

It was an interesting programme. Whilst the EEZ enlargement was clearly of interest to those involved, resulting in long and detailed discussions, I could not detect even a small spark of serious interest. No one even suggested a budgetary first offer. My impression was that those responsible for policing their EEZ were unlikely to have their budgets increased and that somehow they would make use of different types of existing hulls and their crews.

Some research on the charts of Mexican waters revealed an interesting situation: in the waters of the Gulf of Mexico the EEZ was constrained by geographical factors. The Pacific coast was quite different. It was over 1500 miles long and in places 600 miles wide because there are a group of small islands belonging to Mexico about 400 miles offshore. The cold water coastal currents produce huge amounts of good fish which were being plundered by fisher-men from neighbouring countries. I had a long meeting with the admiral, who was head of the navy. Whilst we were clearly interested in the sea-keeping qualities of Flower, he was dead set against any helicopters. Later, my contact, who accompanied me to the meeting, explained that the admiral was a seaman officer. When illegal fishermen were located it was normal practice for the CO of the patrol vessel to have a "negotiation" with the fisherman skipper, and no way would he allow the benefits of this to accrue to an aviator.

As I learned more about naval marketing, it struck me that it was crazy to have a partnership with two German shipyards. They were both excellent shipbuilders but were in fierce competition with each other. It became clear that one reason why they had joined the project was that they regarded P&O as a major customer and could not allow the other alone to be in very close association with P&O. In addition, I was worried about a complete lack of cost control for the project. All three parties just tabled their costs and these were shared on a tri-partite basis. Overall project costs were running at about £200,000 per annum and it was difficult to see how this figure arose because my own costs, including a lot of travel, were only running at about £50,000 p.a.

It was clearly not a runner, and despite the personal cost to me, it had to be stopped. I had a long meeting with Rowland and we went over all the ground I had covered. Rowland agreed with my analysis so I wrote a full report to Douglas Kerr, recommending the project be scrapped. The first reaction came from John Tuke, who appeared in a terrible temper and accused me of just about every crime in the book. The most heinous crime emerged as challenging the validity of a cosy technical partnership with shipbuilders he clearly admired so much. TQMS did not accept my recommend-dations and the project continued for some months before it fizzled out. I estimated that this early demise saved P&O about half a million.

I thought it was about time for my hangman to appear but this was delayed for a time. With Rowland's help, I secured a shipping con-sultancy contract from the EU in Brussels to assist the Bangladesh Shipping Corporation (BSC) in Dacca and this comfortably covered my staff costs for six months or more.

Bangladesh was one of the world's poorest countries and evidence of abject poverty was very visible. Apart from a wish to earn a living for myself, it would be very rewarding if I could make even a tiny improvement to the country's economy. The BSC was a government corporation and I spent a month in Dacca and the port of Chittagong researching the BSC's business. For a number of reasons it was in a very good position to increase the creation of wealth for its citizens. It had a large portfolio of quite different shipping activities and, in the area of earning foreign exchange, its break-bulk cargo liner services to many other counties were the most important. To start with, these services attracted the same freight rates as other more wealthy countries' ships. Bangladeshi merchants were proud of BSC and supportive of its services. Costs were very low since most of its second-hand ships were aid gifts from European governments. Routine docking and repair work was carried out in BSC's own repair yard in Chittagong and most of the seafarers were paid local rates. Like most government agencies, there was a lot of red tape, but in the offices there were many bright young men who had been educated in universities ranging from Moscow to Harvard.

I think my most useful contribution to BSC was to persuade them to adopt a system of profit reporting for each separate shipping service, so that even at the more junior manager level they could see what was happening on almost a daily basis and take action where necessary to improve matters. When I presented the first set of results to MD Captain Shafi he was both startled and a bit alarmed. There was one shipping service operated for another government body that was making enormous profits and he was anxious that his opposite number should not see these results. The one BSC passenger ship in operation was only employed for two months a year in the Haj traffic to Jeddah and lost a great deal of money.

The religious fraternity continued to insist that its flock be allowed to make the holy pilgrimage by sea despite the much lower costs available with aircraft charters that were used from other countries to Jeddah. But at the end of my task, Captain Shafi thanked me very handsomely in the name of his government.

My hangman at last appeared and turned out to be Derek Hall, P&O director and head of Bulk Shipping Division, who told me I would leave the Company's service on 31 March 1980, 35 years to the day after I had joined. It was a blow of course but effected with much courtesy and included a generous redundancy payment, deferred pension rights and a farewell dinner. I could not understand why Derek Hall was tasked with the job, but perhaps it was to prepare him for a similar fate within a year.

Chapter 15. Pennmaritime International Limited

Being made redundant has become part and parcel of life in the last 30 years or so, as the pace of technological and economic life quickens. It is of course a form of rejection which no one likes but it is not the end of the world. It certainly affects people in different ways and in some cases leads to sheer misery, but I was determined not to be one of these.

I had clearly arrived at yet another large alter-course position and Bunty and I needed to take stock. We had many assets to take into account. Most important were our family and many good friends. Lindley and Victoria had both been well educated and had good jobs, which fully supported them. We had a very attractive home which was not costly to run and maintain and the mortgage had been paid off. We were not short of funds from our own savings and P&O's redundancy payment, and did not need to contemplate economising on our life style. Above all, we were both fit and well. A good pension would be available for us both in about ten years.

There was no question of retiring and sitting around because I had always enjoyed working and did not want to stop at the age of 51. It seemed unlikely that anyone would want me as an employee in an industry that was in sharp decline. By now I had a track record in consultancy in the maritime industry, which was the only business I both knew and liked. For the next two years I secured shipping consultancy business, which provided a good income. There was no need to engage separate office space because our house provided a large and comfortable study. However, at the end of two years it became obvious that the shipping consultancy business was in decline. A number of old contacts who had provided consultancy tasks for me had lost their jobs, and when they did get in touch it was to see if I could offer them a job. I did investigate some leads from overseas owners for ship management tasks, but rejected them because they only sought to bring respectability to managing dreadful old tonnage, which should have been scrapped. It was clear that the owners did not understand proper maintenance to class, and there were certainly no funds to pay for it.

As a private individual in a high risk business, I was exposed to being sued for my house and belongings and decided to incorporate a small limited company. In 1980, Pennmaritime International Limited was formed, with an issued and paid up capital of £10,000 and the shares all held in my family. It was one of the best things I ever did and the net worth increased seven fold in the years that followed. It provided me with an income and was very tax effective. The Memorandum of Association was widely drawn so that the Company could engage in just about any business activity, from a soup kitchen to book selling, although I tried neither of these. The original activity was of course maritime consultancy, but other activities were to follow when an opportunity offered.

I personally took over the Pennmaritime accounts and we appointed John A Hyde and Company as Auditors, which they still are. In the early years, income consisted entirely of fees, which was straight-forward enough, but when the Company traded goods and reached a turnover of nearly £300,000 per annum it became more complex. However, one thing I learned at the London Business School was how to understand all-important balance sheets and cash flow statements. From the start I adopted a prompt monthly profit and loss account together with a trial balance, which provided full control, so that the audited account never contained any nasty shocks.

There was another move when I also created a small company pension fund with the help of an insurance company and this also turned out very well. It was a good place to add tax free savings as and when they were available and it was open to other family members apart from me. After a couple of years, I noticed that my guaranteed capital sum from this source was appreciating at 14 percent per annum at a time when my deferred pension from P&O was increasing by only three percent. The higher rate did reduce after some time as interest rates fell generally, but a marked difference still remained and I felt it was time to start asking questions.

Like many other people I believed that in first class companies pension funds were overseen by the Almighty, but this was not the case. Salaried pension department managers considered the funds belonged strictly to them and guarded them with great care. Having checked with my own fund that they could accept a transfer of my funds from P&O, I wrote formally to P&O seeking a transfer.

Absolutely nothing happened for three months, after which I telephoned and was told that a reply would be sent shortly. I was later to learn that sitting on a transfer request for three months was standard practice in the industry. I did manage to achieve the transfer but it took a year, which meant that I had missed an annual window of transfer into my own fund. The great lesson learned was that in the world of money the devil takes the hindermost. There were major upheavals when companies went bankrupt, after having first plundered their pension funds to try and stave off the inevitable, of which Maxwell was the worst case, but happily they were few. There was later to be an attempt to take over my fund, which failed.

Out of the blue a ship management job in South Africa appeared, which at first sight was very attractive. South Africa had two shipping companies, Safmarine, owned by the state and covering the long haul container traffic, and Unicorn, which was privately owned. Unicorn operated a fleet of medium size break bulk ships mainly on the long African coast but in the East they had also extended their services to India and Arabia. With headquarters in Durban, they were owned by a large shipping and forwarding company that moved goods all over Southern Africa.

It was a part of the world I had never seen but there were extensive family links there. In the 1920s no less than three of my Pa's brothers, who were all electrical engineers, had taken their new skills, developed in the old power station at Shoreham in Sussex, to a continent keen to have an electricity supply and its benefits. In a huge country they made a substantial contribution to providing a

P&O ARCADIA.
"My best ship ever."
Arriving at Tilbury from the Clyde, February 1954.
Author on extreme right.

ARCADIA's sea boat launched and setting off.

Approaching PENTAKOTA.

**The tricky bit. About to hook on to ARCADIA with patient on board.
Indian Ocean, 1954.**

BULWARK's helicopters over CHEVIOT saluting the flag.

CHEVIOT, CAVALIER and ROYALIST in a gridiron viewed from BULWARK.
Operation SHOW BOAT, Singapore 1957.

AIRSTREAM (R3) racing (slowly) in the Hong Kong and Macau Interport.

Yokohama YC, ARTEMIS of LONGSTREAM in the foreground.

Staff wedding in Hong Kong. Toasting the bride, Mrs Teng.

Lindley, Victoria (3 weeks old) and Bunty on the beach.

First command. HMS ISIS, sea training tender.

HMS WARSASH, coastal minesweeper 10th MCMS.

**Christening ceremony, HMS AMAZON, first type 21 frigate.
HRH Princess Anne looks on as the youngest rating cuts the cake
with his captain's sword. Southampton 1973.**

**October 1970. Admiral of the Fleet Lord Mountbatten
is principal guest in the wardroom of HMS WESSEX.**

Captain David McCarraher VRD, ADC, hands over command to the author.

**Aboard HMS SOLENT, British Rail present the name plate
from one of their locomotives.**

modern grid, and one headed the Victoria Falls Power Company, which was then one of the world's largest hydro-electric generators. Also present in South Africa were some old P&O colleagues who had migrated to work in the shipping industry.

In London I had a very cordial meeting with the managing director of the Unicorn group. He was looking firstly for a Fleet Director and secondly for an assistant for the whole group. He was impressed with my track record in fleet management and considered that as a Fellow of the Chartered Institute of Transport, I could be of value as Assistant MD. He suggested attractive terms and provided a picture of what these would produce for me locally. He was prepared to look at a basis of employment on a yearly contract basis which seemed appropriate for both parties in the circumstances. I began to get excited.

My excitement was unfortunately short-lived because to take the job I had to migrate to the Republic and did not wish to do this. There was no legal way I could repatriate any earnings out of the country. If I wished to transfer some funds into the country, perhaps for a deposit on a house in which to live, these could not be repatriated. It was one of the factors of life that accompanied apartheid and I would always look upon the UK as my home. There was an illegal way to achieve transferring funds out of the country, and it was often used. It involved purchasing gold metal in the Republic and sending it by (very) safe hand to a bank in Bombay which would exchange it for an international sight draft in pounds or dollars, which could be cashed in London. (Later I often wondered whether Unicorn's Indian destinations were just more than co-incidence.)

It was a great disappointment, but I learned that there were others in the same boat. I had lunch with Sandy Marshall, who, on leaving P&O, had become Chairman of an international engineering company in Slough called Bestobell. As a brand new arrival, he had seen off an unexpected take-over bid by a predator, which certainly demonstrated his qualities. Prior to taking that position, and as soon as his departure from P&O was known about, his first suitor was the substantial Swire Group, which owned shipping and trading activities. These were mainly in the Far East and based in Hong Kong. In recent years, Swire had built up significant shipping and mining activities in Africa and they asked Sandy if he would like to manage them. Sandy knew Chairman Adrian Swire well and had many contacts, including family and other contacts in South Africa, which attracted him to the job. Over lunch he told me that he had to decline for exactly the same reasons as me because even the Swire Group could not reward him outside South Africa and he shared my thoughts about gold bars. The old regime in Johannesburg clearly lost out on some impressive skills and experience through their inward looking stance.

Apart from my own activities, Victoria has added a great deal to Pennmaritime in the area of IT. For a time in the 1980s she was an employee of International Computers Limited, which was the leading British company in the field, where she worked as a salesperson. She was very successful with a dedicated ICL word processor and daisy wheel printer which were selling very well, and principally for the secretaries of top managers. In addition to selling the equipment, she also trained the secretaries in how to use it. This was at a time before the omnipotent desk PC appeared and the equipment sold for about £5,000, with training at an additional cost of £250 per day.

She decided she wanted to have her own business and asked for my help to set it up. We set up a separate division of Pennmaritime called PennLine Systems which kept its own separate accounts. She took office premises in Nottingham and by 1990 the business was thriving, employing three young people who carried out training, tailoring software packages for customers and office administration. I contributed by supervising her accounts until she had learnt how to do them herself. She was able to take a handsome salary out of her business and to contribute to the pension fund, as well as enjoying a quality car. When she married and was about to have her first child we sold the business of PennLine to another trader and quite simply closed the division.

By 2004 she had two children, who were both at school full time, and she was ready to start working again. By this time the IT market for salespeople had become an exhausting rat race unsuitable for a wife, mother and housewife, so she elected to deal in badged promotional goods which are making steady progress. We just opened another division of the Company called Pennline.

Pennmaritime has demonstrated very well the versatility and usefulness of a small family limited company. On two occasions in the last few years I have assisted the widows of old friends liquidate the small companies their husbands had created. My pleas to let the companies lie fallow have fallen on deaf ears, but in both cases their children have later asked me to help them set up a small trading company.

Chapter 16. Warship Salesman

After the Flower project had been discontinued I maintained contact with Andreas Harder, the director of naval shipbuilding at Bremer Vulkan at Bremen-Vegesack on the Weser River. They had won the prestigious contract of lead shipbuilder for six major warships for their government and had decided to market similar ships to navies overseas. It was a huge success to win this order because BV were not perceived to be a naval builder in the same class as Blohm and Voss in Hamburg, who reminded everyone that they had built the BISMARCK, Thyssen Noord See Werke in Emden and Howaldswerke at Kiel. I believed that I could help them with the marketing task and Pennmaritime was invited to assist. In addition to overseas sales visits, I was to contact naval attachés based in London and escort them on visits to Germany. The German navy's scheme of complement for warships was unique, whereas the majority of overseas navies used the Royal Navy's system with which I was familiar and on which I could advise them when it came to accommodation layouts.

BV had been established as a shipbuilder for many years and enjoyed a high reputation with commercial ship owners, both in Germany and overseas. This was particularly the case in the UK and they had delivered a number of large container ships to OCL and the other container consortia. It was only in the last two years of WW2 that they turned their hands to building Type VIIc standard submarines for the old Kriegsmarine. After WW2, and when they resumed production, they concentrated again on merchant ships. With trade recovering and many ships lost in the war there were plenty of orders. When these began to fall off, and especially when low-cost countries in the Far East entered the market, they and other shipbuilders started to look at projects requiring high technology skills. BV was owned by the Thyssen-Bornemesa family, who continued to support it when profitability declined, until matters reached a point where the business had to close.

The chief executive during my time was Doctor Engineer Hans Huchzermeier, who became a towering figure in the industry. This was due not only to winning the naval contract but also his other innovative ideas, and especially the practice of outfitting all the passenger cabins for large ships in a factory ashore and then installing them in blocks. This did away with the old labour intensive practice of outfitting separately each cabin in the ship whilst afloat and alongside a quay, and the concept was adopted worldwide.

Hans Huchzermeier had trained as a naval architect in the 1930s and entered the Kriegsmarine as a constructor officer during WW2. In 1942 he was sent to St. Nazaire in NW France where there was a very large drydock which had been built to dock French Line's transatlantic flagship NORMANDIE, a one-time holder of the Atlantic Blue Ribband for the fastest passage to New York. It could also accommodate the German battleship TIRPITZ which was then in Alten Fjord in Northern Norway.

The German High Command wanted to base TIRPITZ in France so that she would be much closer to her targets, which were the Allies' transatlantic convoys bringing lifeblood from the USA to the UK. They needed a dry-dock for underwater repairs if these became necessary, and constructor officers to supervise the work. The scene was set for an outstanding drama of WW2.

A French naval officer working in the harbour office was secretly a De Gaulle supporter and spied for the Admiralty. He reported to London that he had been ordered to prepare moorings for a large battleship and the Admiralty drew the right conclusions. They decided to mount a raid to destroy the dry dock and selected HMS CAMPBELTOWN, a small destroyer from the USA provided under Lease-Lend, to creep up the river Loire at night and ram the dock gates. The ship was disguised as a German fast patrol boat and packed with explosives. The raid was an outstanding success and the dock was completely destroyed. CAMPBELTOWN was accompanied by a number of small craft manned by demolition parties to destroy pump houses and other equipment, and these were guarded by commandos and other specialist troops. Some of the raiders escaped after the action in the small craft, but others were lost or taken prisoner. TIRPITZ stayed in Alten Fjord, where she was finally destroyed by the Royal Navy using midget submarines and the Royal Air Force using Lancaster bombers and tallboy bombs.

Amongst the specialist troops was a subaltern in the London Scottish Regiment called Ronald Swayne, who survived the raid but was taken prisoner. About 35 years later, Sir Ronald Swayne was Chairman of OCL. At a celebratory dinner in Bremen to mark the delivery of a new container ship Hans Huchzermeier revealed that he had been Sir Ronnie's captor in March 1942, a revelation that amazed everybody including his principal guest.

The order for six large frigates was a major event for the new German Navy because they would be the first large surface warships to be built after WW2. The surface fleet requirement had been met by the transfer of three large destroyers from the USN, whilst diesel submarines and minor warships were built and commissioned. With all the German shipyards short of work the order was given to BV as lead shipbuilder with other yards building hulls and machinery. The important weapon and sensor outfit for all six ships was a sole BV responsibility. The ships would carry the names of six States in the Republic with BREMEN, a Hanseatic City-State, as the first of class.

The ships, and particularly their weapon and sensor outfits, were technically very complex. To provide for this BV built an upper deck mock-up on dry land into which was built all the weapon/ sensor equipment for the sixth ship, so that interfacing them had an early start. This was to prove a good investment when it later came to sea trials and the "setting to work" process. Two years before BREMEN was commissioned, training classes were started for the instructors who would teach the crews how to operate their equipment. BV had to build in equipment sourced from overseas and their own management team had to oversee both specialist suppliers and consultants.

Warship Salesman

The BREMEN class were classified as general purpose frigates equipped to deal with threats on the surface, from the air, and underwater. Four launchers for long range surface-to-surface missiles were fitted, backed up with an automatic 75 mm gun which was also an anti aircraft weapon. On top of the hangar there was also an anti-missile system for both missiles and aircraft. On each side of the ship were three torpedo tubes with anti submarine torpedoes. All of these were controlled by computer controlled surface and air radars and a large sonar dome under the bow. The hangar housed a helicopter which could be deployed in various modes. The hulls were powered by two MTU diesels for cruising at speeds of up to 20 knots, supplemented by two General Electric gas turbines, each of 25,000 shaft horse power which provided about 30 knots. To increase to top speed it was only necessary to open the throttles on the bridge and the gas turbines burst into life immediately. Gone were the days of scrambling to connect in No.2 boiler room.

The ships were intended for both national and NATO roles. In the latter role, and before the wall came down, their first task was to bottle up the Baltic so that the Soviet Navy could not break out into the North Sea and the Atlantic from their bases near Leningrad (St. Petersburg). Thereafter, they would join the other NATO naval forces in the Atlantic, defending the convoys against Soviet submarines.

To prepare for my sales task, I first prepared a marketing plan. There was only one way to go about this, which was to read the current volume of Jane's Fighting Ships, because it lists under "countries" every warship in the world. Its lists are very detailed and show the original country and date of build, in addition to technical details of weapons and sensors fitted, and recent modifications.

For warships, politics and alliances play a major part in governing sales, both new construction and second hand, because they are sales of arms. At the end of WW2 all the British Commonwealth navies were equipped with warships built in the UK, but in the 1970s this had begun to change. The Moscow/Delhi association strengthened and the Indian Navy began to acquire Russian-built ships. Australia purchased destroyers from the USA and took steps to establish naval shipbuilding in its own country. Western European countries mostly had their own indigenous naval ship-builders, whilst those of Eastern Europe were not only in the Soviet Bloc politically but Moscow was a sole supplier. Whilst the BREMEN class frigates announced to the world that Germany was now in the market for major surface ships, it was only a first step on a track record. The success of German diesel submarines and minor warships was certainly helpful but large frigates were another matter.

There were two other major factors that were important in selecting possible customers for large frigates. The first was cost: a budgetary cost for a BREMEN class ship was US$ 200M. A single hull on its own could not be a "fleet in being", and either two or three hulls would be a logical choice. A customer country would also need a strong and effective technical and industrial base for both crews and ongoing maintenance.

Both BV and Blohm and Voss entered the bidding for two countries that had almost simultaneously sought frigate designs and prices - Iran (at that time ruled by the Shah) and Argentina. With the high cost of preparing full designs and prices, the two German ship-builders agreed not to compete for both inquiries, so that BV took Iran and Blohm and Voss took Argentina. There was plenty of non-German competition available. Whilst Iran had only a small navy, its oil revenues were enormous and it could afford to buy in whatever was needed for crewing and maintenance. Work had already started on building a new naval base at Char Behar, in the middle of nowhere but outside the Strait of Hormuz. This was so that large ships would have the proper sea room to deploy effectively. Andreas Harder spent months camped in Teheran servicing the inquiry for ships, and was sure he was making steady progress towards an order, when the Shah was overthrown and everything came to a halt. Blohm and Voss had more success, securing an order for three of their MEKO class frigates. MEKO was a concept of a standard hull and machinery, with different weapon and sensor modules according to customer choice. One ship from this order was ready in the Elbe River for delivery to Argentina in the middle of the Falklands war in 1982!

My own survey suggested two prime country targets - Pakistan and Chile. They both had well run medium-sized navies and the technical/industrial base to support them. I was less certain about their ability to pay, but suspected this was a matter for governments in the end. In the course of my work, I did visit a number of other countries as requested by BV, because they were also interested in quoting for other small warships, and even on a one-off basis.

My old P&O colleague Ahmed Faruque was still managing the Mackinnon Mackenzie Co office in Karachi. He was surprised about my new task but thought a visit was worthwhile, not least because he had just engaged as his assistant the recently retired fleet commander, who knew that replacement ships were under discussion. I went on my own and duly arrived in Karachi at 0300 one morning to find Ahmed's driver waiting for me. Ahmed had invited me to stay in his house for a couple of nights. The driver chatted away politely in good English as he drove and when we arrived Ahmed had long been abed but his bearer and staff were awaiting me. The bearer announced to the driver in Hindi that I was expected in the office at 0930 later that morning and immediately I understood what had been said. It was about 30 years since I had heard Hindi spoken but clearly my Hindi teacher had got it right those many years ago.

Ahmed's new assistant, the Commodore, was introduced and we had a general discussion. They agreed to act locally for BV on terms to be discussed later. Their fleet was aging and relationships with neighbouring India were still fragile. Not long before, the two countries had been at war, at which time all three services had been engaged. During one skirmish, one of the Indian Navy's fast patrol boats had fired two Styx missiles at Pakistan's fleet tanker. The first landed on the main deck but failed to detonate and ricocheted into the sea. The second was heading for the bridge structure and was detonated about 500 yards out by an Oerlikon 20 mm on the bridge wing, which was very good shooting. Whilst Pakistan was reliant on refurbished and modernised destroyer escorts, obtained from the USA, and some submarines, India possessed larger and more powerful ships provided by Russia.

The Commodore and I flew to Islamabad for a few days and I was introduced to the Admirals in the Defence Ministry. It helped that they had all been trained as sub-lieutenants in the Royal Navy's establishments in the UK, as indeed I had, so we had shared experiences. Armed with a wealth of paper provided by Andreas Harder, I gave them a full presentation of the new BREMEN class and the various alternatives on offer. The discussion later went on for a very long time and I was told that they would let me know later if they were seriously interested. It was a very good meeting. Since the diplomatic corps were excluded from the country's alcohol ban, the German military attaché, who was a soldier, provided a very good party in his apartment to which all the senior Pakistani officers came.

A few weeks later Ahmed Faruque sent word that his navy had expressed serious interest and had invited a formal offer for two ships. In Bremen-Vegesack, Andreas Harder and his colleague Herr Müller did a lot of work and invited me to join them for a further visit and presentation.

I knew things were serious when I was instructed to bring a large empty suitcase with me to Germany in which to carry paperwork. We flew direct to Islamabad for a series of meetings at the Defence Ministry. With typical efficiency, BV had provided a complete and detailed design, which took a long time to go through, and clearly impressed the client. For several months there were exchanges of correspondence between the parties, but in the end it did not produce an order. I believe it to be due to budget restraints at a time when Pakistan was spending quite heavily on jet aircraft and battlefield equipment. In due course they purchased from the Royal Navy's Disposal List the surviving Type 21 light frigates of the AMAZON class, which I had met up with before.

Chile was of course a complete change of scene. To start with, after 150 years of democracy it was ruled by a military junta headed by General Pinochet and his colleagues from the Navy, Air Force and

Warship Salesman

National Police. The Navy was most professional, having been founded by Admiral Lord Cochrane in the early 19th century when he took leave abroad from the UK. It was in a state of readiness as the result of a dispute with neighbouring Argentina about mineral rights under the Beagle Channel in Magellanes. This was so serious that even His Holiness in Rome, the jointly agreed arbitrator, could not resolve it. Without exception, every naval officer I met was very pro-British, although they were wary about British arms purchases for a number of reasons. They were very friendly to me personally and I was invited to be an honorary member of their elegant officers club in Viña del Mar. My German boss was also made welcome and had appointed as his agent a local trader whose ancestry was British. The Navy were looking to replace an American 6" cruiser and some British-built destroyers and they were clearly impressed with BREMEN.

One thing I liked very much about Chileans was that they were clearly Chileans at heart, regardless of their European ancestry. This was exactly the opposite of the citizens of Argentina, who put their ancestral loyalties first (including the British). All the Chilean officers I met used Spanish as their first language but most were multi-lingual and used their family language and English fluently. But when they spoke English it was always with a strong hint of their ancestry. The office of Fleet Commander Admiral Storaker, with his accent, might well have been in Norway. Director of Services Vice Admiral Maurice Poisson looked and sounded as if he would be at home on a Paris boulevard. Captain Schwarzenberg ("My friends call me Mountblacken") was clearly of German stock and Captain Pu's words carried the lilt of the Welsh hills where his grandfather had farmed sheep.

The Chilean Navy had its own repair and maintenance company called Aznar, which was located in Talcahuano, and which engaged in commercial work as well maintaining the fleet. The technical staff were impressive and had gained both Bachelor's and Doctor's degrees at the top universities in the USA, especially MIT. They lived for the day when they might have the tools to build their own ships like BREMEN but there were clear budgetary constraints on doing this. The country was not wealthy and the junta had to give priority to social needs, particularly in the light of the fact that many of its poorer citizens were attracted to the politics of their deposed President. After several months of discussions, it became clear they would not buy new hulls in Europe, and they later announced that they were acquiring the Royal Navy's COUNTY class destroyers complete with their Seaslug missile systems. Andreas Harder was very disheartened at not getting an order after so much work and expense and told me that the Royal Navy, through its Disposal List, was his worst enemy. I was thankful to have opted to be paid on a fee basis and not on results.

I certainly got in a lot of sea time during my job with BV, including sea trials of both BREMEN and NIEDERSACHSEN, the next of class. London is an important posting for naval attachés, most of whom were of Captain's rank, and my task was to invite them in a small group for trials and then escort them to Germany. In Germany, BV would make full arrangements for them. We would be met by one or two cars at Hamburg airport and the driver would hand me an envelope with detailed instructions. It would also include two DM1,000 notes (about £600) "for evening entertainment".

Sea trials are conducted by the shipyard to demonstrate that the basic hull and machinery are up to scratch with regard to seaworthiness and speed. They take one or two days and are staged immediately prior to delivery to the customer. The complex weapons and sensors are tested later in what is known as "setting to work", which takes several weeks. Sea trials are usually a festive occasion, and especially when all goes well. The ships turned out well and it was a joy to be at sea in them when creaming along at over 30 knots. I was even invited to take over the bridge for a spell, whilst BV's Trial Master went below for a quick meal. Andreas Harder's favourite post was right aft on the helicopter pad and over the propellers, demonstrating to an admiring audience that a one Deutschmark piece would stand on its edge and not fall flat.

During the "setting to work" programme I made several visits to BREMEN at sea in the Heligoland Bight, accompanied by one or two attachés. There was no scheduled flight to Heligoland so light aircraft and ship's boat were used, or sometimes a helicopter. Each week in the programme was scheduled for five days of different weapon/sensor tasks, but the guide system built ashore in Vegesack had been so successful that most tasks were completed in three days. This left a narrow window - say Tuesday - for getting there in time. Most of the work was with regards to the sensors and their controlling computers. The use of long range weapons was not possible in the limited sea room of the Bight since the long range surface weapons needed firing ranges many miles away. The ship's helicopter was not ready for delivery and the anti-missile system was still in the production stage. We did however see the Oto Melara 75mm gun in use against a target towed by an aircraft and it was impressive. The quick firing gun demolished targets in short order and then started to track up the towing wire towards the aircraft before being stopped.

The BREMEN class setting to work programme was in sharp contrast to that of the Royal Navy. A few years before, HMS SHEFFIELD, first of class of a new class of anti-aircraft destroyers, took more than a year before she was operational. Captain (later Admiral) Sandy Woodward was distraught and frustrated, not least because his important command time of a large ship was spent in a ship that just did not work. Even in the South Atlantic those few years later, the weapons and sensors were still not up to scratch. There was however, from SHEFFIELD in the South Atlantic, one message that was quickly picked up by other navies and that was to eschew aluminium. The sight of her hangar shutter doors blazing merrily after being hit became engraved on many minds, including mine. Almost immediately the sailor's kit lockers, the only aluminium in the BREMEN, were removed and replaced with steel lockers. They should have consulted us (in OCL and Container Fleets) first!

Chapter 17. Plain Bananas

Upon reaching my 54th birthday, and just as I thought that I was to have nothing to do with managing ships for the rest of my working life, I was approached by a headhunter for a ship manager's job. Flattered by such attention, I went for an interview out of interest only, because I was convinced that there were no decent jobs left in the industry and that I was in any case much too old. The interview went well and I left agreeing to put my name forward.

The post was put forward as Managing Director of Geest Line, the company which owned and managed four refrigerated fruit carriers on a weekly service to Barbados and the Windward Islands from Avonmouth at the River Avon's mouth in the Bristol Channel.

The van Geest family were farmers in the Hook of Holland area. Not long before WW2 two of the three brothers, Leonard and John, decided to emigrate to Eastern England to farm there. As farmers they were not conscripted and continued to work their farms throughout the war. After the war they expanded their activities to include trading in imported fresh produce. John also took a long holiday, visiting the Caribbean and particularly the Windward Islands. At that time the import of bananas was largely restricted to the Fyffes company, which sourced the fruit in Jamaica, and John was convinced that they could be cultivated satisfactorily in the Windwards and brought to the UK.   These islands were really desperately poor at that time. The world's sugar supply came more and more from sugar beet which could be grown in temperate climes, and tropical sugar cane became uncompetitive. John believed banana production could improve the islanders' lives, which it certainly did, and much later John was made CBE for his work. He developed the technique of shipping the fruit in cartons on pallets and learnt a lot about being a shipowner. By 1983 he had retired but still maintained an overview of the business. He also interviewed me informally before I joined.

His brother Leonard managed the produce business in the UK and was father of Leonard W and John W, both of whom entered the business. By 1983 Leonard had died and son Leonard W (referred to as just Leonard from here) headed the business assisted by his brother John. They were both farmers at heart and understood very little about shipping.

Following an interview with Leonard in the head office in Spalding, Lincolnshire, I agreed to take on the job and was accepted. I suggested that his company might agree to contract with Penn-maritime to provide my services full time and this was agreed. My office would be in Avonmouth and I would lease a flat locally to be close to the scene because neither Bunty nor I wanted to move home permanently. It was a very good job that we did not.

I started work in Avonmouth and studied the shipping operation carefully. The title of MD was a misnomer because I was really a Fleet Director. The reason for this was that my own commercial picture was incomplete because the revenue (even a theoretical intra-company revenue) accruing from the carriage of bananas was either not known or not divulged by the brothers. I was responsible for the revenue from general cargoes carried from the UK to the Caribbean, and for the small passenger revenue, and of course for all shipping costs.

Not surprisingly, the four sovereign governments in the Windwards wanted a part of the action in the shipping operation, short of owning and managing ships. Geest had wisely agreed to this and formed some sort of association with each country's Banana Association and the trade organisation known as WINBAN with which they were all associated. It was reasonable that this was not disclosed to a newcomer even if it precluded a proper profit target for Geest Line's "MD".

My paramount priority was to ensure that the ships ran well and that one appeared every weekend at Avonmouth with a full cargo of sound fruit. Bananas are very temperature sensitive and variations of even one half of a degree Fahrenheit can cause problems. If the UK market was short of fruit we would be instructed both to arrive on Sunday and to raise the temperature by one degree.

The whole of Geest's banana business in the UK hinged on timely arrivals, since from these there followed road transport to the depots, the ripening process, and delivery to customers just before the weekend on Friday or Saturday. During the time I was at Avonmouth there was never a late arrival and this was the norm. In 1982 Geest Line had transferred discharge operations from Barry, South Wales, to reduce UK road haulage costs to the UK ripening depots, but this move was later reversed.

The ships were fast modern fully refrigerated ships built by Smiths Dock on the Tees and they were fully decked for pallet operations. The two newer ships, GEESTBAY and GEESTPORT, could carry 3,500 tons weight of fruit and their two older sisters 3,000 tons. During the Falklands war GEESTPORT had become a STUFT (Ship taken up from trade) and joined the Royal Navy's fleet train in the South Atlantic, holding refrigerated provisions for them. They were single screw and their diesel engines provided a top speed of 20 knots and a service speed of 18 knots. They were manned by British officers, seamen and engine room ratings from the Windwards, and British catering crew. The islanders were long term Geest Line employees and were members of the National Union of Seamen. They were very good seafarers and kept the ships in sparkling condition.

I was instructed to visit the Caribbean and see things for myself in five islands (four Windwards and Barbados). Barbados was strictly a discharge port for outward cargo. Loading fruit began at St. George's, Grenada, known as the Spice Island, on Tuesday each week, followed by Kingston, St. Vincent, on Wednesday morning. Wednesday night was spent at Vieux Fort, St. Lucia, and Thursday at Castries, St. Lucia. Friday morning saw the ships in Roseau, Domenica, and Friday evening at Portsmouth in the same island. It was a week of fairly hectic cargo work interspersed with short sea passages. All the berths were on the Western (and lee) coasts but the ship handling of a single screw ship was performed by the master without pilots or tugs. It helped that the berths allowed berthing upwind into the Easterly trade wind which could blow quite strongly. I made a few passages in ships which not only helped me to meet the seafarers and see them at work but provided a more attractive alternative to the local inter-island airline, LIAT about which the locals believed that the acronym stood for "Luggage In Another Terminal".

When bananas were first shipped from the Windwards they were unpacked and carried aboard while still on the stem (which was about 4 feet high). Each stem contained a number of hands, each with its fingers which were single bananas. For this type of handling the ships had side doors in each hatch and the stems were passed by the shore gang to the ship gang at the door, who in turn took them and placed them in stow. To ease the handling task they were later packed in boxes which weighed about 30 lbs. The next innovation was to use pallets for the boxes since this not only reduced damage to the fruit but also allowed the use of mechanised pallet carriers. These greatly reduced handling costs, particularly in the UK. To my surprise, in the Windwards I found that two of the ports still loaded loose cartons by hand, which meant at Avonmouth they needed unloading by hand. At Vieux Fort during Wednesday night the cartons were stacked on the quay and the shore gang of women carried them up to the side door where they handed them over to a male member of the ship gang. At Portsmouth there was no alongside berth for the ship which anchored off the tiny port. The cartons were loaded on to pallets in small barges at the pier and towed out to the ship where unbelievably they were then manhandled off the pallets and into the ship by hand.

I made suggestions that the two ports concerned should follow the all-pallet system in the other four ports which worked very well and had been the practice for ages. A changeover was eventually made after lots of tooth sucking but it was a typical example of Geest's lack of understanding about the first principles of improving profitability.

I took a holiday at the end of my official visit and was joined by Bunty and three young friends. I had chartered a 40' sloop and took delivery in Marigot Bay in St. Lucia. We sailed South to the towering Pitons and from there to Admiralty Bay in Bequia, avoiding the main island of St. Vincent, which had an unfortunate reputation for robbery. From Bequia we went on to the truly beautiful Grenadines, and Tobago Cays with its magnificent anchorage protected from the Atlantic only by a submerged reef through which shoals of brightly coloured fish swarmed. It was a most welcome break.

Back in Avonmouth I started on plans to improve the efficiency of the business, with ships' costs as my first target. These were the responsibility of the fleet manager, John Hampton, who had been in the post for twelve years. John was a marine engineer who had been schooled by the old Blue Funnel which guaranteed that he knew what he was doing. The fact that the four ships performed their programmes like clockwork was clear testimony to his professional skills. But like many professional engineers of that era, he had not been greatly involved in overall commercial considerations or been asked to produce budgets. The most important cost that appeared high was the bunker fuel and lubricating oils. With their high speeds the ships were thirsty and no-one had challenged the suppliers' prices; they had merely been accepted. I introduced an old P&O colleague, Peter Sullivan, who was an experienced bunker broker, and in no time at all he brought prices from the same supplier sharply down to a realistic level.

The next cost centre to be targeted was the manning costs. Compared to the numbers borne in similar sized ships of other owners, we were noticeably overmanned. We were hesitant about reducing our Bajan crews because they were not only good but we were well aware of the need for the islanders to earn a living. John Hampton and his personnel manager opened negotiations with the crews to seek a manning reduction. The National Union of Seamen in the Bristol Channel heard of our approach and an official from their head office came forward to negotiate on behalf of the sailors. The ensuing negotiations were both difficult and long winded, but John did achieve the reduction he sought, albeit in a round-about way. It turned out that our sailors were well aware of what was going on in shipping in general and realised it was a time of change.

236

It helped that their UK rates of pay created affluence for them in their home islands.

Without reducing our overall establishment the sailors agreed they would spend fewer days on pay in the ships in future, which was an effective reduction in their annual earnings. As far as I was concerned it was full marks for everybody.

There were other small cost savings available, principally on the catering side, but they were not of the same order as those above. However the overall savings achieved amounted to £1million per annum which was 10 per cent of total ship management costs, and it was provided in a few months. In Spalding, the only person with a smile on his face was the chief accountant since either Leonard did not know about it or did not understand it.

In the outward trade to the islands we were in competition with five established carriers who all provided regular services although certainly not weekly. They appeared only rarely in the Windwards and then on the basis of a low rated large parcel of fertiliser for the plantations with a handful of general cargo at good rates. In the final analysis Geest carried 98 per cent of the general cargo. Barbados was a different matter since it was more affluent than the Windwards but even so Geest carried 45 per cent of the trade. This high percentage was not due to charging lower rates but was entirely due to the speed and timely service every week. There were clear parallels with the old P&O liner service to Japan in the 1960s. The majority of the outward cargoes to the islands consisted of what we called the "grocery" trade, with high value provisions, wines and spirits, and tobacco based goods required for the growing tourist business. Our consignee customers found weekly deliveries attractive since it enabled them to keep stocks low. We had also to bear in mind that Florida was much closer than Europe, and the USA was a top class grocery supplier with a low cost barge service for the sea transport.

In this trade Geest Line was an absolute winner but we still always had vacant space on outward voyages and the tourist trade was only growing slowly. On travelling about, I began to believe that we should take a day out of the ships' Avonmouth stay to include another island discharge port. This would improve ship utilisation and provide additional revenue from the high rated groceries. My first choice for an additional port was St. Johns, Antigua. This was not a banana producing island but it had developed very extensive tourist facilities on a similar basis to Barbados. Antigua in the Leeward Islands is not only picturesque but has an important place in our naval history. In Nelson's time it contained an Admiralty Dockyard which is still there but is now a tourist attraction. In the nearby island of Nevis Captain Nelson met and married a widow, Frances Nisbet.

On a visit to Antigua I met a local man who farmed pineapples on a small scale and mostly for local consumption. He told me that if a weekly shipping service to the UK was mounted he would certainly support it with his fruit. At the time (1984) in the UK fresh pineapples were both scarce and expensive and in the supermarket in Bristol they were more than £1 each. I knew that in earlier days John van Geest had applied his farming and shipping skills to growing pineapples in the Windwards and had seen several farms started that soon produced good fruit. However, not one ever reached the market in the UK because they were all stolen by the islanders and eaten. This did not happen with bananas since they were shipped green and only eaten locally baked as a vegetable, which is much less succulent than a sweet ripe pineapple.

In Spalding my suggestion went down like a lead balloon and I was instructed to seek more cargo for the existing discharge ports. A few months after I left Geest Line I was interested to learn that not only was Antigua included for outward cargo weekly but two other smaller islands would be included on a fortnightly basis.

Although Leonard had told me to report directly to him, when necessary it proved very difficult to contact him. I did not need to report often, but locating him could take up to three weeks and nobody else in Spalding seemed able to assist. He did occasionally appear in Avonmouth which was usually to berate me for not selling more space. At one stage he suggested Geest Line should set up grocery stores on the islands and would not believe me when

Plain Bananas

I tried to explain that this would be a well worn track to disaster. When Blue Funnel changed their name to Ocean Transport and Trading, they immediately lost customers who believed that Ocean would compete with their business and their shipments would be free of any freight charge. I was sure we would see a similar result if we tried it in the islands. In any case we carried 98 per cent of the traffic as it was.

Geest Line was a member of a shipping conference of lines called WITASS. This was a cartel of shipowners who set rates and other conditions of carriage. In the days of cargo liners carrying break bulk cargoes they were commonplace, but the advent of containerisation saw their influence diminish and in many countries price-fixing was ruled illegal and subject to penalties at law. Apart from enjoying some good dinners I was never enthused about conferences because the whole business was two-faced. The members would sit around a table to establish rates which they would all agree to quote, but many would then depart to their offices and cut rates for special customers or offer rebates. I went to one meeting and was soon aware that some things never change so decided that Geest Line would quit WITASS, and Spalding endorsed my action. Apart from giving us complete pricing freedom, this also meant that we could save the fees charged by the conference for its administration. There was absolutely no need for us to cut our rates because our service was impeccable. From time to time we would carry the materials for a construction project on an island funded by an overseas government's aid programme. If this entailed a series of regular shipments over a few months, it justified a special project rate and we did not have to ask conference colleagues for their agreement.

Geest Line's small passenger business needed no attention from me. The ships carried 12 passengers in comfortable double cabins with their own facilities and despite quite high prices the cabins were mostly filled. A three-and-a-half week round trip took in five Caribbean islands and lots of sunshine. There was no casino or flower painting lessons but there was a very good bill of fare and life in a small friendly ship. Some happy customers returned every year

Sea Officer

As time in the job wore on I could sense that I did not fit in, particularly with Leonard. He did in fact invite me to be an employee instead of being provided by Pennmaritime, and went on to suggest that my pension was transferred into Geest's own pension fund. Whilst being anxious about the pension position I did agree that the Geest actuaries should examine it and make proposals for a transfer.

By great good fortune their report stated that my position was incompatible because the transfer value was more than three times the value of any other employee's pension and would give me a theoretical figure of more than 50 years in the Geest fund, which could not work. It also highlighted for me that Geest employees were generally not well remunerated. This was something I also sensed from colleagues who were envious of my independent status.

It was all pointing to an end of my job and there was one particular incident that I believe hastened matters. Leonard had been on holiday with his family in the islands for two weeks during which time he had visited two ships on their voyages. On his return he sent for me and reported that one ship had not offered the usual courtesies required for their Chairman, in that the Master and other senior officers were ashore when he arrived. I offered apologies from Geest Line for this fall from grace and said I would have words with the Master. Returning to Avonmouth I found that the master was at home in South Wales on leave and asked him to call on me in my office. I explained what it was all about and asked for his comment. The answer was quite simple; neither he nor the particular ship had been near the islands during the whole of Leonard's visit. Recovering my poise, I immediately apologised profusely for the mistake. My apology was accepted and I took him for lunch since he was a most steady and reliable master. In the afternoon I managed to speak to Leonard on the telephone and reported events. Leonard was not the slightest bit interested in my report and offered no apology for his mistake. I expressed my disgust, Geest employees just did not do that.

It was not long before I was dismissed, but it was not difficult to understand the reason. After leaving Geest I did keep in touch with a number of ex colleagues, including passing them bits of information about shipping when they requested it. A few years later, John Hampton, who had been an employee for 15 years, was summarily dismissed without warning and poorly paid off after much loyal and efficient service. Happily he found himself a job as Chief Superintendent Engineer with William Cory's in London, who were a very old established British company that operated tugs, barges and bunkering services.

I was very chuffed that he chose me as a reference for his new job, and had a fascinating telephone conversation with his boss-to-be, director Bob Anderson. "Can you tell me about John Hampton?" he asked to which my answer was that he was a Blue Funnel engineer. He repeated his question and to avoid repeating my answer I had to think hard to respond detailing John's many qualities. After all, Blue Funnel Engineers were a breed apart.

Chapter 18. Solar Power

After leaving Avonmouth I returned to my house to work both on shipping tasks when they appeared, which was not often, and to assist Victoria with PennLine Systems. Such shipping tasks as there were proved of little real interest and I did not pursue the business very hard.

I did make contact with an old colleague, Captain Rodney. St J Fancourt, and we worked on several projects together. Rodney's career had been very similar to my own: he left Pangbourne a couple of terms before me and entered Union Castle Line as an apprentice. This company, later called British and Commonwealth, was another long established shipping company with a large fleet of passenger and cargo liners serving South Africa. After about ten years' sea service, he transferred to a company managing cable laying ships as fleet director, where he acquired a great deal of specialist knowledge about the bottom of the sea and how to deal with it in practical terms. His skills included knowing exactly how much telephone cable to ship before laying it across the Atlantic, because it was distinctly embarrassing to run out a mile short of the shore. After several years his employing company was bought out by GEC and he was dismissed so he set up his own company called Ocean Moorings Ltd. He played a major part in establishing how to secure large floating platforms, like oil drilling rigs, to the sea bed with specially designed anchors and other equipment. He was also a Captain RNR, and CO of London Division RNR when I was CO of Solent Division.

Quite suddenly, at the same time, my life underwent a surprising change at age 57. Rodney telephoned me one Sunday afternoon with a long story, which I did not believe for a moment. He had been contacted by an acquaintance, who worked in the world of pension funds and who had in fact set up a pension fund for Ocean

Solar Power

Moorings. The finance man had called from a flat in Aachen, Germany, which was the home of a Siemens engineer, his personal friend. The engineer and another Siemens colleague were employed at a company called Interatom, whose main activity was producing nuclear powered generating stations. The company also produced photovoltaic solar panels and was completing a project for the Greek government using solar panels to power navigational buoys and beacons with lights in the Aegean. They were looking for someone in the UK to assist them in marketing the solar panels. Whilst Rodney was interested, he had no experience of selling goods in Ocean Moorings, whereas he knew Pennmaritime was experienced and he wondered if we would like to assist.

I just could not believe my ears and thought Rodney had either lost his trolley or been heavy handed with the gin bottle before his Sunday lunch. A nuclear engineering company? The Aegean was one thing for sunshine, but what about the North of Scotland? In December the sun is only over the horizon for about seven hours and even then it is likely to be obscured as the storms track in from the Atlantic.

Rodney was completely unperturbed and suggested we should look into the matter carefully. His financial acquaintance was aware that Rodney knew a great deal about the UK manufacturers and users of navigational aids besides which he was a younger brother of the Corporation of Trinity House, who for centuries operated the majority of English lights. There were also light authorities for Scotland in Edinburgh and for Ireland in Dublin. We researched all the information we could lay our hands on. To start with, Interatom, based at Bergisch Gladbach in the Rhineland, turned out to be a department of Siemens power generation division KWU. Within the division there was a small department developing photovoltaic equipment which was manufactured in a Siemens factory in München.

The photovoltaic effect had been discovered by scientists in the 19th century and works quite simply by producing electrical energy when a semi-conductor is exposed to sunlight. The electrical output is so small that the technology was virtually ignored until the 1960s, when interest in space for both unmanned and manned spacecraft emerged. In outer space the sun is always shining and there are no nights of darkness.

There are in fact two types of "solar panels" useful to mankind and many people still confuse them. Photovoltaic modules produce electricity whilst photo thermal panels use solar energy to heat water without any electrical involvement. Photovoltaic modules use cells strung together in series electrically and are usually framed behind armoured glass and sealed against weather at the back.

Rodney arranged an appointment for me to meet the senior electrical engineer of Trinity House and what I was to learn from him completely changed my outlook. Whilst still in a development stage, I learned that the future of powering navigational aids would lie with solar electric power. At the time the aids were powered by acetylene gas, which had been in use for over a century. But this power source was losing appeal, because the cost of the gas was rising steeply, the heavy gas cylinders were cumbersome to replace, and the specialist gas engineers needed to service the equipment were just dying out.

Armed with a great deal of information, we expressed interest to Siemens and a meeting in my study was arranged, with Victoria summoned to add her sales and marketing skills. Reiner Rosendahl and Klaus Poppek, two very large gentlemen from Bergisch Gladbach, arrived with a carry-all full of modules, which they laid out on the carpet glass face up. Bunty appeared with coffee and I was worried that she might tread on the glass but Reiner, sensing my apprehension, stood up and marched all over them in his big boots. At least they appeared to be sailor-proof.

As we all talked on, Rodney and I became more interested. The outcome was that we arranged to visit Germany for another meeting to call on the senior management and to learn more. In January 1987 Siemens decided that their photovoltaic department should become Siemens Solar GmbH with its own directors and Rodney and I arrived in Bergisch Gladbach in really bitter cold to meet them. We agreed that Pennmaritime would be both agent and

Solar Power

distributor in the UK and spent the whole week in Germany as a teach-in to learn about the business, which included a day in the factory in München to witness how monocrystalline solar modules were created in dairy conditions.

There was a great deal to learn about the technical aspects of designing and supplying stand-alone solar generators. Whilst storage batteries were unnecessary in space, on the earth's surface they had to be part of a system. We were given a copy of Siemens Solar's CAD programme which provided information about local insolation values for most parts of the world on a hourly and monthly basis. From this we could determine the size of an array of modules and the battery required to meet a given electrical load. The programme also revealed local shade temperatures, since systems are heat sensitive. I used this programme for more than 15 years and it never let me down. What I designed worked well and without power cuts. The one failure I can recall was caused by President Saddam Hussain. When he decided to torch the Kuwaiti oil fields, the thick black smoke from them rolled over the border into Northern Saudi Arabia and some stations there closed down.

It is extraordinary how well the background that Rodney and I had was suited to hoisting in all this new information. At Pangbourne, Rat Davey's teaching of physics covered many relevant factors, starting with simple DC electrical engineering. As old fashioned navigators using sextants, we instinctively knew where the sun was at any time of the day, month and year for any latitude in the world. Later, when I went out to the market, it was clear that this factor was a closed book to engineers with otherwise impressive qualifications.

Pennmaritime purchased a small stock of modules and controllers from München and started a low key sales campaign. Prospective customers were generally interested, but the navaid market was not quite ready to make the change. The price of modules was high (and still is) and our first customers were yacht chandlers who sold on to yacht owners to charge existing batteries when their boats were idle at moorings. In 1987, our first year, turnover was only £18,000.

But slowly the business grew, and caravans and campers started to use modules. The navaid industry came to life and we ended up powering the navaids of a number of ports, including the long river Humber. The water and gas industries became customers so that they could power remotely their on-site measurement sensors and radio readings back to a computer at their works at pre-set intervals.

Our first big break through came from the maritime area. During the Iran/Iraq war a large number of mines were laid from aircraft in the Gulf and the Strait of Hormuz. These needed clearing and eventually NATO despatched several squadrons of MCM ships to the Gulf, including the Royal Navy's 1st MCMS. Before the arrival on the scene of the Global Positioning System (GPS), Racal Marine Systems (now named Thales) had developed a position fixing system called Hyperfix, which could provide MCM ships with position fixes accurate to five metres at a range of 200 kilometres. This needed a chain of four or five shore stations located accurately but invariably in places miles from anywhere and without electrical power supplies. The Navy had commissioned Racal to build and store five stations for deployment worldwide when required under Racal's management.

Racal had been experimenting with a number of possible power sources, none of which proved attractive. I made a call on their field management office in Paignton, Devon, and provided a demonstration of modules. A fortnight later they telephoned to say they had received orders to deploy in the Gulf and asked if we could provide five solar generators in a week, which included a bank holiday. Fortunately Siemens in München had the modules and controllers in stock, and Racal purchased batteries in the Gulf. But the modules needed a support structure to tilt them up to 50° and secure them to the ground, for which the Siemens lead time was two months.

I designed a structure in aluminium extrusion and my son-in-law Tony Britton, an aero engineer, built all five structures in his garage in four very long days. We took them to Racal New Malden bang on time for a QA inspection which consisted only in making sure that one module would bolt up satisfactorily to the structure. This accomplished, everything was whisked off to Heathrow. Racal were pleased and later placed orders for about 30 more stations along the South coast of the Gulf which were all working well ten years later.

They also put us in touch with their sister company, Racal Survey, in Great Yarmouth. They used a smaller system called Microfix for short term offshore survey work and their requirement was for portable generators that could be easily and frequently transported by air from site to site, and handled with fork lift trucks. For this we developed Pennmaritime Genkits, which consisted of minimal supports, modules and controllers, all packed in strong plywood boxes. Racal Survey in the end ordered 70 Genkits and told us they worked well for them. They also worked well for Pennmaritime because we employed temporary tradesmen and enjoyed both a high margin and added value for our business.

Another early success was to secure an order from Cable and Wireless for the Falkland Islands, in the face of strong competition. After the war in 1982 our lady Prime Minister supported a complete new telephone system with its own earth satellite station and commissioned C&W to provide it. To cover the huge areas involved, they needed to include eight microwave relay stations, set upon tree-less hills covered with scrub. There were no paths, let alone roads, to reach the hilltops and all the equipment had to be dragged through the scrub on sledges for installation.

The batteries selected by C&W were of the wet bloc type, filled with sulphuric acid on site, and had to be sent to Port Stanley by sea, since wet acid is not allowed in aircraft. Individually manufactured by Varta in Germany as single two volt cells they had an expected life of 15 years, and 12 such cells were needed to provide a 24 volt battery to power the radio equipment. C&W insisted upon galvanised steel for the support structures and told us that the constraints imposed by the sledges meant they should be shipped in small pieces for bolting together on site. This we arranged with our steelwork contractor. In service one structure located close to a helipad started to vibrate when the Chinooks were hovering overhead but we suggested that C&W asked for welding assistance from the Navy's repair ship in the islands which solved the problem.

The advent of a new dial-up telephone system proved so popular with the islanders that the load on the repeater stations soared well above predictions. C&W solved this by adding a wind turbine to create a solar/wind hybrid. These increased the generation but the wind force in the Falklands was not kind to the wind turbines. Twelve years later C&W's chief engineer told me that all our equipment was working well. In that time, the only spares required from us were for the charge controllers at a cost of just £12. This was marvellous for the job satisfaction factor but much less so for Pennmaritime's sales ledger.

As the business grew we moved to outside premises. These were certainly not palatial, but provided comfortable offices and a showroom together with storage space for stock and a workshop for creating aluminium structures. At this time there were no suppliers of solar module mounting structures and it was profitable to do it ourselves. We devised a number of mountings for small stations, which consisted of aluminium pipe and galvanised steel scaffold clamps that allowed customers to set the required tilt and orientation of the module. It was hardly rocket science but was used with success and soon copied by our competitors. I did think about a patent but knew this was both costly and longwinded and who on earth would grant a patent on a use for a scaffolding clamp?

With proper premises we also took on two part time staff. David Colley, who had worked with me in New York, took over the leisure industry sales on a commission only basis. He clearly enjoyed being amongst yachts and caravans and was at his best organising and manning our stand at trade exhibitions. Maria Willoughby, after many years of being a private secretary to chairmen and directors, took on the job of office manager and learned a lot of new skills. She did a number of jobs for us, ranging from purchasing to dunning our debtors and even in the latter role could remain bright and polite (which I could not!).

It was vital to keep our costs down because the market was both small and very competitive. To many would-be entrepreneurs the prospect of being in a new and emerging business area, coupled with its attraction as environmentally sound, was apparently irresistible. It just would not support glamorous offices and expensive cars. We saw many come and go, including one whose first business attempt lost him his savings and a bank loan. Undaunted he mortgaged his house for a second attempt and lost that too. Even the big players like Siemens could not make profits out of showpiece large projects sponsored by governments. There were however a small number of young enthusiasts who proceeded carefully and are still there today.

Also beginning to emerge were very ordinary citizens who wanted to go down the environmental road and reduce CO_2 emissions by putting arrays on the roofs of their houses. One theory that was suggested was that if every South facing roof in England was clad with modules, they would together generate annually the same amount of electrical energy as we consumed. This was purely hypothetical because most of it would be generated at both the wrong time of the day and the year, and large scale electricity storage is not yet a practical proposition. But it certainly made many people aware of what might be possible in the future. Some did indeed bite the bullet and spent their savings on equipment.

Roof arrays usually have no storage batteries and are connected to the grid. This means that the householders can import power from the grid when they need it and export power to the grid when their roof is generating and they have no use for the power. The financial considerations are unattractive on their own. Roof arrays have an installed cost of about £6,000 per kilowatt peak (kWp). 1 kWp measures about 9 M2 and in Southern England will generate about 750 kilowatt hours (kWh) per year of AC electricity matched to the grid's characteristics. Householders may be able to save themselves some of the energy they import from the grid at about 9p per kWh and obtain a credit of about 2p per kWh for what they export. An array of 1 kWp will save the emission from power stations of about 344 kilograms of CO_2 per year. The equipment is rugged, has no moving parts and has an expected life of more than 30 years.

Sponsors for roof arrays did slowly emerge and we were involved with some of them. The established Quaker housing associations that provided low cost housing in poor areas supported the concept where derelict buildings were pulled down and replaced. At Ballymena in Ulster the local town council secured millennium funds to build an environmental centre (ecos) which included an array of 12 kWp. However the high costs and poor return discouraged many private house owners from proceeding.

Outside the UK we witnessed other countries, particularly Germany and Japan, subsidising the cost of arrays for private householders by 50 per cent or more. Germany introduced a one thousand roofs programme. When this came to an end they introduced a further such programme, which was followed by a 100,000 roofs programme. In the UK the government sat on its hands despite many pleas for support, until at last in 2004 they announced grants for private householders of typically 50 per cent, as well as grants for public buildings.

This did open the floodgates and several millions of pounds were soon disbursed in grants. It was always very gratifying to witness the delight of private customers with small houses as they saw power being supplied to the grid from their roofs on their export meters.

Pennmaritime continued to pioneer aluminium structures on which to mount arrays of roof modules. These have to be fastened by roof straps between the tiles secured to the rafters of the roof. In the UK there are a large number of different tile types which all need different styles of roof straps. For the earlier arrays there was no supplier of kits of "fixings" that were suitable for the different tile types although they did appear later. In the meantime the Pennmaritime design worked well and was cost effective. Several years later they are still securely in place.

As my 70th birthday approached in 1999, it was time to think about reducing my workload and David Colley was seeking to do the same. My family dropped hints that I had reached a point where I should not be trading goods or handling money. My first thoughts were to locate a small or medium-sized electrical company that might create a photovoltaic department to tack on to their existing business. Our business had reached a turnover of about £300,000 per year, we had a good record with the 240 customers on our list, and more than 400 names on our prospect list. However, I could find no spark of interest at all.

I reported what I was doing to Bernard Bein, then our sales manager in Siemens Solar, München, who took note and asked to be kept advised. We had enjoyed good relationships with him and most of his colleagues throughout our association and earned their respect. Whilst we did not create the sales volume of their German distributors they could see that our UK market share was rising; although it was still a small market.

In the UK we also kept in touch with Siemens plc, which was the UK arm of Siemens AG. Our contact was Tony Wake in the marine department in Sunbury, and we kept him apprised of our progress despite not having a commercial connection. He did however pass news of my forthcoming departure up the line to his bosses at their office in the Manchester area. He duly appeared with one of them who asked to have a look at the totality of our photovoltaic business which we revealed to him. His appraisal revealed that the business was too small for Siemens plc to take in-house in the UK. I thought this was the end of the matter, but for reasons unknown to me the departmental manager decided otherwise and arrived with a small team to take a look at the business and decided they did want to take it in. Bernard Bein was appalled; his experience in other countries with the local Siemens company had always been negative. If Siemens at a top level wanted to take in their own company's business, there was little I could do about it.

On 31 March 1999 we closed our offices and threw a very good party. The next day the photovoltaic department of Siemens plc opened in Sunbury. I then joined them as a part time consultant to be rewarded by a sales commission on results on a reducing basis over the next three years. Siemens had recruited a young sales engineer, Matthew Douch, who was bright and enthusiastic, and I set about training him in photovoltaic technology which he hoisted in well. David Colley and I persuaded just about all of Pennmaritime's customers to purchase from Siemens.

It turned out to be hell on wheels. Apart from recruiting Matthew, who previously had no sales or commercial experience, Siemens plc had made no preparations whatsoever. The work was co-located with Tony Wake. Although not officially involved, he gave enormous assistance to Matthew (and me) in treading a path through the Siemens jungle. A major problem for a small business was the Siemens worldwide computer programme provided by SAP. For the CEO of a major multinational, it provided an instant and daily report of invoiced sales and new orders placed. It worked very well for Siemens' large and successful divisions such as power generation and railway rolling stock, whose staff included those trained at length and great expense in how to use it.

For a tiny photovoltaic department it was a disaster, not least because for any sale a computer driven sales order took 15 minutes to key in. For a customer needing a £25 charge controller it was ridiculous, and there was no (legal) way of accepting payment in cash because a cleared credit account had to be created and this took days. The departmental management had refused to agree to any staff training or programme simplification because SAP's fees were astronomic, and in any case the managers did not know how it worked themselves.

Thankfully (for Pennmaritime's commission!) Matthew kept the sales going, and found new customers but the promised marketing skills of Siemens never put in an appearance. The departmental managers had not an idea of what it was all about. Just over a year on the Siemens plc board decided to close down the Sunbury office. The management in the North West were moved on, and Matthew was sacked. Tony Wake was also retired early, but in a manner not reflecting his long service and the fact he was Siemens first British employee after WW2. Control of the business was transferred to another small department in Manchester, whose knowledge of the business was even less than their predecessors. In six months their sales were almost nil, and those sales made were at distress prices to clear stock. Small customers were ignored. Pennmaritime's

Solar Power

agreement with Siemens plc was terminated early and I set out to obtain compensation. My letters asking for a meeting to discuss this were ignored until I wrote to Siemens' chairman in Germany, after which things started to move. At a meeting in Manchester the matter was resolved but it was difficult because the new department claimed they had no files, and we had to provide copies of documents from our files. It was a disgraceful performance for a major company.

I have no doubt that Siemens plc incurred losses but it was they who decided to take in the business. The saddest thing for me about the whole matter was that what we had built they had destroyed, and I felt strongly that the customer base had been let down.

With the encouragement of Siemens Solar GmbH, I set out to find another UK distributor. The most promising candidate was an established Pennmaritime customer with whom we had dealt for about ten years. A B Butt Ltd were a long established and family owned company in Leicester, who employed about 40 and were engaged in the automotive electrical business for all types of road vehicles, including caravans. Ken Muddimer was then MD and was the owner of a super caravan whose interior décor was up to TITANIC standards. We sold him a small module to fit on the roof and keep his battery charged and he was pleased with his purchase. Butts set about supplying and fitting caravans and campers with modules, and branched out into other photovoltaic applications.

It was the start of a long and happy customer/supplier relationship. In 2001 Ken retired as MD and was replaced by Simon Butt, who was the son of chairman Peter Butt. Simon was soon in control of the whole of the business and was enthusiastic about furthering the photovoltaic business, along with the other activities.

Siemens Solar approved the choice and I accompanied Ken and Simon to München for a meeting with all of Siemens Solar's European distributors. These meetings were always popular, not least because it was possible to discuss matters with other solar people. This meeting was extraordinary because it was announced that Siemens Solar had been acquired by Shell Solar NV and it was the first time the staff of Siemens Solar were told of such a major change. The rationale was that Siemens no longer wished to lose money competing with oil companies whilst Shell wanted Siemens' technical skills to add to their own marketing skills. The Shell Solar MD kept on talking about selling petrol, which was slightly un-nerving to photovoltaic engineers. But now was the time for me to let Simon get on with it.

I continued to support Simon on a diminishing scale for a few years. Initially I instructed him and a colleague on how to design arrays using the Siemens Solar CAD programme. A particular joy was to get in touch with a large number of my old customers and to make sure they knew where they could purchase modules and other equipment. They welcomed the change and a surprising number are still customers today. I passed over all my structure drawings for use in A B Butt's workshops and some are still used.

When the government began giving grants for grid connected arrays for private householders I assisted Simon with designs and some installations, but the time had arrived when I became a liability on a roof. Besides which, Simon had quickly absorbed all the required knowledge and had himself introduced the many improvements in technique necessary to meet the installation rules that came with the grants.

Photovoltaics had provided me with yet another career that fascinated me and produced great enjoyment. I also helped sailors use solar modules for their boats and twice visited Tenerife before the start of the transatlantic rowing races to Barbados. In each case about 30 competitors rowed 14' two handed boats for about 2,900 miles and they needed solar modules to power their equipment which included GPS, water makers and other equipment. It was also great fun assisting many of the competitors in their preparations to brave the Atlantic in their small craft.

Chapter 19. Reflections

It was very saddening to witness the end of P&O because for more than 150 years it had provided so much service to its customers, including the nation. It had also provided well managed employment, taxes to Her Majesty's Government, and business for suppliers, and even dividends to shareholders. In the end the British shipping nemesis was unstoppable. The arrival on the scene of Honorary Commodore Lord Jeffrey Sterling as chairman brought hope that he could continue its existence and he certainly made a huge effort to do so, at a time when most other British ship owners had thrown in the towel. Whilst his business skills and experience had been acquired elsewhere, it did not take him very long to learn which end of a ship went first, and to join the list of outstanding P&O chairmen. At the last pensioner's lunch before his retirement, he recalled that, a few years previously, the company had eleven operating divisions and 85,000 employees.

What had happened to change the scene so dramatically? It was surely the relentless demands of the financial community for ever more profits without regard to any other consideration. That community has a lot to answer for. In insisting that money is their only god so much else is destroyed. Too many people do not enjoy their boring computer-orientated work, and the rich/poor gap is much too great. The recent run on a UK bank has demonstrated very clearly both extraordinary greed and irresponsibility, together with the fact that no one on either side believes a single word of the other, with very good reason.

Surely the last 50 years have demonstrated that capitalism is the most successful type of society in which to live, and for providing economic growth. The great Communist experiment was an economic and social disaster. Even socialism, with its caring aspirations, was economically stagnant. Free enterprise is a precious freedom but if it cannot regulate itself, Governments must do so, starting at the top and not the bottom. Some of the activities of directors who break monopoly and competition laws, or who plunder their publicly owned companies, are deeply detested by the community, and they should be dealt with as individuals, not as part of a body corporate. The new law which allows individual directors to be sued by shareholders is perhaps a step in the right direction, but private shareholders may be reluctant to sue very wealthy directors.

The P&O house flag still flies where it should not, in ships owned by others. What I and many other ancient mariners find unnerving is the sheer size of cruise ships, and their passenger capacity. In the transport world there are always accidents, and these will continue. When CANBERRA, with about 3,000 on board, became a floating hulk in the 1960s, we were extremely lucky that she was in tranquil waters, close to other ships, and the Malta dockyard. How on earth will we bring 5,000 souls from the middle of a storm in a large and empty ocean to a safe place? Matters are not helped by a cruise line's statement that once their ships are at sea they are a law unto themselves and no one else.

The cross-Channel ferries still belong to P&O but cannot make the profits required. At Dover there is too much competing capacity with Eurotunnel's trains, which are a loss maker but government supported. Without denigrating the tunnel's engineering achievement, I have always supported the bridge concept for both trains and road vehicles. A bridge would not need the huge annual operating costs of ships and shuttle trains, and the use of so much land. The motorway bridges over the Great Belt in Denmark and the Gorge du Tarn in France prove it can be done, and they seem to work well for all types of traffic.

The Royal Naval Reserve is still in existence, albeit in a very different shape from 50 years ago. The new shape provides many of the skills needed in the 21st century, but seafaring in small ships is no longer the priority. Like many others of my time I did not join to be

Reflections

a press officer, although today they are an important part of the Navy.

In the current deadly conflict against our dedicated enemies, fighting ships have to take a back seat, although the Royal Marines are right at the forefront. All three armed services, together with their reserves, are being overtaxed and leant upon by a government engaging in a serious war with insufficient funds and broad public support. It looks as if it will take a very long time to succeed.

We are an island nation, and will still need ships and sailors for several more decades. There is no black magic in living in a ship, but it is quite different to living ashore. As far as the Merchant Service is concerned I believe it to be quite wrong that they now sit in classrooms to complete their nautical studies to a master's level until they are about 22 years of age. They then have to achieve three years sea time as apprentices before becoming a third mate. Apart from anything else, at this age they rightly need greater financial consideration than is required for people four years their junior, and this places an economic burden which many inter-national employers cannot accept. Surely sea officers need to spend a lot of time at sea.

There is perhaps another way to encourage young men and women to become part of the corps of sea officers that an island nation needs, and this involves the Royal Navy. It would require recruit-ting undergraduates at the maritime technical colleges as sub lieutenants RNR, and paying them a retainer when they served in merchant ships, which would help to bridge the gap between the commercial and military salaries. In time of war this would provide sea officers for both commercial ships and warships. It would allow the Royal Navy's officers to concentrate on fighting the ships, at which they have always excelled, whilst providing them with the ship management skills available from masters and mates, which they also need. It really did work brilliantly two centuries ago, and in two world wars since; we often seem to forget former skills that had proved so successful.

SEA OFFICER APPENDICES

Appendix 1.
Bibliography.

Baker, Richard	Dry Ginger	W H Allen	1977
Bedser, Alec & Eric	Our Cricket Story	Evans Brothers	
Blake, George	Bi Centenary 1956	Collins	1956
Campbell, Cdr A B	Yarns of the Seven Seas	Pitman	
Costello & Hughes	Battle of the Atlantic	Book Club Assoc	1977
Course, Capt A G	Painted Ports	Hollis & Carter	1961
Davis, Jim	You and Your Ships	Memoir Club	2006
Gilbert, Martin	Second World War	Wiedenfeld	1989
Hague, Arnold	Destroyers for G Britain	Greenhill	1990
Hough, Richard	Former Naval Person	Wiedenfeld	1985
Kemp, Peter, Editor	Oxford Companion to Ships and the Sea	Oxford U P	1976
Kennedy, Ludovic	Pursuit	Collins	1974
Kerr, George F	Business in Great Waters, P&O WW2 History	Faber & Faber	1951
Mahan, Captain A T	Life of Nelson	Sampson, Low	1897
Marshall, Sandy	Taking the Adventure	Michael Russell	1999
Massie, Robert K	Castles of Steel	Jonathan Cape	2003
Oman, Carola	Nelson	Hodder & Stoughton	1947
Padfield, Peter	Beneath the House Flag of P&O	Hutchinson	1981
Padfield, Peter	Doenitz, Last Fuehrer	Victor Gollanz	1984
Penney, Capt Stephen	River Thames and Approaches	J D Potter	1898
Pocock, Tom	The Young Nelson in the Americas	Collins	1980
Symonds, RA Sir Wm	Memoirs	Longmans	1858
Various	Jane's Fighting Ships	Jane's	
Woodward, Ad Sir Sandy	One Hundred Days	Harper Collins	1992
Worcester, G R G	The Floating Population in China	Vetch & Lee	1970
Ziegler, Philip	Mountbatten	Collins	1985

PENINSULAR AND ORIENTAL STEAM NAVIGATION COMPANY

AVENUE 8000. CABLES: PENINSULAR LONDON   TELEGRAMS: PENINSULAR STOCK LONDON

Please address reply to
THE MANAGING DIRECTORS

OFFICERS' DEPARTMENT.
REF: LRH/DL.

122, LEADENHALL STREET,
LONDON, E.C.3,
4th April,1945.

Cadet M.D.Penney,
  "Cornerways",
    Massetts Road,
      HORLEY, Surrey.

Dear Sir,
        We have to request you to report to Captain G.Bridge at the
offices of our Agents, Messrs. General Steam Navigation Company, 95,
Bothwell Street, Glasgow on Tuesday, 10th April, prepared to join a
steamer as Cadet. It will be necessary for you to commence to travel
on Monday, and we enclose voucher for your rail journey, dated accordingly
which should be presented at the railway booking office and exchanged
for a ticket.
        Kindly acknowledge the receipt of this letter.
        We are, dear Sir,
          Yours faithfully,

For the Managing Directors

Appendix 2.
First P&O ship appointment.

BROADLANDS,
ROMSEY,
HAMPSHIRE.
SO5 9ZD.

TELEPHONE
ROMSEY 3333

19th October, 1970

Dear Penney,

I am writing to thank you as President, and all the members, of the Wardroom Mess of H.M.S. Wessex very much indeed for the really splendid 'Trafalgar Night Dinner' to which you invited me last Friday.

You certainly have a tremendous spirit bubbling up in your Mess and they formed the most encouraging audience to talk to.

I am afraid I had to recast my speech a bit as the evening went on when I realised they didn't want to hear too much serious stuff nor did they want too long a speech.   I hope it turned out all right in the end.

I do admire all that the RNR are doing under the present difficult conditions and send you my best wishes for your future success.

yours sincerely

Mountbatten of Burma

Appendix 3.
Letter from an Admiral of the Fleet.

From ADMIRAL SIR EDWARD ASHMORE, GCB DSC ADC
First and Principal Naval Aide-de-Camp

MINISTRY OF DEFENCE
MAIN BUILDING WHITEHALL LONDON SW1A 2HB

Telephone 01-218 2656 (Direct Dialling)
01-218 9000 (Switchboard)

No. 200/10   12th February 1975.

Dear Penney,

    I am glad to inform you that Her Majesty
The Queen has been graciously pleased to
appoint you as Naval Aide-de-Camp. Your
appointment will take effect from 1st March 1975.

    If Aides-de-Camp are required, duty of
attendance will be assigned in rotation as
far as possible. I should be glad, therefore,
if you would keep me informed of any change
in your address during the period of your
appointment.

Yours sincerely,

Edward Ashmore

Captain M.D. Penney, RD, RNR.

Appendix 4.
Letter from the First Sea Lord.

P&O Building Leadenhall Street London EC3   Telephone 01-283 8000

2nd September 1971

Dear Michael

Many thanks for your note and for sending
your good wishes to my wife and myself. We
both appreciate this very much.

I remember Bodley's cabin well on account of
the toys which you recall. I am glad that
you remember one particular interview in his
cabin since it was a turning point in your
career, and I am very glad to have had some
hand in it. I send you my best wishes for
its and your future success.

Yours sincerely

D. J. Anderson

M D Penney Esq
Planning Division
P & O Building

Appendix 5.
Letter from Sir Donald Anderson.

Appendix 6.
The Tunnage of Ships.

There is a great deal of confusion and ignorance about how ships are measured. With the exception of tankers and bulk carriers the majority of merchant ships are measured by their Gross Registered tonnage, (GRT) which has nothing whatsoever to do with weight and all to do with the enclosed volume of ships whereby 100 cubic feet equals one ton.

Tankers and bulk carriers are measured in long tons weight of 2240 lbs, (or metric tonnes of 1000 kilograms, about 2200 lbs) which is not what they weigh but the weight of cargo they can lift.

The size of warships is usually measured by their actual weight, which is also their displacement ("Eureka" said Archimedes in his bath) in tons or tonnes, and includes all their fuel, fresh water, ammunition, stores and ship's company with their gear.

For merchant ships in the XII century it all began to take shape. In 1152 King Henry II of England married Eleanor, daughter of the king of France, whose dowry from her Pa was the province of Aquitaine which contains the best vineyards in the world. On their bridal night King Henry produced English wine from Hampton-on-the-Thames to toast his bride.

"For heavens sake, Henry" said Eleanor, "your English wine is rubbish, and I have brought with me a tun of best Bordeaux reuge." A tun was a barrel which measured overall about 40 cubic feet and needed about 100 cubic feet inside the curved shape of a ship to stow it ("Bung up and bilge free, if you please Mister Mate" said the master). So a ship that could stow ten tuns totalling 400 cubic feet needed 1000 cubic feet of space inside her hull and below deck. Her GRT was thereby 10 tons.

No wonder the TV announcers and journalists get it all wrong and particularly when Cunard's website claims that QUEEN MARY 2's GRT is 151400 gross tonnes. What must our late queen think!

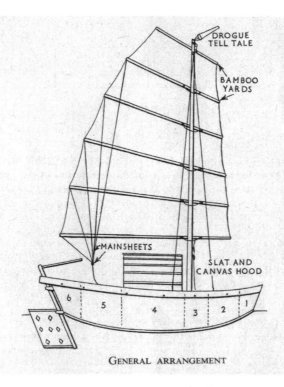

DROGUE
TELL TALE

BAMBOO
YARDS

MAINSHEETS

SLAT AND
CANVAS HOOD

6 | 5 | 4 | 3 | 2 | 1

GENERAL ARRANGEMENT

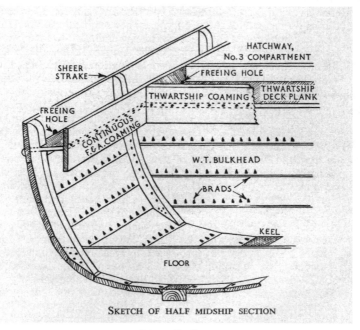

HATCHWAY,
No. 3 COMPARTMENT

SHEER
STRAKE

FREEING HOLE

THWARTSHIP COAMING

THWARTSHIP
DECK PLANK

FREEING
HOLE

CONTINUOUS
F & A COAMING

W.T. BULKHEAD

BRADS

KEEL

FLOOR

SKETCH OF HALF MIDSHIP SECTION

Appendix 7a.
Small junks built in Hong Kong.

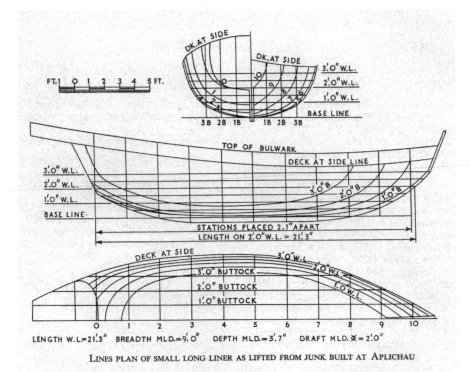

FT.1 0 1 2 3 4 5 FT.

DK.AT SIDE

DK.AT SIDE

3'.0" W.L.
2'.0" W.L.
1'.0" W.L.
BASE LINE

3B 2B 1B 1B 2B 3B

TOP OF BULWARK

DECK AT SIDE LINE

3'.0" W.L.
2'.0" W.L.
1'.0" W.L.
BASE LINE

3'.0" B
2'.0" B
1'.0" B

STATIONS PLACED 2.1" APART
LENGTH ON 2'.0" W.L. = 21'.3"

DECK AT SIDE

3'.0" W.L.
2'.0" W.L.
1'.0" W.L.
3'.0" BUTTOCK
2'.0" BUTTOCK
1'.0" BUTTOCK

0 1 2 3 4 5 6 7 8 9 10

LENGTH W.L.=21'.3"   BREADTH MLD.=9'.0"   DEPTH MLD.=3'.7"   DRAFT MLD. ⊠ = 2'.0"

LINES PLAN OF SMALL LONG LINER AS LIFTED FROM JUNK BUILT AT APLICHAU

Appendix 7b.
Small junks built in Hong Kong. Built value about £40 in 1958.

Index: People

Sea Officer

Index: People

Sea Officer

Index: People

Index: Ships

Index: Ships